Protecting the Rights of People with Autism in the Fields of Education and Employment

Valentina Della Fina • Rachele Cera
Editors

Protecting the Rights of People with Autism in the Fields of Education and Employment

International, European and National Perspectives

Springer Open

Editors
Valentina Della Fina
Institute for International Legal Studies
National Research Council (CNR)
Rome, Italy

Rachele Cera
Institute for International Legal Studies
National Research Council (CNR)
Rome, Italy

Co-funded by the PROGRESS Programme of the European Union

This publication has been produced with the financial support of the PROGRESS Programme of the European Union. The contents of this publication are the sole responsibility of the authors and can in no way be taken to reflect the views of the European Commission.

ISBN 978-3-319-36733-0 ISBN 978-3-319-13791-9 (eBook)
DOI 10.1007/978-3-319-13791-9

Springer Cham Heidelberg New York Dordrecht London

Softcover reprint of the hardcover 1st edition 2015

Printed on acid-free paper

Springer International Publishing AG Switzerland is part of Springer Science+Business Media (www.springer.com)

Foreword

The Convention on the Rights of Persons with Disabilities (CRPD) and its Optional Protocol were adopted on 13 December 2006 at the United Nations Headquarters in New York, and opened for signature on 30 March 2007. They entered into force on 3 May 2008.

The CRPD is unique in its complexity for many reasons. It encompasses both civil and political rights, and economic, social and cultural rights; it includes rights established in previous instruments, but extends them by prescribing the content of the rights and the obligations of Contracting Parties. Furthermore, it contains a new set of rights such as those concerning accessibility, personal mobility or habilitation and rehabilitation, as well as it introduces new topics such as the identification of the persons with disabilities, the concept of reasonable accommodations and the obligation of Contracting Parties to cooperate in the field of disability.

Fundamental rights for all people with disabilities, education and employment are regulated in Articles 24 and 27 of the CRPD and are key areas for the social inclusion of persons with autism. Their relevance has been highlighted by the UN Secretary-General in the message of 2 April 2014 on World Autism Awareness Day recalling that 'Schools connect children to their communities. Jobs connect adults to their societies'.

Consolidating a research area of the Institute for International Legal Studies (ISGI) of the Italian National Research Council (CNR), this book focuses on the analysis of the content and scope of obligations enshrined in these fields by the CRPD, in order to evaluate their implementation at national level from the perspective of people with autism.

The volume emerges from the study carried out by ISGI within the European Project 'Promoting equal rights for people with autism in the field of employment and education', conducted in partnership with Autism-Europe (A-E). Such Project aimed at improving the knowledge and understanding of the CRPD implementation in the fields of inclusive education and employment through the study carried out by ISGI on Articles 24 and 27 and a compendium of best practices in the field of employment prepared by A-E. The Project also promoted the exchange of concrete best practices with the aim of encouraging their replication in other countries. In this vein, the research activities have been coupled with the initiatives for dissemination of the results of the Project, such as the Final Conference, held in Turin on 29 November 2014 during the Italian Presidency of the EU, with the participation of a wide range of relevant stakeholders, including policy-makers.

Following such researches, the present legal study identifies legislative models for implementing Articles 24 and 27 of the CRPD consistent with its principles and obligations and suggests the priorities to be incorporated into domestic legislations. In this vein, the book provides an in-depth assessment of domestic legislative, judicial and administrative practice of the EU Member States having developed laws on the rights of the persons with autism especially in the fields of inclusive education and employment. A chapter is also dedicated to the protection of people with autism in the framework of the Council of Europe and the European Union.

Unique for its legal perspective focused on the rights of people with autism and their inclusion in the fields of education and employment, this book is a useful source of consultation for the community of professionals, academics, scholars and advanced students dealing with international human rights law; practitioners; government legal advisers and policy-makers interested in disability issues; trade unions; representatives of DPOs and other NGOs.

Rome, Italy — Valentina Della Fina
Rome, Italy — Rachele Cera

Contents

Contributors

Lucia Cajola Chiappetta is Professor of Special Education and Pedagogy at University Roma Tre, Rome, Italy.

Rachele Cera is ISGI-CNR Researcher, expert in international cooperation and legal protection of vulnerable people.

Valentina Della Fina is ISGI-CNR Senior Researcher, has a consolidated scientific background in the fields of international human rights law and law of international organizations.

Marco Fasciglione is ISGI-CNR Researcher, legal adviser and trainer in international law field, with specific experience in international human rights law, international economic law, and corporate responsibility.

Evelyne Friedel is Vice-President of Autism-Europe (President 2008–2011); Partner of an international law firm, Doctor of Laws, Attorney at law at the Paris and Brussels Bars.

Giuseppe Palmisano is Director of the ISGI-CNR, Full Professor of International Law and President of the European Committee of Social Rights (Council of Europe).

Introductory Remarks on the Rights of People with Autism to Education and Employment: The Convention on the Rights of Persons with Disabilities & the European and National Perspectives

Evelyne Friedel

Autism-Europe has the great honour of introducing this publication on the protection of the Rights of People with Autism in the fields of education and employment from international, European and national perspectives.

All families having children with autism as well as self-advocates have understood for quite a long time that dealing with autism and ensuring the defence of their fundamental rights requires international exchanges of good practices, under an evidenced based medicine approach, and an international advocacy initiative above purely national lobbying, under the so-called rights based approach.

1 Historic Perspective: Continuing Advocacy by Autism-Europe for Adapted Legal Instruments

From a historical perspective, we should recall the following steps which, during the last 20 years, undoubtedly permitted a better definition of the fundamental rights to education and to employment of people with autism.

As early as 1996, a Charter for persons with autism was drafted by Autism-Europe and adopted by the European Parliament as a written declaration. Although this Charter outlines the rights of people with autism in Europe, it is not legally-binding for the Member States of the European Union.[1]

[1] European Parliament, Charter of Rights of persons with autism, Declaration, May 9, 1996. Charter available on the site of Autism-Europe, presented at the 4th Autism-Europe Congress, Den Haag, 10 May 1992, adopted as a written declaration by the European Parliament on 9 May 1996.

E. Friedel (✉)
Autism-Europe, Bruxelles, Belgium
e-mail: e.friedel@taylorwessing.com

V. Della Fina, R. Cera (eds.), *Protecting the Rights of People with Autism in the Fields of Education and Employment*, DOI 10.1007/978-3-319-13791-9_1

Although, the European Social Charter of 1996 is a general human rights instrument, its Article 15 defines specific rights for people with disabilities. On the basis of this Article 15, the first collective complaint in Europe for the defence of the right to education of people with autism was lodged by Autism-Europe in 2002.[2]

The Committee of Social Rights of the Council of Europe rendered its decision on 4 November 2003. France was found to have failed to fulfil its educational obligations to people with autism under the European Social Charter.[3]

Subsequent to this landmark decision, the Committee of Ministers of the Council of Europe adopted in 2009 a Recommendation on the education and social inclusion of children and young people with autism spectrum disorders on the basis of the work achieved by an ad-hoc committee in which Autism-Europe actively participated.[4]

The 2002 collective complaint has also been at the origin of a second complaint lodged in 2012 by the European organisation *Action européenne du Handicap*.[5] The decision rendered by the Committee of Social Rights on 11 September 2013 confirmed and reinforced the decision issued 10 years previously.[6]

Finally, Autism-Europe was actively involved, along with the European Disability Forum, in the adoption of the UN Convention on the Rights of Persons with Disabilities. The UN Convention is the very first international treaty dedicated to people with disabilities.

This Convention was adopted on 13 December 2006 and opened for signature on 30 March 2007. It entered into force on 3 May 2008. Autism-Europe worked with the European Disability Forum to advocate for a European Disability Strategy 2010–2020 for ensuring the implementation of the Convention among the EU member states. In 2014, it was ratified by most of the European countries. The European Union itself also ratified the Convention. The States which have only signed the UN Convention are not legally bound thereby, but are obliged to refrain from acts that would defeat or undermine the treaty's objective and purpose. The States which have ratified the Convention are legally bound by it and must ensure that its national laws and policies comply with the Convention.

Regarding the rights of people with autism, and from both a European and an international perspective, we are of the opinion that should be taken into account not only the principles set forth by the UN Convention, but also the case law

[2] Collective Complaint no. 13/2002, International Association Autism-Europe (IAAE) v. France.

[3] Council of Europe, European Committee of Social Rights, Decision on the merits, 4 November 2003. Decision available on the site of the Council of Europe.

[4] Council of Europe, Committee of Ministers, Recommendation CM/Rec (2009) 9 to Member States *on the education and social inclusion of children and young people with autism spectrum disorders*, 21 October 2009. Recommendation available on the site of the Council of Europe.

[5] Collective Complaint no. 81/2012, *Action européenne des handicapés* (AEH) v. France, available on the site of the Council of Europe.

[6] Council of Europe, European Committee of Social Rights, Decision on the merits, 11 September 2013. Decision available on the site of the Council of Europe.

rendered by the Council of Europe applying the European Social Charter. To date, the Council of Europe is indeed the sole international organisation having enacted clear guidelines on the rights of people with autism and how they need to be applied in order to be effective.

The interaction between the UN Convention and the Council of Europe decisions and recommendations is an approach ensuring an effectiveness of the rights to education and to employment of all people with autism at the national level in Europe and outside Europe. Indeed, the rights to education and to employment of people with autism are in practice regulated by national legislations.

2 Scope of the Substantive Rules Set Forth by the European and International Instruments Targeted at the Defence of the Rights of People with Disabilities

Indeed, as far as substantive law and effectiveness of rights are concerned, what are the rules to be retained in order to ensure the effectiveness of the rights of all people with autism?

As we know, the spectrum of autism is wide. At one end of the spectrum, people with autism are severely disabled. At the other end, we find people with Asperger syndrome who benefit from the highest capabilities. The UN Convention states that all people with disabilities are 'entitled to all the rights and freedoms set forth therein, without distinction of any kind'. It emphasises the need to promote and protect the human rights of all people with disabilities, including 'those who require more intensive support' as might be the case for many low functioning people with autism. All people with autism deserve education and employment. Education and employment must be defined and adapted for each person with autism. The legal instruments, such as the UN Convention and the European Social Charter do provide and permit so.

Twenty years ago, Article 15 of the European Social Charter of 1996 already stated that for 'ensuring to persons with disabilities, irrespective of age and the nature and origin of their disabilities, the effective exercise of the right to independence, social integration and participation in the life of the community', the States undertake, 'to take the necessary measures' to provide them with 'guidance, education and vocational training in the framework of general schemes wherever possible or, where this is not possible, through specialised bodies, public or private', and 'to promote their access to employment through all measures tending to encourage employers to hire and keep in employment persons with disabilities in the ordinary working environment and to adjust the working conditions to the needs of the disabled or, where this is not possible by reason of the disability, by arranging for or creating sheltered employment according to the level of disability. In certain cases, such measures may require recourse to specialised placement and support services (...)'. It is worth underlining that this Treaty is especially targeted at responding to the needs of all and surely takes into account the wide variety of disabilities, as we know it in the world of autism.

Ten years later, Articles 24 and 27 of the UN Convention define the principles to be complied with for ensuring the full education and full employment of people with disabilities. Pursuant to Article 24 of the Convention on the right to education, the States must ensure that people with disabilities have equal access to education systems at all levels, including lifelong learning and vocational training. The States must also ensure that reasonable accommodation is provided to people with disabilities, not only through technical assistance, but also human assistance to enable access to education. Teachers must also receive specific training. Pursuant to Article 27 of the Convention, the States must enable people with disabilities to exercise their right to work and employment. This includes taking appropriate steps to ensure that reasonable accommodation is provided to people with disabilities in the workplace. The States must of course also employ people with disabilities in the public sector.

Notwithstanding certain approaches retained by some stakeholders or politicians, Articles 24 and 27 do not exclude special education and sheltered employment. Believing so is in fact a legal mistake. Articles 24 and 27 of the UN Convention must not be subject to a summary reading and its interpretation must not lead to a legal loophole. Retaining that pure inclusion is the sole solution promoted by Articles 24 and 27 would on the contrary exclude many people with severe mental disabilities to whom mainstream education or employment might not only be inadequate but also aggressive. Articles 24 and 27 of the UN Convention do not ban special educational services and sheltered and supported employment.

The scope of Articles 24 and 27 must be read in light of the whole UN Convention. In particular, Article 3 recalls the following principles:

- Non-discrimination: to reach non-discrimination, positive measures such as supported or sheltered employment can be implemented;
- Full and effective participation and inclusion in society: inclusion does not exclude the possibility for regular companies to subcontract work to sheltered services; such contracting processes between the companies and the sheltered services under fair commercial conditions do constitute effective participation and inclusion, as any other subcontracting; then, through supported and sheltered employment services, people with disabilities do effectively participate in the society;
- Equality of opportunity: does not mean “identity of opportunity”;
- Respect for difference: specific educational services and sheltered services positively respond to this respect;
- Accessibility: these services permit an effective and adapted access to society.

Article 5 on equality and non-discrimination stresses that: ‘In order to promote equality and eliminate discrimination, States Parties shall take all appropriate steps to ensure that reasonable accommodation is provided’. It also adds that ‘specific measures which are necessary to accelerate or achieve de facto equality of persons with disabilities shall not be considered discrimination’. What is meant by 'reasonable accommodation'? Pursuant to Article 2 of the UN Convention, 'Reasonable accommodation means necessary and appropriate modification and adjustments not imposing a disproportionate or undue burden, where needed in a particular case, to ensure to persons with disabilities the enjoyment or exercise on an equal basis with others of all human rights and fundamental freedoms'.

In fact, said provisions do encourage positive measures which might be needed for highly mentally disabled people for whom pure inclusion in mainstream school or in the open labour market might be ineffective with no respect of their abilities and differences. The notion of equality does not mean identity of measures and does not impede having recourse to positive measures which in the meaning of the UN Convention are to be specific measures. The issue is not so much to retain or ban special education or sheltered employment services but to carefully determine to whom such services must be offered and to guarantee that such services must always remain positive and support measures.

Although the alternative of specific services must not be excluded, it remains imperative that States promote and develop opportunities for children and adults with autism to receive education in mainstream schools and to work in the open labour market, inclusive and accessible to all.

3 National Measures for the Rights to Education and Employment

Because of the variety of the needs, and because of the obligation to guarantee the rights of each person with autism, Kari Steindal quite correctly underlined, 'A society that can cope with autism can deal with all other forms of disability. If Europe cooperates in helping people with autism and helps to meet the huge demands of this disability, it will be better equipped to support all other forms of disability'.[7]

As a matter of fact, it is the responsibility of national legislations to implement the right to education and to employment of people with autism and severe disabilities. In practice, the latter do not always enjoy positive discrimination, in terms of the adequate or appropriate support they are entitled to, in order to enjoy the effectiveness of their rights.

[7] Council of Europe, Interview of Kari Steindal, 'A society that can cope with autism can deal with all other forms of disability'. Interview available on the site of the Council of Europe. Kari Steindal is educationalist and principal adviser to the Autism Unit of the National Autism Network of Norway, University of Oslo.

3.1 Positive Measures and Effectiveness of the Right to Education

The 2003 and 2013 decisions rendered by the European Committee on Social Rights[8] and the 2009 Recommendation of the Committee of Ministers of the Council of Europe[9] constitute an interesting guidance for ensuring, at the national level, the effectiveness of the right to education of people with autism.

The States must guarantee the right to education, at all ages, to children and adults with autism 'in particular by providing for the establishment or maintenance of institutions and services sufficient and adequate for this purpose'.

The golden rule is that children with autism should be given regular and specific teaching in mainstream schools wherever possible.[10] Schooling options, in no specific order, should be available to meet the diverse needs of the children.

The specialised institutions must ensure, through their internal organisation and their working methods, that guidance, education and vocational training are given priority over the other functions and duties that they may be required to perform under national law.[11]

Education itself must be based on detailed assessments identifying the needs and strengths of each child or adult. In order to meet individual needs, personalised plans must be defined and regularly reviewed with the person, his/her family and the professionals at stake. Said plans must facilitate the transitions within the education system and to adulthood and the employment. Support and opportunities for social inclusion are to be provided in whatever situation best fits the current needs of the person with autism.

Training and continuing programs must also be introduced for professionals involved in the education of children and adults with autism. Finally, research must always be pursued in order to constantly retain the best and most adapted educational and inclusion strategies.

---

[8] Decisions rendered in 2003 and 2013 subsequent to the Collective Complaint no. 13/2002, International Association Autism-Europe (IAAE) v. France, and to the Collective Complaint no. 81/2012, *Action européenne des handicapés* (AEH) v. France.

[9] As indicated above, this Recommendation was the result of the work achieved by the ad-hoc committee directed by Kari Steindal and which permitted an efficient exchange of good national practices. Recommendation CM/Rec (2009) 9 of the Committee of Ministers to Member States on *the education and social inclusion of children and young people with autism spectrum disorders* adopted by the Committee of Ministers on 21 October 2009. Recommendation available on the site of the Council of Europe.

[10] Article 15 of the European Social Charter of 1996.

[11] Collective Complaint no. 81/2012, *Action européenne des handicapés* (AEH) v. France, available on the site of the Council of Europe, para 111.

3.2 *Positive Measures and Effectiveness of the Right to Employment*

States must promote and develop opportunities for persons with disabilities to work in a labour market which is open, inclusive and accessible to them. Pursuant to Article 27 of the UN Convention, people with autism have the right to employment in inclusive settings and the right to reasonable accommodation and support to enable them to work effectively.

To enable people with autism to gain employment and fulfil their potential at work, adapted support is indispensable. This support should always be tailored to each person's individual needs and depends also on the nature of the enterprise concerned. Numerous approaches for providing this support exist. Innovative practices include work experience programmes, adapted recruitment processes and specific forms of support in the workplace. Support in the workplace means adjusting the job description, working hours, workplace communication practices and physical work environment. Providing assistance with transport to and from work and using assistive technologies are also support means to be retained. As underlined by Autism-Europe, 'one of the most significant emerging forms of support for people with autism at work is the practice of having identified support people such as 'job coaches' or other staff members who are designated to assist a person with autism with the difficulties they encounter (...) Given that like all other people, the needs and abilities of people with autism in relation to employment can change over time, support should also be provided on an ongoing and/or as required basis, from preparation for employment through to retirement'. Positive emphasis must be placed upon the abilities of people with autism rather than their disability.[12]

If the principle of inclusion in the open labour market must be the rule, sheltered employment services must not be excluded. As sensibly and realistically underlined by Arthur O'Reilly,[13] recalling the International Labour Organisations and the Council of Europe positions:

> It is generally accepted that for some disabled persons, open employment may not be a practicable option, for various reasons. In calling for measures to promote employment opportunities for persons with disabilities, ILO Recommendation No. 168 states that such measures should include "appropriate government support for the establishment of various types of sheltered employment for disabled persons for whom access to open employment is not practicable". The UN Standard Rules on the Equalization of Opportunities for Persons with Disabilities states that while the aim should always be for persons with disabilities to obtain employment in the open labour market, 'for persons with disabilities

---

[12] Autism-Europe (2014).

[13] O'Reilly (2007). Dr Arthur O'Reilly is the former Assistant Director General of the Irish National Training and Employment Authority (FAS), and former Chief Executive of the National Rehabilitation Board and National Disability Authority. He was the President of Rehabilitation International and former Chairman of CEDEFOP, the European Centre for the Development of Vocational Training. Dr Arthur O'Reilly has also worked as consultant to the European Commission, OECD, UNIDO and ILO.

whose needs cannot be met in open employment, small units of sheltered or supported employment may be an alternative' (Rule 7 (7)).

As ILO Recommendation No. 168 implies, there are possibilities for different types of sheltered employment (. . .)

"When government officials are asked to present their system of sheltered employment to foreigners (. . .), they will sometimes refer exclusively to organizations providing productive work (in industry or services) to persons with disabilities who have an employment contract and receive a wage. Other officials (. . .) may want to include organizations where productive work is certainly not the only and often not even the main aim and where persons with disabilities have no employment contract and receive no wages, but only a bonus in addition to their disability pension. Other interested parties, such as workshop organizations or organizations of and for people with disabilities, may share this view or disagree." (. . .)

The Council of Europe (1992) also uses a broad definition of sheltered employment.

"Sheltered employment should be open to people who, because of their disability, are unable to obtain or keep a normal job, whether supported or not; it can cover a number of diversified situations, amongst which are sheltered workshops and work centres. Sheltered work should have a double purpose: to make it possible for people with disabilities to carry out a worthwhile activity and to prepare them, as far as possible, for work in normal employment. To this end, all ways of facilitating the passage from supported to ordinary employment should be devised, such as: the setting up of sheltered work sections in work centres or work centres in sheltered workshops; the setting up of sheltered work sections or work centres within ordinary firms; individual or collective detachment of workers in sheltered workshops or work centres to ordinary firms."

3.3 National Duty in Response to the International Legal Instruments

Despite the complexity and cost for enforcing the rights to education and employment of people with autism, the States must, in the name of positive discrimination, take measures that allow achieving the objectives pursued by the international and European legal instruments which prohibit all forms of discrimination, direct and indirect, the latter arising when people with autism are given 'inappropriate treatment'.

References

Autism-Europe (2014) Autism and work: together we can – a report on good practices in employment for people with Autism from across Europe. Pasparta Publishing, Prague

O'Reilly A (2007) The right to decent work of persons with disabilities. International Labour Office, Geneva

Evelyne Friedel is Vice-President of Autism-Europe (President 2008–2011); she is Partner of an international law firm, Doctor of Laws, Attorney at law at the Paris and Brussels Bars; Evelyne is also the author of the first collective complaint for the defense of the right to education of people with autism, lodged by Autism-Europe in 2002 before the Council of Europe.

The Protection of People with Autism in the Framework of the Council of Europe and the European Union

Giuseppe Palmisano

1 The Protection of People with Autism Within the Wider Framework of International and European Rules on the Rights of Persons with Disabilities

At the level of the European institutions and supranational organizations—namely, the Council of Europe and the European Union—*ad hoc* legal rules or hard law instruments specifically aimed at affirming and protecting the rights of people with autism, imposing on States obligations to respect, protect and promote such rights, in particular in the field of education and employment, do not currently exist.

The special situation and needs of people with autism find rather legal recognition and protection within the wider framework of the rules and legal instruments concerning the rights of persons with disabilities, as well as within the scope of application of the general principle of equality and non-discrimination.

Considering such a wider framework, the most important and comprehensive legal instrument to be taken as a point of reference is, of course, the 2006 United Nations Convention on the Rights of Persons with Disability (CRPD). This Convention elaborates in detail the rights of persons with disabilities and sets out a code of implementation. States parties to the Convention have indeed engaged themselves to develop and carry out policies, laws and administrative measures for securing such rights and abolish laws, regulations, customs and practices that constitute discrimination against persons with disabilities. In addition, the CRPD provides for a monitoring mechanism aimed at assessing the implementation by States of the obligations arising from the Convention in their respective domestic

G. Palmisano (✉)
ISGI-CNR, Rome, Italy

Institute for International Legal Studies, National Research Council (CNR), Rome, Italy
e-mail: giuseppe.palmisano@cnr.it

V. Della Fina, R. Cera (eds.), *Protecting the Rights of People with Autism in the Fields of Education and Employment*, DOI 10.1007/978-3-319-13791-9_2

legal orders and practices. But, above all, the Convention sets up all the rights and guarantees referred to persons with disabilities according to a 'social', inclusive approach to disability, and not a medical and 'assistential' approach. In other words, the approach of the CRPD is convincingly based on the awareness that 'disability results from the interaction between persons with impairments and attitudinal and environmental barriers that hinders their full and effective participation in society on an equal basis with others' (Preamble to the Convention).[1]

With regard to the education and employment, the relevant provisions of the CRPD are Article 24 and Article 27, respectively. They are indeed impressively accurate and detailed provisions, at least if compared to the usual wording of other human rights treaty provisions concerning education or employment.

It is worth noting that the CRPD is not only a 'universal' convention; it has also the value of a European legal instrument. In fact, not only the very large majority of European States have ratified the Convention,[2] but since December 2010 the European Union as such is a party to it. This means that the Convention can be considered and treated as forming part of the law of the Union, which is obviously not without consequences also from the point of view of the domestic law of EU Member States.

But moving to the very specific European regional level, the protection of the rights of persons with disabilities is provided for by two important human rights instruments: the European Social Charter and the Charter of Fundamental Rights of the European Union.

The European Social Charter (ESC) is a legally binding treaty for the protection of social rights, which is embedded in the institutional framework of the Council of Europe.[3] Article 15 of the Revised Social Charter is expressly devoted to 'the right of persons with disabilities to independence, social integration and participation in the life of the community'.

---

[1] On the CRPD see, *inter alias*, Arnardóttir and Quinn (2009), Marchisio et al. (2010), and Schulze (2010).

[2] A part from Finland, Ireland and the Netherlands, all other member States of the European Union have ratified the Convention.

[3] The European Social Charter has been signed in Turin more than 50 years ago, in 1961, but it has progressively changed by virtue of a process of institutional reform started in the late 1980s and continued during the 1990s of the last century. This process took the form of three Protocols, adopted in 1988, 1991 and 1995, and the Revised Social Charter, in 1996. In 1988 came the first additional Protocol which added new rights. In 1991, it was adopted the Amending Protocol improving the supervisory mechanism; and in 1995 another additional Protocol, providing for a system of collective complaints, was adopted. The culmination of this reform process came in 1996 with the adoption of the Revised Charter, which added a number of new rights, while at the same time incorporating the basic content of the 1961 Charter and its Protocols. To date, 43 out of the 47 member States of the Council of Europe have ratified either the 1961 Charter or the Revised Charter. 10 States have ratified only the 1961 European Social Charter, and 33 States are parties to the Revised Charter. The countries that have not yet ratified the Charter at all are Liechtenstein, Monaco, San Marino and Switzerland.

The Charter of Fundamental Rights of the European Union (CFREU) has been adopted within the framework of the European Union and, according to Article 6 (1) of the Treaty of Lisbon, has—since 2009—the same legal value as the EU Treaties. Under the Chapter of the Charter devoted to 'Equality', there is a provision—Article 26—concerning specifically the issue of 'Integration of persons with disabilities', and Article 21, on 'Non-discrimination', expressly includes disability among the prohibited grounds of discrimination.

Both the ESC and the CFREU are hard law instruments, and both recognize the rights of persons with disabilities in the fields of education and employment, and the correspondent obligation for European States to protect and ensure such rights. In particular, Article 15(1) and (2) of the Revised European Social Charter states:

> With a view to ensuring to persons with disabilities, irrespective of age and the nature and origin of their disabilities, the effective exercise of the right to independence, social integration and participation in the life of the community, the Parties undertake: 1. to take the necessary measures to provide persons with disabilities with guidance, education and vocational training in the framework of general schemes wherever possible or, where this is not possible, through specialised bodies, public or private; 2. to promote their access to employment through all measures tending to encourage employers to hire and keep in employment persons with disabilities in the ordinary working environment and to adjust the working conditions to the needs of the disabled or, where this is not possible by reason of the disability, by arranging for or creating sheltered employment according to the level of disability. In certain cases, such measures may require recourse to specialised placement and support services.[4]

The CFREU is much less detailed and demanding. According to Article 26: 'The Union recognises and respects the right of persons with disabilities to benefit from measures designed to ensure their independence, social and occupational integration and participation in the life of the community'.[5]

2 International and European Soft Law Instruments Concerning the Protection of People with Autism

In addition to these hard law instruments and provisions concerning, in general, the rights of people with disabilities (including persons with autism), there are also—at the international and European level—some soft law instruments dealing with the specific issue of the rights of people with autism. In particular, declarations of principles and resolutions adopted by European or international organizations which do not have legally binding force, but nonetheless have a normative tone.

Starting from the international–universal level, it is worth mentioning the Resolution 67/82 adopted by the UN General Assembly on 12 December 2012, on 'Addressing the socioeconomic needs of individuals, families and societies

[4] On Article 15 of the European Social Charter see Palmisano (2013), pp. 337–361.

[5] On Article 26 of the CFREU see O'Brien (2014), pp. 709–748.

affected by autism spectrum disorders, developmental disorders and associated disabilities'. This Resolution, which recalls *inter alia* some preceding resolutions adopted by the World Health Organization and the so-called 'Dhaka Declaration on Autism Spectrum Disorders and Developmental Disabilities' (adopted by civil society organizations from South-Asia and South-East Asia, on 25 July 2011), significantly calls upon UN Members States: 'to enhance access to appropriate support services and equal opportunities for inclusion and participation in society, by providing, as appropriate, training to public administrators, service providers, carers, caregivers, families and non-professionals on the needs and rights of persons with autism spectrum disorders' (para 1); and 'to ensure inclusive education system at all levels and lifelong learning, as well as to promote vocational training and skills development programmes for persons with autism' (para 5).

But also some Resolutions adopted in the framework of the WHO are relevant, in particular the very recent Resolution WHA67.8 of 24 May 2014, in which the World Health Assembly has urged States 'to develop or update and implement relevant policies, legislation, and multisectoral plans, supported by sufficient human, financial and technical resources to address issues related to ASD and other developmental disorders, as part of a comprehensive approach to supporting all persons living with mental health issues or disabilities'.

At the European level, the first and most wide-ranging soft law document on the protection of people with autism is the 'Charter for persons with autism', which was originally drafted and presented by Autism-Europe more than 20 years ago, in 1992, and which has been adopted by the European Parliament on May 1996.

This Charter points out, first of all, the guiding principle of best interests of the person with autism, along the lines and model of the principle of best interest of the child, established by the 1989 UN Convention on the Rights of the Child. And then it lists a number of rights, concerning all fields of life. The provisions stating such rights are remarkably worded, in a way that the peculiar needs of persons with autism are taken into an appropriate account. Considering the thematic area of education and employment, I wish just to recall, as examples, points 3, 6 and 10 of the Charter, that is: '3. The right of people with autism to accessible and appropriate education'; '6. The right to the equipment, assistance and support services necessary to live a fully productive life with dignity and independence'; '10. The right to meaningful employment and vocational training without discrimination or stereotype'.

In the framework of the Council of Europe, some resolutions and recommendations adopted by the Committee of Ministers should be stressed. In particular, the Resolution of 12 December 2007 and the Recommendation of 21 October 2009, both 'on the education and social inclusion of children and young people with autism spectrum disorders'. It is worth noting that such acts have been prepared by an *ad hoc* committee—'the Committee of Experts on the Education and Integration of Children with Autism'—which was established on 2004, in the aftermath of a

Decision of the European Committee of Social Rights concerning the violation in France of the rights of people with autism.[6]

The Committee of Experts was charged with exchanging information on the definition of autism and related statistics, examining the services provided to children with autism, particularly within the education system, sharing information on experience in the implementation at national level of a coherent policy for this particular group, drawing up recommendations to governments to further education and integration of children with autism. The Committee submitted a substantial report, drafted by Professor Rita Jordan from Birmingham University.

Some points of the Resolutions of the Committee of Ministers of the Council of Europe deserve indeed to be highlighted.

First of all, they affirm the principle that people with ASD have the right to be guaranteed full enjoyment of all human rights and fundamental freedoms, and that failure to promote the rights of people with autism and to ensure equality of opportunities is a violation of their human dignity. From this perspective, Governments are called upon to encourage education and social inclusion of children and young people with autism, by involving non-governmental organisations representing children and young people with ASD and their families in the implementation and monitoring of the measures adopted to that effect.

And then the Resolutions list a number of specific actions that States should take in order to ensure effective respect for, and promotion of the rights of peoples with autism. In this respect, the following passages could be mentioned by way of example: 'States should provide a legal framework, which ensures the right of children and young people with autism to receive education - within general schemes wherever possible - that is appropriate to their needs, is non-discriminatory and works towards social inclusion. There is a need to ensure that resources are sufficient for the full implementation of relevant legislation'; 'Following diagnosis, education for children and young people with autism should be based on detailed assessments that identify the needs and strengths of each individual. Steps should be taken to ensure that services dealing with young children are aware of these problems as early as possible'; 'Research should be carried out in support of the educational, therapeutic and inclusion strategies, because reliable information helps to identify new problems which must be addressed, to develop solutions and to obtain satisfactory results'.

In addition to the above mentioned European soft law instruments, concerning specifically the protection of persons with autism, it is important to recall the European Action Plans or Strategies concerning disability in general.

In this regard, it is worth recalling both the 'European Disability Strategy 2010–2020: A renewed Commitment to a Barrier-Free Europe', which is a Communication of the European Commission to the other political institutions of the EU (adopted on November 2010), and the 'Council of Europe Action Plan to promote the rights and full participation of people with disabilities in society: improving the

---

[6] See Sect. 4.

quality of life of people with disability in Europe 2006-2015', which is a Recommendation of the Committee of Ministers of the Council of Europe adopted on April 2006. Such instruments cover of course all the situations and categories of disabilities, including autism; and they propose to national authorities significant actions to be taken also in the fields of education, vocational training, and employment, aimed in particular at: promoting inclusive education and lifelong learning for pupils and students with disabilities; enabling people with disabilities to earn their living on the open labour market; and eradicating discrimination on grounds of disability in Europe.

3 The Rights of Persons with Autism Before the Court of Justice of the European Union and the European Court of Human Rights

The current picture of the European legal rules and soft law instruments which are directly relevant for the protection and promotion of the rights of people with ASD is not very rich or satisfying, indeed. The existing European 'legislation' concerning expressly autism is clearly poor and not developed enough.

However, it is important to see what such rules and instruments imply and require in terms both of State legal obligations and of rights to be invoked by individuals or groups before European judges or monitoring bodies.

In this regard, it is worth considering the jurisprudence and views of the European bodies and courts which have been established to monitor and assess respect for, and implementation of, the above mentioned—few—rules by European States.

Starting from the judicial organs and institutions of the European Union, unfortunately there is not so much to say about their role in the protection of the rights of persons with autism. As mentioned above, in the framework of the EU law the main rule to which refer for the protection of people with autism (or other kind of disabilities) is Article 26 of the Charter of Fundamental Rights. But we still do not have any case law or jurisprudence of the Court of Justice on Article 26. This is presumably due, on the one hand, to the fact that the Charter entered into force, as a legally binding instrument, only 5 years ago; but it also due, on the other hand, to the inherent limited scope of application of the Charter.

In fact, the Charter does not establish any new power or task for the Union: it has to be respected by the institutions and bodies of the European Union only when applying already existing EU law and rules, and is legally binding for Member States only when they are implementing Union law or acts (Article 51 of the Charter). As a consequence, there are not many situations in which Article 26 of the Charter can be fruitfully invoked by individuals or groups to obtain respect for, or promotion to the rights of people with autism (or other kind of disabilities).

A meaningful example of this state of affairs is the recent case of a petition lodged to the European Parliament on September 2013 by the 'Diamant Association', alleging that the right of persons with autism to education without discrimination and on the basis of equal opportunity is not respected in France, and asking the European Parliament to take steps to ensure that persons with autism in France are not treated in psychiatric clinics but integrated into specialized schools. The European Parliament requested information on this issue from the Commission. The Commission replied that 'The competencies of the Union are limited to contributing to the development of quality education by encouraging cooperation between Member States and supporting and supplementing their actions. ... Only where Member States are implementing Union law can the Commission assess whether a national law or measure is compliant with the United Nations Conventions on the Rights of Persons with Disabilities. [...] On this basis ..., it does not seem that the issues the Petitioner raises are related to the implementation of European Union law. For this reason, the European Commission is not in a position to follow up on them. It is for Member States, including their judicial authorities, to ensure that fundamental rights are effectively respected and protected in accordance with their national legislation and international human rights obligations'.

And the final answer of the Parliament to the Petition was that 'The situation raised by the petitioner does not fall within the scope of existing EU law'.

A part from the Charter of Fundamental Rights, there are of course other norms and acts of the European Union which could be usefully referred to, interpreted and applied in order to properly ensure the rights of persons with autism, taking into account their peculiar situation. A good example is the 'Employment Equality Directive' (Directive 2000/78/EC), which prohibits discrimination on the ground of disability in the field of employment, occupation and vocational training. The way in which this Directive has been interpreted and applied by the European Court of Justice in some landmark rulings can clearly have a positive impact also on national legislations and practices concerning the employment and vocational training of people with autism.[7] From this perspective, are worth mentioning the *HK Denmark* judgment of 11 April 2013 with regard to the notion of disability and the categories of persons which are covered by the Directive, and to the meaning of 'reasonable accommodation' as including not only material but also organizational measures; and also the judgment of 4 July 2013 in the case *Commission v. Italy*, still with regard to the meaning of 'reasonable accommodation' and the obligation for all employers to take concrete measures allowing persons with disabilities to have effective access to employment, to participate and advance in employment, and to be trained.

Moving from the European Union to the Council of Europe, let us starting with European Court of Human Rights. To tell the truth, to date no direct contribution of the Court to the protection of persons with autism can be found or mentioned. There are of course some judgments concerning persons with disabilities which can be

[7] See the chapter by M. Fasciglione, in this volume.

relevant also in the specific perspective of the protection of people with autism. This is the case, for example, for two old decisions concerning the right to education of disabled children, where the Court condemned the compulsory placement of children with disabilities in special nursing homes against parents' wishes (*Graeme v. UK*, Commission's decision of 5 February 1990, and *Persson v. Swefen*, of 2 July 1993). And this is also the case for a number of judgments where the Court conducted a review of the measures taken by the authorities with respect to the specific circumstances and needs of the prisoners with disabilities or with chronic illnesses.[8] These cases point to the fact that disabled prisoners were disadvantaged in comparison to their non-disabled inmates and the appropriate steps were not taken to remove that disadvantage which caused them suffering and distress beyond that associated with detention. In other words, the failure to provide reasonable accommodation to prisoners with disabilities resulted in them being subjected to inhuman and degrading treatment.

Something new about the application of the European Convention on Human Rights to the specific situation and needs of autistic persons could maybe come in the next future from the assessment by the Court of a very recent application submitted by Mental Disability Advocacy Center (MDAC) against the Czech Republic: a case concerning a child with mental disability and the alleged violation of the right to equal access to education (Article 2 of Protocol No. 1 to the Convention) in conjunction with the right not to be discriminated against (Article 14 of the Convention). According to the applicant, the latter right would in particular include, for children with disabilities, the right to reasonable accommodation and inclusive education. It will be interesting to see what the Court will say in this regard.

[8] See Price v UK, Application no. 33394/96, judgment of 10 July 2001; Vincent v France, Application no. 6253/03, judgment of 24 October 2006; Mouisel v France, Application no. 67263/01, judgment of 14 November 2002; Khudobin v Russia, Application no. 59696/00, judgment of 26 October 2006; Xiros v Greece, Application no. 1033/07, judgment of 9 September 2010; Kupczak v Poland, Application no. 2627/09, judgment of 25 January 2009; Grori v Albania, Application no. 25336/04, 7 July 2009; Logvinenko v Ukraine, Application no. 13448/07, 14 October 2010; Raffray Taddei v France, 36435/07, judgment of 21 December 2010; Vasyukov v Russia, Application no. 2974/05, judgment of 5 April 2011; Vladimir Vasilyev v Russia, Application no. 28370/05, judgment of 10 January 2012; Artyunyan v Russia, Application no. 48977/09, judgment of 10 January 2012; Grzywaczewski v Poland, Application no. 18364/06, judgment of 31 May 2012; DG v Poland, Application no. 45705/07, judgment of 12 February 2013.

4 The Protection of People with Autism in the Framework of the Collective Complaints Procedure Before the European Committee of Social Rights

But apart from and beyond the jurisprudence of European Court of Human Rights and its possible impact on the protection of the rights of persons with autism, much more directly relevant to the protection of such persons are, up to now, some decisions taken by the European Committee of Social Rights, in the framework of the so-called collective complaints procedure provided for by the European Social Charter.[9] There are in fact two important decisions of the Committee concerning precisely the violation of the rights of persons with autism, as established by the above mentioned Article 15 of the European Social Charter.

We refer namely to Decision 13/2002 of November 2003 in the case *Autisme-Europe v. France*, and to the more recent Decision 81/2012 of September 2013, in the case *Action Européenne des Handicapés (AEH)*, still versus France.[10]

In *Autisme-Europe v. France*, the European Committee of Social Rights found that France failed to fulfil its educational obligations to persons with autism, mainly on the grounds that the proportion of children with autism being educated in either general or specialist schools was much lower than in the case of other children, whether or not disabled, and that there was a chronic shortage of care and support facilities for autistic adults.

This decision is indeed important, and not only because it has publicly qualified the inacceptable situation in France as being in violation of European legal rules

[9] The collective complaints procedure was inserted into the Social Charter system with the Additional Protocol of 9 November 1995. To date, only 15 States (out of the 43 States Parties to the European Social Charter) have accepted it. According to this procedure, four categories of organisations may lodge complaints, alleging that a State Party is in breach of the Charter: firstly, international organisations of trade unions and employers organisations; secondly, non-governmental organisations which have consultative status within the Council of Europe and have been put on a special list; thirdly, the trade unions and employers' organisations in the country concerned; and fourthly, national non-governmental organisations (this last category is only entitled to submit complaints if the State Party concerned has expressly agreed to it; to date, only Finland has accepted this option). Complaints are examined by the ECSR, which, if the complaint is declared admissible, proceeds to decide on the merits of the case, that is whether the situation is in conformity with the Charter or not. The decision is taken on the basis of an exchange in writing of arguments between the parties. If necessary, the Committee may also decide to hold a public hearing where arguments are presented orally by the parties. Finally, the ECSR transmits its decision to the Committee of Ministers of the Council of Europe, which adopts a resolution and may invite the State concerned to take the necessary measures to bring the situation into conformity with the Charter.

[10] The European Committee of Social Rights has adopted important decisions also in other cases concerning the rights of persons with disability. See, namely, the decisions of collective complaints 41/2007, *Mental Disability Advocacy Centre v. Bulgaria* (3 June 2008), and 75/2011, *Fédé ration international des droits de l'homme v. Belgium* (18 March 2013).

and obligations. It is important especially as it has clarified the contents and scope of the protection that States must guarantee to persons with autism.

In this respect, some statements in the decision deserve to be highlighted:

- States shall use a proper definition of autism in their legislation and official documents, and not an improper restrictive notion. According to the European Committee of Social Rights, the point of reference for the national definitions should be the one adopted by the World Health Organization.
- States shall take not merely legal action but also practical action to give full effects to the rights recognized to people with autism. This means, for example, an obligation to provide for adequate statistics with which to assess the situation of persons with autism and to rationally measures progress through time. But this mainly means the obligation for States to adopt concrete measures and modalities of funding for care and support facilities, within a reasonable time and to an extent consistent with the maximum use of available resources.
- Disability has to be considered a prohibited ground of discrimination, even if it is not expressly listed among the prohibited grounds of discrimination in the relevant provision of the European Social Charter (Article E). As a consequence, indirect discrimination on the ground of autism is also prohibited. This means that there is a violation when a State does not take steps to ensure that rights and advantages that are open to all (like education) are genuinely accessible also by and to persons with autism.[11]

Coming now to the Decision of September 2013 in the case *Action Européenne des Handicapés (AEH) v. France,* the European Committee of Social Rights found that France failed to fulfil its educational and training obligations to children and adolescents with autism on the grounds, *inter alia*: that France does not ensure that such children and adolescents are educated primarily in mainstreams schools; that it does not ensure that the work done in specialized institutions caring for children and adolescents with autism is predominantly educational in nature; and that the defective schooling of adolescents with autism has the consequence of not allowing their access to vocational training.

What are in this decision the most interesting statements from the point of view of clarifying contents and meaning of State obligations to adequately protect persons with autism?

- First of all, by referring itself to the definition of autism given by the WHO, the Committee reaffirms very clearly that autism is not a temporary disease but a disability. Therefore, considering the stable and permanent nature of all disabilities, assistance must be arranged by States, when necessary, for all part of the schooling and training of persons with autism.
- In so far as assistance in mainstream schools is concerned, States have to provide for a continuous service of such assistance throughout the school life of children

[11] For a more detailed analysis of the decision see Palmisano (2013), pp. 354–356.

and adolescents with autism, in order to allow them to attend such schools. If such assistance is not adequately arranged, this does hamper school careers of autistic persons, provoking a process of driving away such persons from mainstream schools, which is contrary to the obligation to provide autistic persons with education within the framework of general schemes.

- The obligation to take the necessary measures to provide persons with autism with guidance and education, means that States have also the obligation to ensure that specialized institutions caring for autistic children or adolescents give education priority over other (medical, therapeutic or social) functions and activities, without leaving to education just a subsidiary role.
- The State obligation to adopt positive measures to provide persons with autism with guidance, education and training is not satisfied by merely elaborating and adopting adequate Action Plans, but it requires that such Plans are put into practice and implemented within a reasonable time.
- Moreover, the State obligation to implement positive measures to provide autistic persons with education cannot be satisfied by merely subsidizing travel to other States were children and adolescents with autism can be accommodated in specialized institutions functioning according to appropriate educational standards; it rather requires financing and organizational measures to implement these standards within specialized institutions active in the State territory.
- Last but not least, in the specific field of autism (and, more in general, of disability) indirect discrimination occurs also when an apparently neutral provision or practice—like public budget restrictions in social policy matters—ends up in putting the persons in question at a particular disadvantage, as they are more likely to be dependent on community care, funded through the State budget, in order to live independently and in dignity. Public budget restrictions cannot therefore be equally applied to the field of autism and disability, since this would result in a difference in treatment indirectly based on disability.

5 By Way of Conclusion

At the end of this brief survey on the legal protection of people with autism at the European 'supranational' level, we can just come back to what has been emphasized at the very beginning of these reflections.

It is true, in fact, that we still do not have a set of European rules or a European normative instrument specifically devoted to the protection of autistic persons. And it is also true that nothing is seriously going on in such direction: it is not realistic to expect European States or European political institutions to draft and adopt in the very next years a European convention or a hard-law act on the rights of peoples with autism.

However, this does not mean that there are no legal sources and rules, at the European level, which one can refer to in view of obtaining from States adequate consideration and respect for the specific needs and rights of autistic persons, as well as positive measures and actions to ensure that such persons fully and effectively enjoy their fundamental rights, like the right to education or to work and employment. In this sense, let us just refer, once again, to the CRPD, the ESC, the CFREU, to some EU Directives, and of course to the principle of non-discrimination.

With this in mind and in view of achieving some progress and improvements in the European Union—within Member States—in the field of protection of autistic persons, what would be needed is not so much a new European 'legislation' or a normative instrument dealing specifically with autism. Much more important than this would be, in our view, if the already-existing European rules and principles were properly applied by States, in all their implications and practical requirements.

As the experience of the European Committee of Social Rights in applying Article 15 of the ESC shows well, what is really important is to push State institutions and authorities to put into practice their existing obligations with regard to the protection of autistic persons, and to carefully monitor actions or omissions of States in this field, by rigorously assessing and emphasizing when they, contrary to their obligations, do not do anything, or do not enough to ensuring to persons with autism the exercise of their rights and participation in the life of the community.

In this respect, the advocacy action carried out by civil society associations or by European NGOs—like Autism-Europe—is extremely important, as it allows European monitoring bodies or courts to deal with concrete cases concerning the application by States of the legal rules which require them to ensuring autistic persons the effective exercise of their rights. Also research projects and comparative studies on the possible measures and best practices to give full effect to the rights of persons with autism are very useful, as they do provide competent European monitoring bodies and courts with the proper guidance to assess whether or not States and public authorities are acting in conformity with their obligations towards people with autism.

References

Arnardóttir OM, Quinn G (eds) (2009) The UN Convention on the rights of persons with disabilities: European and Scandinavian perspectives. Martinus Nijhoff Publisher, Leiden/Boston

Marchisio S, Cera R, Della Fina V (eds) (2010) La Convenzione delle Nazioni Unite sui diritti delle persone con disabilità. Commentario. Aracne, Roma

O'Brien C (2014) Article 26. In: Peers S, Hervey T, Kenner J, Ward A (eds) The EU Charter of fundamental rights – a commentary. Hart Publishing, Oxford/Portland, pp 709–748

Palmisano G (2013) I diritti delle persone con disabilità nel Sistema della Carta sociale europea. In: Colapietro C, Salvia A (eds) Assistenza, inclusione sociale e diritti delle persone con disabilità. Editoriale Scientifica, Napoli, pp 337–361

Schulze M (2010) Understanding the UN Convention on the rights of persons with disabilities: a handbook on the human rights of persons with disabilities. http://www.hiproweb.org/uploads/tx_hidrtdocs/HICRPDManual2010.pdf. Accessed 21 Nov 2014

Director of the ISGI-CNR, Full Professor in International Law (University of Camerino) and President of the European Committee of Social Rights (Council of Europe).

Domestic Laws and National Plans or Strategies for the Protection of the Rights of People with Autism: An Appraisal

Valentina Della Fina

1 Introduction

The recognition of autism in psychiatry in 1943 by Dr. Leo Kanner[1] and Hans Asperger's studies in the mid 1940s marked the beginning of the scientific studies on autism.[2] In 1979, Wing and Gould introduced the concept of autism spectrum disorder (ASD) covering a range of levels and severities, and characterized by qualitative impairments in social interaction, communication, understanding and imagination.[3] The ASD is a complex lifelong developmental disability which impacts on all aspects of individual's life and on several public sectors (education,

[1] See Kanner (1943). Kanner used the expression 'infantile autism' to describe a psychiatric syndrome, characterized by disturbances of social relationships, limited use of language to communicate, and fixed repetitive interests and routines.

[2] See Asperger (1944). The article was translated into English only in 1991, see Frith (1991). Individuals with Asperger's syndrome have impairments in social interactions but with no significant language or cognitive development delay, nor lack of age-appropriate self-help skills. For these reasons, they may be well integrated in their community.

[3] See Wing and Gould (1979). Under the fifth edition of the American Psychiatric Association's Diagnostic and Statistical Manual of Mental Disorders (DSM-5) published in 2013, ASD is the only overarching diagnosis and Asperger's syndrome is no longer a separate label, see American Psychiatric Association (2013). Differently, under DSM-IV, patients could be diagnosed with four separate disorders: autistic disorder, Asperger's disorder, childhood disintegrative disorder, or pervasive developmental disorder not otherwise specified. The DSM-5 is the manual used in the United States (US) and Anglophone countries by clinicians and researchers to diagnose and classify mental disorders.

V. Della Fina (✉)
Institute for International Legal Studies of the Italian Research Council (ISGI-CNR), Rome, Italy
e-mail: valentina.dellafina@cnr.it

V. Della Fina, R. Cera (eds.), *Protecting the Rights of People with Autism in the Fields of Education and Employment*, DOI 10.1007/978-3-319-13791-9_3

health, welfare, justice[4] and others). The very nature of its pervasiveness makes the ASD different from other conditions. Indeed, ASD covers a broad group of disorders that share core deficits but with a wide range of differentiated degrees of disabilities and impairments.

The World Health Assembly, the plenary organ of the World Health Organization (WHO), in the Resolution WHA67.8 concerning 'autism' of 24 May 2014 has affirmed that 'autism spectrum disorders are developmental disorders and conditions that emerge in early childhood and, in most cases, persist throughout the lifespan and are marked by the presence of impaired development in social interaction and communication and a restricted repertoire of activity and interest, with or without accompanying intellectual and language disabilities; that manifestations of the disorder vary greatly in terms of combinations and levels of severity of symptoms'.[5]

Currently, ASD is the fastest-growing serious developmental disability in the United States (US) affecting 1 in every 68 children, while in the European Union (EU) 1 in every 150.

A number of studies indicate that behavioral and educational interventions, particularly those that begin in early childhood, lead to positive improvements in children with ASD with regard to behavioral problems, acquisition of new skills and greater social integration.[6] It is now accepted that the quality of life of individuals with ASD and their families are much enhanced when timely, appropriate and effective support is ensured, and adequate health, education, and social care services are provided.

In some countries these factors have contributed to make ASD an issue of public interest which has impacted on policies and laws. Legislation may play a key role in providing special support and services for individuals with ASD and their families, and in safeguarding autistic people from discrimination and social exclusion on the grounds of disability irrespective of the underlying impairments (whether physical, mental, intellectual or sensory). This role has also been recognized by the World Health Assembly in the above-mentioned Resolution on autism that recommended to Member States 'to develop or update and implement relevant policies, *legislation*, and *multisectoral plans*, supported by sufficient human, financial and technical

---

[4] See, for instance, the Bill introduced in the United Kingdom on 'Hate Crime (People with Learning Difficulties and Learning Disabilities) Act 2014'. The Bill requires police forces to register hate crimes committed against people with learning difficulties and learning disabilities, including autism.

[5] The Resolution was co-sponsored by more than 50 countries and supported by all WHO members, including the US. The Resolution, even if not legally binding, is relevant because WHO countries have underlined the importance of addressing autism and other developmental disorders in national policies and legislations, and have established a clear set of actions to be undertaken to support individuals, families and communities affected by them, see more at: http://www.autismspeaks.org/science/science-news/who-publishes-autism-resolution#sthash.DkJ099LS.dpuf. For all websites, last access 31 October 2014.

[6] See National Autistic Society for National Initiative for Autism: Screening and Assessment (NIASA) (2003), p. 89.

resources to address issues related to ASD and other developmental disorders, as part of a comprehensive approach to supporting all persons living with mental health issues or disabilities'.[7]

Similarly, the European Committee of Social Rights (ECSR) in the decision of September 2013 on the case *European Action of the Disabled (AEH) v. France* underlined that having regard to the definition of autism given by the WHO in the ICD-10,[8] autism is not as a temporary disease, which could therefore be cured, but is a disability which has stable and permanent nature. For the Committee such a nature affects the form of protection that States must accord to people with autism, in the specific case children or adolescents with autism 'must be educated in citizenship' and 'human assistance must be arranged for all or part of their schooling'.[9]

2 The Legal Recognition of Autism in National Laws

At domestic level, national laws protecting the rights of people with disabilities are the first sources of statutory obligations for States to guarantee fundamental rights of persons with ASD and provide them targeted services and support. However, from a legal point of view, the needs of persons with ASD are better satisfied if autism is recognized as a specific form of disability with lifelong impairments. Indeed, the inclusion of autism among the disability categories established by law may be a first step to reinforce the rights of people with autism in the domestic legal order.[10]

In the EU, some countries have included autism among the disabilities recognized by law.

In France the Law no. 96-1076 of 1996 amended the Law no. 75-535 of 1975 ('Disabled Persons Policy Act') by recognizing autism as a form of disability

[7] See para 1.2 (italic added).

[8] See ICD-10 Classification of Mental and Behavioural Disorders adopted by the World Health Organization (WHO) in 1993 (http://www.who.int/classifications/icd/en/GRNBOOK.pdf). The ICD-10, widely used in the European countries, is under revision. The French Federation of Psychiatry developed an alternative classification system the CFTMEA (Classification française des troubles mentaux de l'enfant et de l'adolescent), first released in 1983, and lastly updated in 2012. http://www.psychiatrie-francaise.com/Data/Documents/files/CFTMEA%20-%20R-2012.pdf.

[9] See para 80 of the decision.

[10] For the relevance of a normative definition of autism in the field of employment, see the chapter by M. Fasciglione, in this volume.

requiring a multidisciplinary taking care which must take into account the specific needs and difficulties of the person concerned regardless of the age.[11] The Law no. 2005-102 of 11 February 2005 'For equal rights and opportunities, for the participation and the citizenship of people with disabilities' does not mention autism but contains a legal definition of disability that reads as follows: 'a disability constitutes any activity limitation or participation restriction to life in society that a person may undergo in her/his environment, due to a significant, lasting or permanent alteration of one or more functions, be it physical, sensory, mental, cognitive or psychological, due to multiple disability or due to a disabling health condition'.[12] This notion has been criticized to be more restrictive compared with the WHO's definition according to which 'disability is the result of the interaction between individual characteristics and that of the environment' and the concept of disability enshrined in Article 1(2) of the Convention on the Rights of Persons with Disabilities (CRPD) of 2006 modeled on the human rights approach.[13] With regard to ASD, Autism France has proposed to include in the Law no. 2005-102 'autism and ASD as a specific disability' and to define the 'cognitive disability and its place within autism'.[14] The critical observations on the notion of disability in the Law no. 2005-102 and the proposal to introduce the concept of autism in the French legislation show the role that normative definitions may play in safeguarding the rights of people with ASD.

The relevance of a broader notion of disability that encompasses autism is also evidenced by the case of Northern Ireland. By the Disability Discrimination (Northern Ireland) Order 2006 and the Autism Act (Northern Ireland, NI) 2011

[11] 'Toute personne atteinte du handicap résultant du syndrome autistique et des troubles qui lui sont apparentés bénéficie, quel que soit son âge, d'une prise en charge pluridisciplinaire qui tient compte de ses besoins et difficultés spécifiques. Adaptée à l'état et à l'âge de la personne et eu égard aux moyens disponibles, cette prise en charge peut être d'ordre éducatif, pédagogique, thérapeutique et social', see the so called Loi Chossy 'Loi n. 96-1076 du 11 décembre 1996 modifiant la loi n. 75-535 du 30 juin 1975 *relative aux institutions sociales et médico-sociales et tendant à assurer une prise en charge adaptée de l'autisme'*.

[12] 'Constitue un handicap, au sens de la présente loi, toute limitation d'activité ou restriction de participa-tion à la vie en société subie dans son environnement par une personne en raison d'une altération substan-tielle, durable ou définitive d'une ou plusieurs fonctions physiques, sensorielles, mentales, *cognitives* ou psychiques, d'un polyhandicap ou d'un trouble de santé invalidant' (see Loi n. 2005-102 *pour l'égalité des droits et des chances, la participation et la citoyenneté des personnes handicapées* du 11 février 2005, JO n. 36 du 12 février 2005, p. 2353).

[13] The French concept of disability seems still to reflect a vision that burdens unequally the individual's impairment ('due to . . .an alteration of function'), even if it takes into account the various dimensions of disability (impairment, activity limitations, and social participation restrictions) and includes mental, cognitive or psychological conditions, see ANED (2009), p. 4. On the concept of disability in the CRPD see Sect. 3 in this chapter.

[14] See Autism France, Bilan de la loi de 2005 pour l'autisme. www.autisme-france.fr/offres/file_inline_src/577/577_P_21066_4.pdf. It is interesting to recall that also the ECSR in its decision on the merits of 4 November 2003 in the case *Autism-Europe v. France* pointed out 'the restrictive definition of autism used in French official documents' (submitted during the procedure) in relation to the definition of autism adopted by the WHO.

the Disability Discrimination Act (DDA) 1995 was amended in order to include ASD within the legal concept of disability. The DDA prohibits discrimination against disabled persons in a range of circumstances, including employment, transport, and the provision of goods, facilities and services. Only 'disabled persons', as defined in Section 1 of the DDA and associated schedules and regulations, are entitled to the protection provided under the Act. In particular, Section 1 of the DDA affirms: '(1) Subject to the provisions of Schedule 1, a person has a disability for the purposes of this Act if he has a physical or mental impairment[15] which has a substantial and long-term adverse effect on his ability to carry out normal day-to-day activities. (2) In this Act-disabled person means a person who has a disability'.

Schedule 1, para 4(1) of the DDA establishes that an impairment is to be taken to affect the ability of the person concerned to carry out normal day-to-day activities only if it affects one of the activities listed in the same paragraph. Social relations, which affect in particular people with ASD, were not included. For this reason, the Autism Act (NI) 2011 added in this list the following activities: (a) 'taking part in normal social interaction; or (b) forming social relationships'.

Through this amendment also social impairments have to be considered under the terms of the Act, allowing people with ASD to fall within the provisions of the DDA and appeal against a form of discrimination. This modification removed the ambiguity, originated by some case law, as to whether ASD could fall within the definition of disability contained in the DDA. The case of *Hewett v Motorola* decided by the United Kingdom Employment Appeal Tribunal in 2004 is particularly significant in this respect.[16]

The case involved a person whose Asperger's syndrome was not considered by an employment tribunal to fall within the definition of disability in the DDA 1995. For the Employment Tribunal of Bristol the Asperger's syndrome produced on Mr. Hewett adverse effects on his ability to participate in human interaction, social relationships and communication, 'however, those are not matters listed in paragraph 4 of schedule 1 DDA 1995 and therefore, not matters the tribunal is able to take into account. The tribunal does not find that the condition from which Mr. Hewett suffered had a substantial and long-term effect on his ability to carry out normal day-to-day activities by reference to those matters set out in paragraph 4 of Schedule 1 to the Act'.

Mr. Hewett appealed and the Appeal Tribunal concluded the following: 'We have not found this an easy case to determine as to whether this experienced

[15] The definition covers both physical and mental impairments. Physical impairments include those affecting the senses such as sight and hearing, heart disease, diabetes, epilepsy. Mental impairments include learning disabilities and mental ill health.

[16] *Hewett v Motorola* 2004, UKEAT/0526/03: http://www.bailii.org/uk/cases/UKEAT/2004/0526_03_1602.html. This is an appeal against a decision of an Employment Tribunal of Bristol of 29 April 2003. The appellant, employed as a Firmware Engineer, claimed to be unlawfully discriminated against in breach of section 5(1) of the DDA 1995 and that the respondents had failed to make reasonable adjustments to the employment arrangements, to provide training supervision and assistance, and to modify the procedures for assessment.

Chairman and Tribunal fell into error in their approach, but after considerable consideration, we are unanimously of the view that their approach to the concept of 'understanding' was at fault in failing to acknowledge that someone who has difficulty in understanding normal social interaction among people, and/or the subtleties of human non factual communication can be regarded as having their understanding affected and that concept is not limited simply to an ability to understand information knowledge or instructions... In conclusion, therefore, we are of the view that the Tribunal was in error in not accepting that the Appellant's ability to understand was affected by his impairment'.[17]

This case highlights the difficulties in defining the effects of the ASD under the terms of a disability legislation and the necessity to amend the DDA 1995 in order to broaden the scope of the definition of disability in a way which would encompass autism, and avoid the discretion of the courts regarding the interpretation of rules.[18] Also in the United States case law concerning judicial protection against discrimination in the workplace involving people with ASD shows the difficulties of courts to qualify 'social interaction' a 'major life activity' under the American Disability Act (ADA)[19] and to recognize autism as a disability for the purposes of the ADA.[20]

In addition to national disability legislations which include autism, definitions are also contained in specific acts and national plans or strategies on autism adopted by some European Member States.

The Autism Act (Northern Ireland) 2011, in the section 4(1) affirms that the term 'autism' comprehends 'autism, Asperger's syndrome, Rett's syndrome, Heller's syndrome or any pervasive developmental disorder not otherwise specified'. The definition is consistent with the ICD-10 classification of Pervasive Developmental Disorders (PDDs-F84) and is broaden enough to facilitate access to services and support provided in the Northern Ireland Autism Strategy (2013–2020). The Autistic Spectrum Disorder (ASD) Strategic Action Plan for Wales (2008–2018) also contains the concept of ASD which conforms with the ICD-10. According to this definition 'the term ASD is used to describe the group of PDDs characterized by qualitative abnormalities in reciprocal social interactions and in patterns of communication and by a restricted, stereotyped, repetitive repertoire of interests and activities'.[21] The ASD Strategic Action Plan specifies that there are a number of

---

[17] See paras 24 and 25 of the judgment.

[18] See also the case of Ireland, the Autism Bill 2012 provides an amendment of the notion of disability contained in the Employment Equality Act 1998 and in the Equal Status Act 2000 in order to include autism.

[19] To be entitled of the ADA judicial protection a person must be found to have 'a physical or mental impairment that substantially limits one or more major life activities of such individual'. For the definition of disability as emended in 2008, see ADA Amendments Act of 2008, PL 110-325 (S 3406), 25 September 2008. http://www.eeoc.gov/laws/statutes/adaaa.cfm.

[20] *Morgenthal v. AT&T*, No. 97 Civ. 6443 (DAB), 1999 U.S. Dist. LEXIS 4294, at 8 (S.D.N.Y. Apr. 5, 1999) cited in Caruso (2010), note 192.

[21] See Chapter 2 of the Strategic Action Plan. http://wales.gov.uk/strategy/strategies/autism/asdplane.pdf?lang=en.

definitions of autism but the Welsh Assembly Government for the purpose of the Plan has adopted that of the WHO as 'the use of the terminology of ASD denotes the fact that there are a number of subgroups within the spectrum of autism'. The Danish National Autism Plan (2008) affirms that 'ASD is a term used to denote the problems known as PDDs and which include highly differentiated levels of reduced social, verbal and intellectual functional abilities. People with ASD may have other disorders or conditions. This is known as comorbidity and may require special treatment, e.g. medical'.[22] In the Hungarian National Autism Strategy (2008–2013), autism is defined as 'a neurological development disorder which is the result of the permanent disorder of the central nervous system and/or a complex behavioural syndrome characterised by behavioural and developmental differences. It is a lifelong disorder and the basic disorder cannot be influenced by treatment according to our present knowledge'.[23] The Scottish Strategy for Autism (2011) refers to 'autism' as 'a lifelong developmental disorder more commonly referred to as autism spectrum disorder (ASD) but also known as autism spectrum condition (ASC). ASD affects people differently with some individuals being able to live independently. Others will need very specialist support'.[24] Finally, with regard to England, it is interesting to observe that in the Autism Act 2009 the definition of ASD has not been included because 'As research and experience refines the understanding of autism, so the range of characteristics will change'. Nevertheless, 'the intention is that definitional issues will be dealt with in the autism strategy, which, as it has to be kept under continual review, will allow for changes to be made much more quickly in response to new developments than if the definition were to be included in primary legislation'.[25] Then, the 2010 Strategy specified that the term 'autism', in line with the approach to terminology adopted by key autism representative organisations, was used as an umbrella term for all conditions (autistic spectrum disorder, autistic spectrum condition, autistic spectrum difference and neuro-diversity), including Asperger syndrome.[26]

Outside the EU, the Individuals with Disabilities Education Act (IDEA) of 2004, the US federal education law on special services for children with disability, contains the definition of 'autism' that reads as follows: '(i) Autism means a developmental disability significantly affecting verbal and nonverbal

[22] See National Autism Plan-a summary (2008), p. 6.

[23] See Hungarian National Autism Strategy, Annexes I. The Strategy further specifies the triad of autism and its characteristics.

[24] See Scottish Strategy for Autism, p. 7.

[25] See Autism Act 2009, Explanatory Notes. http://www.legislation.gov.uk/ukpga/2009/15/notes/division/5/1. As for the United Kingdom it is important to recall that the concept of 'impairments' contained in the Equality Act 2010 includes ASD as specified in the 'Equality Act 2010, Guidance on matters to be taken into account in determining questions relating to the definition of disability', p. 9.

[26] The updated Strategy for adults with autism in England (2014) affirms that the term 'autism' is used to refer to 'all diagnoses on the autism spectrum, including Asperger syndrome, high functioning autism, Kanner or classic autism' (Appendix A).

communication and social interaction, generally evident before age three, that adversely affects a child's educational performance. Other characteristics often associated with autism are engagement in repetitive activities and stereotyped movements, resistance to environmental change or change in daily routines, and unusual responses to sensory experiences. (ii) Autism does not apply if a child's educational performance is adversely affected primarily because the child has an emotional disturbance, as defined in paragraph (c)(4) of this section. (iii) A child who manifests the characteristics of autism after age three could be identified as having autism if the criteria in paragraph (c)(1)(i) of this section are satisfied'.[27]

In order to receive special education and related services children with autism must meet requirements under the IDEA and States' definition of the term autism, not always coincident with the federal one.[28]

3 Protecting the Rights of People with Autism Through Specific Legislations and the Role of the CRPD

In 1996, the European Parliament adopted, in the form of a written declaration, the Charter for Persons with Autism which states that people with autism should have the same rights enjoyed by all EU citizens, where such be appropriate and in the best interest of the person with autism, and that these rights should be enhanced, protected and enforced by appropriate legislation in each State.[29] The Charter recommended that diagnostic services, individualized education, family support, housing, vocational training and lifelong care should have been adequately addressed and appropriate services provided at domestic level.

After 18 years of the Charter's adoption, the protection of the rights of people with ASD within the EU Member States is far from being uniform and satisfying. Among the European countries substantial differences exist with regard to the legal framework in favour of persons with ASD revealing that only a short number of countries has implemented the recommendations of the European Parliament.

---

[27] See Public Law 108-446. Autism was added to the IDEA in 1991, see Caruso (2010), p. 52.

[28] For the purposes of special education services, States have adopted national definition of autism. See, for instance, the Nebraska State Definition of Autism, Rule 51 (92 NAC 51.006) contained in the Nebraska state plan for autism spectrum disorders, revised January 2013 http://www.mindbank.info/item/3935. For up-date data on the percentage of population with autism by year and age group under IDEA and the national projects addressed to children with autism in the US, see the 35th Annual Report to Congress on the Implementation of the Individuals with Disabilities Education Act, 2013. http://www2.ed.gov/about/reports/annual/osep/2013/parts-b-c/35th-idea-arc.pdf.

[29] The Charter was proposed by Autism-Europe that presented it at its 4th Congress (Den Haag, 10 May 1992).

Indeed, only few European countries have developed specific autism legislation or national autism plans and strategies,[30] while some EU Member States have adopted *ad hoc* measures in favor of people with ASD in sectoral laws above all relating to education,[31] health and social care. In general, sectoral laws are more limited in scope than autism plans, for at least a couple of reasons: firstly, they focus only on a specific group of persons with ASD (children, young people or adults); secondly, they address the needs of people with autism only in determinate fields (i.e. education, health and others) even if of great impact on their lives, their families or carers. However, when these laws combine with national autism plans, the domestic legal framework for the protection of people with ASD is more complete and extensive, meeting the needs of a wider range of persons and producing positive effects at domestic level in terms of their inclusion in the society.

As it was rightly observed, 'the post-modern concept of neuro-diversity, with its promise of inclusion and its philosophical acceptance of variation, may find in autism a perfect home'.[32] The full inclusion and participation of disabled persons in the society, including people with autism, is the cornerstone of the human rights approach to disability enshrined in the CRPD. The Convention marks the passage from a medical model of disability to a social one, recognizing that disability is an evolving concept resulting from the 'interaction between persons with impairments and attitudinal and environmental barriers that hinders their full and effective participation in society on an equal basis with others'.[33] In its articles, the CRPD establishes the human rights and fundamental freedoms of persons with disabilities whose fully enjoyment must be guaranteed without discrimination in order to remove all the barriers that obstacle their participation as equal members of society. In the Preamble, States parties recognize, among others, 'the need to promote and protect the human rights of all persons with disabilities, including those who require *more intensive support*',[34] such as people with ASD who need lifelong services and support.

Indeed, the CRPD is an international instrument that may contribute at the domestic level to the reinforcement of the rights of people with disabilities, including those of individuals with ASD. Its legal relevance in the field of autism has been also underlined by the World Health Assembly that, in the Resolution on autism of May 2014, has recalled the CRPD, together with the Universal Declaration of Human Rights of 1948, the United Nations General Assembly (UNGA) resolution 62/139 declaring 2 April as World Autism Awareness Day and the UNGA Resolution 67/82 on addressing the socioeconomic needs of individuals,

---

[30] See Sect. 4 in this chapter.

[31] See the chapter by R. Cera, in this volume.

[32] See Caruso (2010), p. 9.

[33] On the concept of disability in the CRPD see, among others, Della Fina (2010), pp. 17 ff.

[34] Italic added.

families and societies affected by autism spectrum disorders, developmental disorders and associated disabilities.

The role of the CRPD in ensuring the protection of the rights of persons with ASD and their social inclusion in domestic legal orders is confirmed by some best practices concerning EU Member States. In this context, it is worth mentioning the Northern Ireland Autism Strategy (2013–2020) and Action Plan (2013–2016) which have been expressly developed in accordance with the CRPD to support the values of dignity, respect, independence, choice, equality and anti-discrimination for people with autism, their families and carers. The provisions of the Convention have informed the issues, the strategic priorities and the actions provided in the Strategy and in the Action Plan.[35] Another relevant case is the Danish National Autism Plan (2008) which recalls the CRPD, pointing out that the Convention requires States parties to set up guidelines and action plans to ensure that people with functional disabilities, such as ASD, are not put in a position of disadvantage regarding their participation in society.

At the national level the CRPD implementation may therefore strengthen the human rights of people with ASD through the adoption of specific laws or plans which should take into account the fundamental rights of persons with disabilities enshrined in the Convention. This aspect may result particularly relevant in the framework of the EU, considering that the Union and most of its Member States ratified the CRPD.[36] In order to achieve an effective implementation of the Convention, the EU adopted the 'European Disability Strategy 2010-2020: A Renewed Commitment to a Barrier-Free Europe'[37] focused on eight main areas of action (accessibility, participation, equality, employment, education and training, social protection, health, and external action) having great impact also on the life of people with ASD. The EU Strategy identifies actions at EU level to supplement the national ones with the aim to empower people with disabilities so that they can enjoy their rights, and benefit fully from participating in society and in the European economy.

---

[35] See Sects. 6 and 7.

[36] For the EU see Council Decision 2010/48/EC *concerning the conclusion, by the European Community, of the United Nations Convention on the Rights of Persons with Disabilities* of 26 November 2009, O.J. L 23/35. As of 31 October 2014, Finland, Ireland, and Netherlands did not ratify the CRPD.

[37] COM(2010) 636 final, Brussels, 15.11.2010.

4 National Autism Plans and Strategies in the EU Member States

In the EU context, autism plans and strategies have been adopted only by few States namely Bulgaria, France, Denmark, Hungary, and within the United Kingdom, England, Wales, Northern Ireland and Scotland.[38] All these plans have a legal basis in so far they are provided in a legal act or have been adopted on the initiative of a Government or a department.[39]

One of the first European countries to adopt rules in favour of people with autism is France. French government has started regulating autism since the mid-1990s by a series of acts of different legal nature.[40] Following the enactment of the Law no. 2005-102 of February 2005 and the interministerial circular of 8 March 2005 on the Policy for taking care of persons with autism and PDDs,[41] France adopted its first Autism Plan for the period 2005–2007. Later, two additional plans are followed: the Autism Plan 2008–2010 and the third Plan covering the years 2013–2017.

In Denmark, *the National Autism Plan* (*NAP*) was first published in 2006, only in Danish, as a guide for the new municipalities. In 2007, following the reform and the merger of the municipalities the responsibility to establish and run services for people with ASD was assigned to them.[42] Some municipalities started to base their

---

[38] In 2008, the Dutch Government requested a report on ASD to the Health Council of the Netherlands which was published in 2009 with the title 'Autism spectrum disorders: a lifetime of difference' (http://www.gezondheidsraad.nl/en/publications/healthcare/autism-spectrum-disorders-lifetime-difference). On the contents of these plans and strategies in the fields of education and employment see Sects. 6 and 7.

[39] Under this aspect, the autism plans and strategies examined differ from those prepared by autism representative organisations. These latter may be an input for policy makers and a useful tool to identify priorities and objectives to be realized at domestic level but they have not a legal status, except in the case they are adopted by a government.

[40] See the interministerial circular of 27 April 1995 concerning therapeutic, pedagogical, and educational care, and social inclusions of children, adolescents, and adults with autism (circulaire AS/EN n. 95-12 du 27 avril 1995 *relative à la prise en charge thérapeutique, pédagogique et é ducative et à l'insertion sociale des enfants, adolescents et adultes atteints d'un syndrome autistique*); the Law no. 96-1076 which has recognized autism as a form of disability; the Circulaire DAS/TSIS n. 98-232 du 10 avril 1998 *relative à la formation continue et à l'adaptation à l'emploi des personnels intervenant auprès des enfants et adultes présentant un syndrome autistique*. Other relevant provisions concerning the right to education for people with autism are contained in the Code of Social Welfare Action and in the Education Code.

[41] See Circulaire interministerielle n. DGAS/DGS/DHOS/3C/2005/124 du 8 mars 2005 *relative à la politique de prise en charge des personnes atteintes d'autisme et de troubles envahissants du dé veloppement* (*TED*).

[42] Administratively, Denmark is divided into 5 regions and 98 municipality areas. Municipalities are charged with the treatment of and support for people with ASD. The municipalities must maintain and develop an organisation that, in case of suspected ASD, ensures the primary examination, assessment of development and diagnostic considerations. The regions are responsible for specialized assessment of children and young people.

autism policy on the NAP which was published in English as a shorter guide in 2008.[43] The Plan is the result of a collaboration between the National Board of Social Services under the Ministry of Social Affairs, Children and Integration,[44] and autism representative organizations, such as the Danish Autism Society. The NAP adopts a lifelong approach, providing guidelines for best practices in diagnosis, care and treatment for people with autism in all stages of life from children to the elderly.[45]

In Hungary the 5-year *National Autism Strategy* (2008–2013) was commissioned by the Ministry of Social Affairs and Labour and prepared by experts under the supervision of the Hungarian Autistic Society.[46] The Strategy was provided in Section IV/3 of the Government Decree no. 1067/2007 on the implementation of the National Programme of Disability Affairs and the medium term implementation schedule for the period 2007–2010. The purpose of the Strategy is to improve care for persons with ASD by developing specific services, including those in the fields of education, training and employment.

An advanced legal regime in favour of people with ASD, mainly focused on adults, has been developed in England. The Autism Act 2009 is the first autism specific legislation adopted in Europe. The Act is the legal basis of the *Fulfilling and rewarding lives: the strategy for adults with autism in England* of March 2010 and its updated version of April 2014 (called *Think Autism*), and its guidance, *Implementing fulfilling and rewarding lives: statutory guidance for local authorities and NHS organisations to support implementation of the autism strategy* of December 2010, currently under public consultation.[47] The Autism Act 2009 specified the statutory duty to prepare and publish the Strategy to meet 'the needs of adults[48] with autistic spectrum conditions by improving the provision of relevant services by local authorities, National Health Service (NHS) bodies and NHS foundation trusts' (Section 1).

Within the United Kingdom plans to improve services for people with autism have been developed in Wales, Northern Ireland and Scotland. The Welsh

---

[43] Since the publication of the original six NAP reports in Danish, requests for a shorter version in English have been posed, also to share knowledge and experiences internationally, see Danish National Centre for Autism and the National Board of Social Services (2008).

[44] The National Board of Social Services is charged with ensuring that social and welfare initiatives are put into practice by local authorities, including those addressed to persons with disabilities (http://www.socialstyrelsen.dk/om-os/about-us).

[45] http://www.autismeurope.org/files/files/link-autism-56-en-lowres.pdf.

[46] The English translation of the Hungarian Autism Strategy is published in Autism-Europe (2009). Currently the Strategy is under revision.

[47] The revised guidance should be published at the end of 2014 after the public 'consultation on new statutory guidance for local authorities and NHS organisations to support implementation of the Adult Autism Strategy for England' https://www.gov.uk/government/uploads/system/uploads/attachment_data/file/371869/Autism_Statutory_Guidance_Consultation_Draft_Guidance.pdf.

[48] The Act extends to (that is, forms part of the law of) England and Wales, but applies only in relation to England. Section 4(1) of the Act specifies that 'adult' means a person who is aged 18 or over (and, accordingly, 'child' means a person who is under the age of 18).

Assembly Government adopted the *Autistic Spectrum Disorder Strategic Action Plan for Wales* (2008–2018) which sets out specific and measurable actions during a period of 10 years to improve services for children, young people and adults with ASD. The overall objective is 'to set the direction to improve the commissioning and delivery of services so that individuals with ASD are supported to reach their full potential in all aspects of their lives whatever their age, wherever they live, whatever their gender, social or ethnic background'. As for Northern Ireland, on 26 June 2008 the Health Minister announced his intention to develop a Strategic Action Plan for ASD Services across the nation. Consultation on the draft Strategic Action Plan closed on 12 December 2008 with a positive response. The *ASD Strategic Action Plan* (2009–2011) was published in 2009 covering a broad range of actions aimed at improving health and social care services to meet the need for children, adolescents and adults with ASD, their families and carers.[49] The Action Plan provided for an ongoing monitoring by the Health and Social Care Board and an evaluation to ensure effective implementation and to inform the need for any future resource allocation from 2011/2012 onwards.[50] In 2011 the Autism Act (Northern Ireland) was enacted, providing the statutory obligation to develop a strategy for autism not less than two years after the passing of the Act.[51] In 2013 the Autism Strategy (2013–2020) and Action Plan (2013–2016) were adopted. In Scotland the 10-year *Scottish Strategy for Autism*, published in 2011, addresses the entire autism spectrum and the whole lifespan of people living with ASD. The vision at the basis of the Strategy 'is that individuals on the autism spectrum are respected, accepted and valued by their communities and have confidence in services to treat them fairly so that they are able to have meaningful and satisfying lives'.[52]

As for Bulgaria, in 2012–2013 the Ministry of Health prepared a document titled 'Measures to improve care for helping people with autism and ASD, and their families' based on an analysis of existing legislation, policies and services for persons with autism. In August 2013 this document was approved by the Minister of Health and is considered a sort of national autism plan. Main priorities of the plan

[49] Department of Health, Social Services and Public Safety, Autism Spectrum Disorder (ASD) Strategic Action Plan 2008/09–2010/11, June 2009. http://www.dhsspsni.gov.uk/asd_strategic_action_plan.pdf. In April 2009 also the multidisciplinary Regional ASD Network Group charged with the implementation of the ASD Strategic Action Plan started working in coordination of Local Health and Social Care Trust (HSCT) ASD networks.

[50] The Action Plan follows the publication of a series of documents including the Independent Review of Autism Services, the recommendations of the Bamford Review relating to ASD and its Equal Lives Report, and other local, national and international work, see Autism Spectrum Disorder (ASD) Strategic Action Plan 2008/09–2010/11, DHSSPS, June 2009, p. 10. Cf. Kelly et al. (2007) and Maginnis (2008).

[51] The Autism Act (NI) 2011, which received Royal Assent on 9 May 2011, came into operation on 9 August 2011.

[52] The Strategy was developed by the Scottish Government working in partnership with the Convention of Scottish Local Authorities (COSLA), the two national autism organisations, and a wide range of stakeholders.

are: early diagnosis and detection of ASD in the primary outpatient care units; early intervention; providing comprehensive and integrated community services, including education; application of modern therapeutic methods; personnel training and training programs; measures for employment; raising awareness about autism among professionals and the public. The scheduled activities are implemented through an inter-institutional interaction, in partnership with associations of the sector and the involvement of people with ASD and their families. The plan, covering the years 2013–2016, provides mechanisms for its coordination and monitoring.[53]

It is also worth mentioning the case of Ireland where the Autism Bill 2012 was introduced in the Dáil Éireann (the Assembly of Ireland), with the aim to place a statutory obligation on the Government to adopt an autism strategy to meet the needs of adults with ASD in the accessibility to services, employment and social inclusion, and the needs of families and carers by setting out a clear directive towards family support service development. The Bill proposes a system of accountability and scrutiny relating to ASD service provision, an autism awareness campaign, including an information website, poster campaign, media strategy, and the provision of autism awareness training for all professionals who frequently deal with adults with autism. The Bill also states that the autism strategy shall be published not less than two years after the passing of the Act.[54]

Also in Italy a kind of autism plan called ‘Progetto nazionale autismo’, to be developed at national and regional levels, has been proposed by a national working table on autism set up in 2007 by the Ministry of Health (‘Tavolo nazionale di lavoro sull’autismo’), but to date it has not yet been adopted.[55]

Remaining in the European context, Autism-Europe and other associations[56] have also proposed a European Strategy for Autism in consideration of the increas-

---

[53] A translated text of the plan is not available. The information has been taken from the Bulgarian Ministry of Health, National Center for Public Health and Analyses. http://hph-bg.ncphp.government.bg/en/mejd-d-t-2/1020-southeast-european-autism-network,-sean.html.

[54] See ‘Proposed Bill provides for first national strategy on autism’. http://www.thejournal.ie/autism-bill-ireland-823778-Mar2013/. As of 31 October 2014, the Bill was not passed. The Cabinet Committee on Social Policy, together with Government Departments and the National Disability Authority (NDA), are examining the issues arising from the Bill to ensure that the proposals dovetail appropriately with the actions in favour of people with ASD undertaken under the National Disability Strategy, see Statement from Dr. James Reilly, T.D., Minister for Health on World Autism Awareness Day April 2nd, 2014. http://www.merrionstreet.ie/index.php/2014/04/statement-from-dr-james-reilly-t-d-minister-for-health-on-world-autism-awareness-day-april-2nd-2014/.

[55] For Italy see the chapter by L. Chiappetta Cajola, in this volume.

[56] On 6 November 2012, Autism-Europe organized the seminar ‘Towards an Autism Strategy for Europe’ at the European Parliament to present successful national strategies for autism and discuss the possibility of a Europe-wide strategy for autism. http://www.autismrpphub.org/sites/default/files/resources/brussels6novreport_jan2013.pdf.

ing incidence of people diagnosed with autism in the continent and the need to coordinate policy approaches at national and European levels.[57] According to the proponents, the European Strategy for Autism should identify the most urgent needs to be met for people with autism (such as diagnosis, early interventions, and research) and enshrine the fundamental human rights of the persons with ASD in conformity with the CRPD.

In this regard it is important to underline that the EC adopted the European Strategy for Disability 2010–2020 in the form of a communication to the European Parliament, the Council, the European Economic and Social Committee, and the Committee of the Regions.[58] The European Autism Strategy could follow this precedent for recommending to EU Members States a set of domestic actions to address the needs of people with ASD. From this point of view, a European Autism Strategy may be a useful instrument to enhance the protection of persons with ASD within the EU and the domestic legal orders.

5 National Autism Plans Adopted Outside the EU

In the last years, also outside the EU autism plans have been developed. The cases of the US, Canada and Australia are worth mentioning.

In the US, a federal autism legislation has been developed to regulate relevant fields that impact on the life of people with ASD and their families, such as health, social care, education, research, screening, and treatment.[59] In 2009, the Interagency Autism Coordinating Committee (IACC), a federal government advisory panel, has released the Strategic Plan for Autism Spectrum Disorder Research

[57] The European Commission (EC) has specifically included ASD in its public-health work plans since 2005, but the EC actions are mainly focused on providing information on autism, defining indicators and coordinating public health research. http://ec.europa.eu/health/major_chronic_diseases/diseases/autistic/index_en.htm.

[58] The communications, as it is known, are not legally binding and usually contain action plans or legislative proposals.

[59] In these last fields, the US legislation may be considered an example of good practice. The Children's Health Act of 2000 (Health Act) explicitly identified autism as a major target of research (Public Law 106-310 Sec. 1004 (2000), Division A, Title I). Then, the Combating Autism Act of 2006, signed by President Bush on 19 December 2006, expanded the activities related to autism research, surveillance, prevention, screening, early detection and intervention, and treatment, with a funding of about 1 billion dollars over five years for ASD. The Combating Autism Act of 2011, signed into law by President Obama on 20 September 2011 (Public Law 112–132), ensured that the programs established under the Combating Autism Act of 2006 continued for an additional three years, authorizing 693 million dollars federal investment in autism research, treatment and services through fiscal year 2014. Lastly, the Autism Collaboration, Accountability, Research, Education and Support (CARES) Act of 2014, signed by President Obama on 8 August 2014, has authorized 1.3 billion dollars for fiscal years 2015–2019 to fund ASD research, services and support activities (Public Law 113–157).

containing recommendations to federal agencies and Congress on needs and opportunities to improve research in the field of autism.[60]

The US Government funds States to develop autism plans to improve services, as well as investing in research, public awareness, and expanding training programs for health professionals.[61] In conformity with federal legislation, national autism plans have been adopted, among others, by Michigan, Nebraska and Texas. In Michigan, the *ASD State Plan* was published in 2012 with the purpose to identify best practice in supporting individuals with ASD of all ages, review practice across key priorities areas, identify gaps, and make recommendations for improving services and outcomes for individuals with ASD and their families.[62] The ultimate goal of the Plan is to create a solid understanding of the needs of all individuals with ASD, from birth through adulthood, in order to identify, access, and coordinate resources. Among the key priorities areas of the Plan are education and training, and under the focus area 'Adult Supports and Services' employment is considered a tool to include adults with ASD in society.[63]

The *ASD Nebraska State Plan*, published in 2000 and revised in 2013, is limited to the field of education and has the objective to inform education personnel, administrators, parents, educators, and other professionals, on services provided by the Nebraska ASD Network. This latter has been developed by the Nebraska Department of Education to provide consultation, training and technical assistance to local school districts, educational service units and parents of children with ASD.[64] The *Texas State Plan for Individuals with ASD* (2010–2014) was adopted by the Texas Council on Autism and PDDs in 2010.[65] The State Plan has the purpose to create a statewide infrastructure that promotes the coordination of research and the delivery of timely, appropriate and cost-efficient services to people

[60] http://iacc.hhs.gov/strategic-plan/2009/index.shtml.

[61] http://www.hhs.gov/autism/factsheet_autism_support.html.

[62] Key priorities areas are: infrastructure-system, service, and resource coordination; family engagement and involvement; early identification and intervention services; educational supports and services; adult supports and services; physical, mental, and behavioral health care; training and professional development. http://www.michigan.gov/documents/autism/ASDStatePlan_2_19_13_Final_414143_7.pdf.

[63] The Plan recommends to give people with ASD access to a variety of employment opportunities, including supported, competitive and customized employments (see the Plan, p. 42).

[64] Nebraska school districts must assure that all children with ASD have a free and appropriate public education (FAPE) under IDEA, which includes special education and related services that meets their unique needs. In 2002, five ASD Regions were established across Nebraska to provide support for schools and families impacted by ASD.

[65] The Texas Council on Autism and Pervasive Developmental Disorders (TCAPDD) was established by legislation in 1987 adding the Chapter 114 to the Human Resources Code (Interagency Council on Autism and Pervasive Developmental Disorders Act of 1987). Its mission is to advise and make recommendations to State agencies to ensure that the needs of persons of all ages with autism and other PDDs and their families are addressed and that all available resources are coordinated to meet those needs.

with ASD.[66] The Plan follows a practical approach and is structured under four goals: (1) services to children to age 5; (2) services to individuals ages 6–22; (3) services to individuals age 23 and older; and (4) research and statewide infrastructure. For each goal specific objectives and strategies are identified, including those in the fields of education and employment.

In Canada individual members of the Senate requested an enquiry on federal funding for ASD treatment and the need for a national ASD strategy at federal level. In the final report of the enquiry published in 2007, the Standing Senate Committee on Social Affairs, Science and Technology recommended that 'The federal government, in collaboration with the provinces and territories, establish a comprehensive National ASD Strategy; all stakeholders, including individuals with autism, be consulted on the components that should be part of the Strategy, such as treatment, research, surveillance, awareness campaigns, community initiatives, education, respite care for families, etc.; and, the Strategy include child, adolescent and adult treatments and supports'.[67]

After the publication of the Report also Autism Society Canada, together with other associations, asked the Federal Government to build a National Autism Strategy in order to provide minimum standards such as: establish a national surveillance mechanism to effectively track individuals with ASD; define minimum standards of service and treatments and professionals across the country to ensure equal access to services across Canada; promote autism awareness through a national awareness campaign targeted at individuals, health care professionals, and first responders (fire, ambulance, and others).[68]

A federal ASD Strategy has not yet been adopted, but since Canadian provincial and territorial governments are responsible for delivering health and social services within their respective jurisdictions, some provinces have developed autism plans. These are the cases of the *Nova Scotia ASD Action Plan* (2011) and the *Manitoba five-year Plan to help Manitobans with ASD and their families* (2011). In April 2011, Nova Scotia adopted the Plan designed to support children, youth and adults with ASD and their families through a phased-in approach. The Plan is focused on five key areas: (1) intervention and support services for families with preschool children diagnosed with ASD; (2) supports for school-aged children with a diagnosis of ASD; (3) supports for adults with ASD and their families; (4) skills training and awareness; and (5) partnerships to support programming and services.

[66] The State Plan was reviewed and approved by the Texas Council on Autism, its ex-officio state agency members and Regional Advisory Task Force in 2010.

[67] See Standing Senate Committee on Social Affairs, Science and Technology (2007), point I of the Final Report.

[68] See 'Collective Voice of the Autism Community in Canada Calls on Government to Take Steps to Establish National Autism Strategy' (Ottawa, Ontario, Nov. 5, 2007). Autism Society Canada is a national umbrella organization of provincial and territorial societies and has proposed to collaborate with the Federal Government to outline a National Autism Strategy. http://www.parl.gc.ca/Content/HOC/Committee/411/FINA/WebDoc/WD5138047/411_FINA_PBC2011_Briefs%5CAutism%20Society%20Canada%20E.html; http://www.autismsocietycanada.ca/.

Furthermore, the Plan has provided a funding of 4 million Canadian dollars for intervention and support services in the field of education.[69] The Manitoba ASD Plan, launched by the Manitoba government in June 2011 for a period of five years, is focused on support and services for children with ASD and their families. It also provides services for young people and adults in order to ensure them access to education and employment training programmes, promote opportunities for developing life skills, help to find and keep jobs, and live independently.[70]

Also in Australia the Federal Government has adopted specific autism legislation providing public resources to fund initiatives in support of children with ASD and their families.[71] Currently, each State has developed its own legislation including, in some cases, autism national plans. The Victorian Government committed to outline an Autism State Plan during the State election in 2006. In that occasion, with *Addressing Disadvantage*, the Victorian Government undertook to 'develop an Autism State Plan in partnership with Autism Victoria, to build new and better approaches across government for meeting the growing and complex needs of people with autism and ASD'.[72] In 2009, the Victorian Government adopted an Autism State Plan, in recognition that ASDs are becoming more prevalent and demand on services and support is growing, and that ASDs have particular features that distinguish them from other conditions. The Plan identified six priority areas for the next ten years to be addressed in short, medium, and longer term Plan's implementation: (1) make it easier to get support; (2) strengthen the ASD expertise of the workforce; (3) extend and link key services and supports especially during transition; (4) enhance and provide appropriate educational opportunities; (5) facilitate successful participation in the community; and (6) develop a robust evidence base about ASD.[73] In 2013, the Government also issued the Victorian State Disability Plan (2013–2016) in which one of the strategies provides better support for people with ASD.[74] Also the Queensland Government announced the intention to develop an autism plan but, at the current stage, it has not been released.[75]

---

[69] See Autism Spectrum Disorder Action Plan. Progress Report-Spring 2012. http://www.ednet.ns.ca/files/reports/Autism_Report_final.pdf.

[70] See Thrive! A 5-year Plan for helping Manitobans with autism spectrum disorder and their families. The text is available in the website of the Plan http://www.gov.mb.ca/fs/thrive/.

[71] For a synthesis of autism federal initiatives, see Roth (2013). Concerning services and support to people with ASD and their families in Australia, see O'Reilly and Wicks (2013).

[72] See Autism State Plan, May 2009, p. 9.

[73] The Plan was developed after a statewide consultation undertaken in October and November 2007.

[74] http://www.dhs.vic.gov.au/__data/assets/pdf_file/0009/749862/Victorian-state-disability-plan-2013-2016-180113.pdf.

[75] See Roth (2013), p. 25.

6 National Autism Plans and Strategies in the EU Member States: Actions and Services in the Field of Education

From the consultation processes preceding the adoption of the national autism plans and strategies it is emerged that people with ASD face a variety of common challenges for accessing services arising across a wide range of fields, including education and employment. For their relevance in terms of inclusion of autistic people in society such sectors are priority areas in all national autism plans and strategies, although it is evident that actions and services to address the needs of people with ASD differ depending on the domestic legal order and the existing network of social, health, and educational services in each Member State. It is therefore necessary to analyze each autism plan and strategy in order to identify good practices.

The autism plans and strategies will be examined according to the chronological order of adoption.[76]

6.1 Denmark

The *Danish NAP* of 2008 contains a series of recommendations to municipalities to meet the needs of people with ASD during their lifetime. The approach followed is based on the respect of human rights of persons with ASD as enshrined in the CRPD ratified by Denmark in 2007, in particular the right to inclusion and participation in society that should be guaranteed through adequate services. The NAP recognizes that efforts for people with ASD should be based on the fundamental respect for the individual and, in the case of relatively high functioning people with ASD, personalized support in relation to employment and education.

The needs of people with ASD changes during lifetime, for this reason the NAP identifies the following phases: preschool age, 0–6 years old; school age, 6–17 years old; youth, 15–35 years old; adult life, 20–65 years old; and old age, from 60 years old. For each phase, recommendations are given.

With regard to children with ASD before the age of 6, the NAP emphasizes that they often have quite severe difficulties and need a substantial support. The pedagogical efforts are therefore based on specialized services, in the form of specialized day-care institutions, special groups in the framework of the day-care or individual support in a normal day-care institution. In these cases, the NAP recommends early interventions to be initiated as soon as possible after ASD has been identified. In recognizing that to date there is no documentation concerning a particular form of treatment or method that is more effective than others, the Plan recommends a structured pedagogical, learning and behaviour oriented approach.

[76] The chronological order will be also used in Sect. 7 in this chapter. The Bulgarian plan has not been examined because a translated text in English or French was not available at the time of writing.

Interventions should be intensive with an individually organized specialist-pedagogical effort on a daily basis and an important role of family. According to the NAP, counseling in the home and courses on ASD should be offered to the parents and the family should be an important partner for the municipality. In the evaluation of the child's need for support the NAP requires to take into account the child's functional level, while all interventions for preschool should be carried out only by professionals with specific knowledge of autism.[77]

As for school age, the NAP outlines that the number of children with ASD is significantly higher in the later school years than during the early years of schooling because most children are not diagnosed until they reach school. At the same time, the school age is the phase of life in which the need for support varies more.[78] For these reasons, the NAP recommends that many different types of services should be made available for children with ASD, both in the framework of school, spare time, respite care and residential homes, and that services should be highly individualized and specifically adapted. The NAP gives a series of detailed advices on the methods to follow concerning the relationship with autistic children, pointing out that all pedagogical efforts should be based on the understanding of the cognitive nature of the functional disability and attention should be paid to the development of independence in all regards.

Concerning youth, the NAP specifies that is a phase of life during which a person usually develops his/her identity and gains independence, but a high number of people with ASD never achieve these objectives. However, also for persons with autism youth often represents a period of changes (i.e. changing in daily activities from school to work or day-initiatives, education at all levels) and for these reasons the NAP recommends to ensure to young people with ASD the necessary support to be evaluated on the basis of the individual's functional level. A mentor or a support/contact person (often parents) may represent the right way to compensate the difficulties young people with ASD encounter in this phase of life. As for education, the Plan requires that young people with ASD should have the possibility of a flexible course of education, regarding both duration and contents, because many young people with ASD try out several educations before deciding on one.

[77] See also the recommendations concerning assessment (NAP, pp. 12–13).

[78] The Public School Law, LBK no. 521 of 27 May 2013 has no specific chapter on special education, instead it is mentioned in most of the chapters (sections 3, 4, 12, 19, 20, 21, 22, 40, 42, 44, 47, 49, 51 and 57 of the Public School Law). Special education is an integrated part of the Danish public school system. However, in 2008 the Danish Ministry of Education launched the school development project 'Less special education, enhanced professionalism and increased inclusiveness' with the aim to maintain pupils in mainstream education and reduce the reference to special education. An Appeal Board for special education was set up as an independent authority, acting on complaints of every kind concerning local special education for pupils who need extensive support in the teaching or instruction in special classes or schools.

With regard to adult life, according to the NAP education institutions should ensure the necessary adjustments and support for persons with ASD as provided by law.[79] Furthermore, access to education and continuous learning should be guaranteed and individuals with ASD should have the right to try their possibilities on the regular labour market.[80]

6.2 Hungary

The *Hungarian National Autism Strategy* (2008–2013) aims at improving the quality of life of the population affected by ASD by setting out medium-term targets and tasks in the following fields: early screening and diagnosis, education, adult training, employment, and family support. The Strategy requires, first of all, a national map of autism accessible services and a map of missing services in several sectors, including education, in order to improve regional services and design new forms of services.[81]

In the framework of the Strategy training an appropriate number of professionals has a key role in order to improve the quality of the services.[82] The professional training is strictly linked with the field of education to which the Strategy dedicates the Chapter 5 entitled 'Improving Autism-specific Development and Educational Services'. The Strategy points out that children and adults with autism require individualized, disability-specific development, training and education throughout their entire lifetime. In order to meet these requirements, the Strategy recommends an improvement of services both in quantitative and qualitative terms. It is recognized that the traditional form of education, based on spoken language, social communication and learning in a group, is not appropriate for people with autism in most cases. Autism-specific training/education must meet individual requirements and a high number of individual lessons is indispensable for successful learning. For these reasons, the Strategy recommends to increase the professional per child ratio in order to have one special educational needs teacher and two assistants for a group of six to eight pupils with ASD, and at least one trained

---

[79] Law on Vocational Education (LBK no. 439 of 29 April 2013) in Section 29 provides for students who need it, special education and other special educational assistance. The more detailed Guidance rules (chapter 4) establish that students are entitled to have their ongoing support needs identified and relevant actions implemented throughout their schooling.

[80] For the NAP's recommendations in the field of the employment see Sect. 7 in this chapter.

[81] The national autism services map must take into account the qualitative aspects of the existing services that, in the sector of education, are indicate in the following: level of education of experts, applied methods, number of students with autism and others.

[82] To this purpose in the Chapter 3 it is envisaged to set up an Autism Professional Workshop (APW), a provisional consultation organization charged with the creation of a system of intensive professional training and further education. In the APW the health sector (psychiatry, psychology), pedagogy/special needs education and the social field are represented.

professional per mainstream school and one assistant for two children participating in mainstreamed education.[83]

Furthermore, the Strategy requires the codification and the implementation of 'autism-specific qualitative criteria for each level of the educational system' that is the establishment of general criteria (professional requirements, professional/child ratio and others) for a high standard of autism-specific education. These criteria should lead to more standardized and better monitored services, higher level quality of services, a reduction of regional and quality differences between the services, more adequate services that meet the individual requirements of children with autism.

In the field of education, the Strategy considers a priority to offer accessible autism-specific services at secondary and primary schools and requires professional support to schools for the inclusion of pupils with ASD in mainstreamed schools for the entire period of public education. In order to realize this objective special tasks for each educational level are identified.

As for 'Early Development, Nursery, Nursery Schools', the Strategy points out that a comprehensive, complex and multidisciplinary early intervention is crucial and recommends to raise to 25 h (instead of 2–6 h) the weekly professional services. The objectives are to ensure early, intensive and disability-specific services to infants diagnosed with autism, improve the quality and quantity of the available services and reduce the number of children who do not get any services. For Primary Education the tasks are indentified in the following: detailed codification on the operation of special autistic groups (not a system of regular lessons; education based on individual lessons; training and education issues; the question of how to divide and unite groups); more specific legal regulation on the professional and organisational requirements of integration; creation of a comprehensive and coherent administrative and documentation system.

With regard to 'Improving Access to Secondary Education and Vocational Training', the Strategy refers to the above-mentioned 'common strategic tasks in education' that must be applied in secondary education as well. The purpose is the creation of disability-specific services for students with autism of secondary school age which are missing. As for 'Supporting Students with Autism in Higher

[83] Regarding education and training of disabled persons in the Hungarian legal system, the Equal Opportunities Act (Act XXVI of 1998) in the Section 13 states: (1) 'It is the right of the person living with disability to take part in early development and care corresponding to his or her condition and depending on age, to kindergarten training, school training and education and development preparation for such education, in keeping with the provisions of the Act on Public Education'; (2) 'If it is advantageous for development of the capabilities of the person living with disability - in keeping with the opinion of the expert and rehabilitation committee set up for this purpose – the person living with disability shall take part in kindergarten training and school education together with other children and pupils, in the same kindergarten group or school class'. The Act on National Public Education (Act CXC of 2011) provides two choices for children with disabilities: education in special schools or in regular pre-schools and schools. The Act addresses to children/students with special education needs, including those having autism spectrum disorder (Section 4, para 23).

Education', the goal is to offer help and support, preparing higher education facilities. Consequently, a series of tasks are identified such as: professional assistance and consultancy offered to people with autism studying at higher education facilities to help them fit in; offering information and assistance to the person with autism to register as a student with special needs within the higher education and to choose the form of help needed; and peer helping programs. It is interesting to observe that the Strategy emphasizes that the goal and the tasks of this chapter conform with the Resolution ResAP(2007)4 on *Education and Integration of Children with Autism* adopted on 12 December 2007 by the Committee of Ministers Council of Europe that recommended to Member States to take into account in their policies, legislation and practice a set of principles, listed in the Annex of the Resolution, to ensure social inclusion and inclusive education to children and young people with autism.[84]

In the Chapter 6 entitled 'Adult Training' the Strategy aims at creating an opportunity for the target group of autistic people with mental disabilities to have access to training once they terminate the schooling age and giving them the opportunity to continuously develop their adaptation skills. In order to realize these objectives, the Strategy requires that adults with autism must have access to both general and vocational training. This latter must be available within the public educational system and/or within the framework of adult training and market-oriented. Training has the objective to teach adults with autism independence skills, and prepare them for work and employment. In this field, the Strategy also foresees the launch of a model program for autism-specific adult training based on general training (lifelong learning, preparation for independence, developing communication and social skills) and special training.[85]

Finally, in order to meet the requirements in the fields of education and training the Strategy recommends to train autism-specific professionals, define training levels, and establish training programs (Chapter 7).

6.3 Wales

The *Autistic Spectrum Disorder Strategic Action Plan for Wales* (2008–2018) has the purpose 'to set a clear direction of travel for the development of services in

[84] See also Recommendation CM/Rec(2009)9 of the Committee of Ministers to Member States *on the education and social inclusion of children and young people with autism spectrum disorders* adopted by the Committee of Ministers on 21 October 2009.

[85] The Strategy also lists the contents of the model program. In 2010, in Hungary the education system was changed, including all sectors of education and training general/public education, vocational education and training (VET), higher education. VET is now governed by the Act CLXXXVII of 2011 on Vocational education and training and by the Act LXXVII of 2013 on Adult Training (http://www.eqavet.eu/gns/what-we-do/implementing-the-framework/hungary.aspx).

Wales by ensuring that specific and measurable actions are undertaken and, on the basis of evidence of prevalence and need, commissioning interagency services at local, regional or national levels as appropriate. It also aims to broaden the understanding of ASD and its prevalence in Wales'.[86] The approach followed is to improve services, offered by government and the voluntary sector, for children, young people and adults with ASD, and their families, in the fields of health, social services and education.

The Strategic Action Plan (Action Plan) builds on a wide range of existing policies, strategies, and guidance for people with ASD in Wales. In the field of education, the Education Act 1996 states children's right to inclusive mainstream education if it is appropriate and parents agree.[87] In 2002 the Welsh Assembly Government issued the Special Education Needs (SEN) Code of Practice for Wales based on the principle that the SEN of children will normally be met in mainstream schools or early education settings.[88] Within the Action Plan the publication 'Quality Standards in Education for Pupils with ASD' by the Welsh Assembly Government is considered a key action point. In 2010, a small task and finish group (comprising representatives of local authorities, special schools, voluntary organizations and parents) was established to update the original draft document in order to ensure compliance with the Action Plan. The Welsh Assembly Government is still working to deliver it.[89]

The Action Plan also provides measures to raise awareness of ASD in the schools and to train teachers to improve ASD awareness. Raise awareness and

---

[86] The actions outlined in the Plan cover a number of key broad areas: (1) mapping prevalence, needs and services; (2) commissioning services; (3) transitional arrangements; (4) services for adults; (5) awareness raising, information and training; and (6) resources.

[87] See also Education Act 2002 and Education Act (Wales) 2014.

[88] The Code defines SEN as follows: 'Children have special educational needs if they have a learning difficulty which calls for special educational provision to be made for them'. The Code suggests the adoption of a range of strategies that recognize the various complexities of needs, the different responsibilities to assess and meet those needs, and promotes common recognition of the continuum of SEN' http://www.npt.gov.uk/PDF/sen_sen_summary.pdf. See Welsh Assembly Government (2007), p. 22. The Welsh Government proposed a reform of the current Special Educational Needs framework. In May 2014, a White Paper was published to set out proposals to introduce a new legislative framework for supporting children and young people with 'additional learning needs' (see http://wales.gov.uk/topics/educationandskills/schoolshome/curriculuminwales/additionaleducationalneeds/additional-learning-needs-reform/?lang=en). With regard to funding for education, the Welsh Assembly Government has secured 1.5 million pound, commencing 2008/2009, to provide support to children and young people with SEN, including those with ASD, as they move through school and to further education or the workplace. In 2007/2008, £1.7 million (recurring) was allocated by the Welsh Assembly Government to local authorities to children with SEN and children's social services. This funding remains year on year for local authorities to draw on.

[89] The Standards should include an overview of ASD, Local Education Authority (LEA) policy; identification and assessment; multi-agency support and collaboration; intervention; pupil participation; supporting parents and carers; education provision including managements and training; self-evaluation tool for schools. See Thomas (Deputy Minister for Social Services) (2010).

understanding of ASD are one of the key elements in ensuring that individual's needs are fully identified and assessed. In this regard, the Action Plan emphasizes that assessment is an ongoing process that is designed to identify each person's individual strengths as well as difficulties. For children, social services are the lead agency in the 'Framework for the Assessment of Children needs and Their Families', issued by the National Assembly for Wales on 2001 in order to provide a systematic basis for collecting and analyzing information to support professionals on how to help children and families, and the SEN Code of Practice should also be used where appropriate.[90]

The Action Plan contains a specific part dedicated to 'Transition planning and preparation for adulthood and employment' (Chapter V, Part B) where, under 'Transitions for children and young people', it is recognized that 'transition, and the associated changes in life circumstances, can provoke extreme anxiety in people with ASD, and their families and carers. Existing policies outline a number of approaches authorities may adopt to seek to ensure a smooth transition between pre-school services, mainstream school and special school and post school learning and adult services'.[91] As for transition from primary to secondary education, the Action Plan specifies that it tends to have an educational focus in conformity with the procedures outlined in the SEN Code of Practice for Wales. With regard to 'Transition from school to further education', the Action Plan requires a partnership between schools, Careers Wales[92], further education and higher education institutions, employers and carers. Transition should be planned well in advance and the plans should have regard to the views of pupils and parents in leading to an assessment of individuals' needs. For pupils with ASD this may involve using a phased or gradual move to the new service or provision. Specific measures are indicated for the transition of young people (or adults) from school to further and higher education[93] which requires cooperation among schools, Careers Wales, post-school education, training providers, employers and carers. In this context, the 14–19 Learning Pathways[94] aim to ensure that all young people, including those

---

[90] See Action Plan, Chapter 5, point A 'Services for Children and Young People'.

[91] The Action Plan recalls that the Welsh Assembly Government has convened a Multidisciplinary Transition External Reference Group to take forward the recommendations made by the Education, Lifelong Learning and Skills Committee in their review of SEN, with part three focused wholly on transition. Also the National Service Framework for Children, Young People and Maternity Services (Welsh Assembly Government 2005) contains a specific chapter on transition.

[92] Career Choices Dewis Gyrfa Ltd (CCDG) is a subsidiary of the Welsh Government, established on 1 April 2013, to provide all age, independent and impartial careers information, advice and guidance service for Wales (http://www.careerswales.com/en/).

[93] The Adult Task and Finish Group, set up in October 2008 in conformity with the Action Plan (para 11.1) is charged to explore and make recommendations on a series of priority areas for adults, including, employment, higher and further education. The Report of the Group of October 2009 is available at http://www.asdinfowales.co.uk/resource/p_a_Adults_Task___Finish_Group_Report_Formatted_English_Version_February_2010.pdf. See also http://www.assemblywales.org/NAfW%20Documents/specialist_provision_-_e.pdf%20-%2024052010/specialist_provision_-_e-English.pdf.

[94] See Welsh Assembly Government, 14–19 Learning Pathways Guidance, 2006. www.learning.wales.gov.uk.

with learning difficulties, receive learning provision that is flexibly tailored to meet their individual needs and aspirations.[95]

Finally, it is important to recall that all the 22 Local ASD Action Plans adopted in implementing the Action Plan for Wales include a focus on education and address the need for a range of educational provision locally.[96]

6.4 England

The Strategy for adults with autism in England (2010) was underpinned by the fundamental principles of equality and human rights and based on the Government's vision for transforming the lives of and outcomes for adults with autism which affirmed: 'All adults with autism are able to live fulfilling and rewarding lives within a society that accepts and understands them. They can get a diagnosis and access support if they need it, and they can depend on mainstream public services to treat them fairly as individuals, helping them make the most of their talents'.[97]

Government reaffirmed this vision in the updated version of the Strategy published in 2014 (2014 Strategy) which takes into account the progress made in improving support for adults with autism in England since 2010, the legislative developments in relevant sectors, such as special educational needs (SEN), and the results of the review of the Autism Strategy undertaken in 2013/2014 in conformity with Autism Act 2009.[98] The 2014 Strategy identifies 15 Priority Challenges for Action listed under three wide themes: (1) An equal part of my local community; (2) The right support at the right time during my lifetime; and (3) Developing my skills and independence and working to the best of my ability.

The field of education is firstly treated under the Priority Challenge for Action no. 4 with regard to the reasonable adjustments that all public organizations, as schools, are required to make in order to ensure that services are accessible to

[95] Working with local education authority (LEA) networks, the 14–19 Learning Pathways set out to provide appropriate opportunities and experiences for young people of all abilities to develop necessary core life and vocational skills, with the help of personal and learning coaches support and career guidance.

[96] See Welsh Assembly Government (2011), p. 45.

[97] The 2010 Strategy focused on five core areas of activity: (a) increasing awareness and understanding of autism among frontline professionals; (b) developing consistent pathways for diagnosis in every area, followed by the offer of a personalised needs assessment; (c) improving access to the services and support which adults with autism need to live independently; (d) helping adults with autism into work, and (e) enabling local partners to plan and develop appropriate services for adults with autism.

[98] See 'Think Autism – Fulfilling and Rewarding Lives, the strategy for adults with autism in England: an update, 2014'. This updated Strategy specifies that requirements for local authorities and NHS bodies from the 2010 Strategy still apply. Indeed, *Think Autism* does not replace the original Strategy but rather it is build on its themes (see para 1.8).

persons with disabilities, including people with autism.[99] The 2014 Strategy recognizes that without reasonable adjustments many services can be inaccessible for adults with autism, for this reason some good practices are recommended also for educational settings, such as providing quiet or low-light areas.[100] The 2014 Strategy also recalls that the Disabled Student Allowance (DSA) supports people with autism with the academic aspects of university life, in particular funding a note-taker for lectures, electronic equipment and software, social skills training, travel training, and 1:1 support.[101] The 2014 Strategy also recommends reasonable adjustments for physical environment and for services and behavior of frontline staff who must be trained to this purpose.[102]

In the Priority Challenge for Action no. 11, the 2014 Strategy points out that the needs of adults with autism may be significantly influenced by their experiences within education and children's services. Indeed, the Strategy recognizes that 'transition from school to college and beyond into adult life from children's services into adult services is an important time for many young people with autism and their families'. Consequently, it recommends that good transition planning developed by schools should bring together education, health and social care staff when a young person has complex need, while better transition planning for the move to further education and universities should be developed to support people with autism to lead independent lives and fulfill their potential. In this context, the 2014 Strategy recalls the legal changes introduced by the Children and Families Act 2014 that improves transitions from adult life for young people with special educational needs and disabilities (SEND), by providing new forms of protection for those with SEN in further education. The Act introduces a single Education, Health and Care (EHC) plan for 0–25 year olds, in place of the statements of SEN (mentioned in the 2010 Strategy) and Learning Difficulty Assessments.[103] When a young person with an EHC plan is expected to leave education, the local authority must agree the support he/she needs to engage with adult services and provision. The Act also includes duties on local authorities to maintain support for young

[99] Under the Equality Act 2010, educational and training institutions may not discriminate on the ground of disability and are required to make 'reasonable adjustments'.

[100] In the communications, a reasonable adjustment could be avoiding ambiguous questions, not pressurizing adults with autism in conversation and being aware of sensitivity to touch, ensuring essential documents and forms are available in accessible formats, in particular, easy read and formats that take account of sensory issues, in their choice of colours.

[101] For the services offered by the DSAs see https://www.gov.uk/disabled-students-allowances-dsas/overview.

[102] The 2014 Strategy recommends that quality autism awareness training should be included within general equality and diversity training programmes across all public services. Autism awareness training is set out in the Priority Challenge for Action no. 9 (see the 2014 Strategy, pp. 27–28).

[103] EHC plans are more person-centered and put greater emphasis on long term outcomes for young people. The annual reviews of support have to consider progress made against agreed outcomes within the plan, and from year 9 onwards must include a focus on preparing for adulthood.

people with EHC plans who become NEET (not in education, employment or training), and reengage them in education.[104] Furthermore, the Act improves the transition of young people with autism from school, through college and into adult life.

The 2014 Strategy also recalls that further education colleges and providers can also arrange an assessment for those people aged 19 and over who do not have an EHC plan but who self-declare a learning difficulty and/or disability.[105] The Department for Business Innovation and Skills (BIS) provides Learning Support funding to colleges and providers to help them meet the additional needs of people with learning difficulties and/or disabilities so that they can participate fully in education and training. The role of education is also emphasized under the Priority Challenge for Action no. 14 with regard to the development of skills and independence of adults with autism where it is underlined that education and training have a direct impact on the skills and ability to live independently, to enter into and remain in employment and to lead a socially inclusive life.[106] To this purpose, some colleges and universities provide appropriate services. Further education and training have also a key role in enabling adults with autism to improve their life skills and be as independent as possible.

6.5 Scotland

The 10-year *Scottish Strategy for Autism* (2011) is build on the idea that a strategic action is needed both nationally and locally because autism impacts on the whole life experience of people and their families who need to be supported by a wide range of services such as social care, education, housing, employment and other community based services. The Scottish Strategy is underpinned on some relevant

[104] The Department of Education (DfE) funds the Autism Education Trust (AET) with £1.5 m over two years from 2013 to 2015, to provide tiered training across early years, schools and further education. The Autism Education Trust is dedicated to coordinating, supporting and promoting effective education practice for all children and young people on the autism spectrum (http://www.autismeducationtrust.org.uk/about-aet.aspx).

[105] A learning difficulty means that a person has difficulties in a specific area (see the case of dyslexia) while a learning disability may affect all aspects of life (http://www.autism.org.uk/about-autism/related-conditions/learning-disabilities.aspx). DfE funds 'Ambitious about Autism', with £660,000 over two years from 2013 to 2015, to work with the Association of Colleges and four general further education colleges on transitions into further education for young people with autism (para 11.3 of the 2014 Strategy).

[106] Under the Equality Act 2010, educational and training institutions may not discriminate on grounds of disability and cannot refuse trainees on this ground alone. Training providers (including employers) are required to make 'reasonable adjustments' and must not to treat disabled learners 'less favourably'. There are wide variety of providers, including mainstream and special colleges, specific residential vocational training courses, apprenticeships and other work-based schemes.

values that are considered to be at hearth of the act and must address the behaviour of all those who are responsible for implementing it, such as: dignity, privacy, choice, safety, realizing potential, equality and diversity. It is important to observe that all the mentioned values conform with the principles enshrined in the CRPD that the Scottish Strategy expressly recalls under the issue 'Independent living'.

The Strategy identifies 13 goals divided into 3 parts: (1) Foundations (by 2 years) with five goals; (2) Whole-life journey (by 5 years); (3) and Holistic-personalised approaches (by 10 years) with respectively four goals.[107] Education is expressly mentioned in the goal no. 3, under the second part 'Whole-life journey', which requires 'Consistent adoption of good practice guidance in key areas of education, health and social care across local authority areas'.[108] In the recommendation no. 18 the role of education is linked with the transition planning. In particular, it is recommended that 'good practice transition guidance is developed, building on from existing educational guidance, in order to support the lifelong challenges facing people with autism as they make daily and life-stage transitions'.

Education is then treated in the Chapter 2 of the Scottish Strategy under the item 'Autism Lifelong: the school years' where it is underlined that when changes concerning the various stages of schooling or day-to-day transitions involve a child or a young person with additional support needs, the education authority and other agencies should take into account the way in which these changes affect the provision of additional support. To this regard it is important to recall that the Standards in Scotland's Schools Act (2000) places the duty on education authorities to secure 'that the education is directed to the development of the personality, talents and mental and physical abilities of the child or young person to their fullest potential' (Article 15). This Act establishes that education must be provided in mainstream schools, except in certain defined circumstances listed in Article 15 (3). Moreover, with the Education (Additional Support for Learning ASL) (Scotland) Act (2004) the concept of 'additional support needs' in substitution of 'special educational needs' has been introduced in the Scottish legal order.[109]

---

[107] The Strategy lists 26 recommendations for improving services and access to services for people with autism to be implemented at national and local levels.

[108] An inspection on educational provision for children and young people with ASD across Scotland has identified good practices in relation to the work of education authorities and schools and other professional practice supporting pupils with ASD. However, the inspectors suggested to pay more attention to approaches to learning and teaching, and to targets set out in individualised educational programmes. Furthermore, those with responsibility for delivering services to pupils with ASD should ensure consistency in the quality of services provided, and teachers and support staff should be provided with high quality training to enable them to meet the needs of pupils with ASD (see the Scottish Strategy, p. 53). In order to fill the gaps concerning training of professionals involved in the education, health care and support of people with autism, Scotland has developed several initiatives and projects since 2004 (see the Scottish Strategy, p. 55).

[109] Under Article 1 'A child or young person has additional support needs for the purposes of this Act where, for whatever reason, the child or young person is, or is likely to be, unable without the provision of additional support to benefit from school education provided or to be provided for the child or young person'. See also 'The Supporting Children's Learning Code of Practice' of 2005

As for transition of children and young people, the Scottish Strategy recommends to ensure early and timely planning in conformity with the Supporting Children's Learning Code of Practice which sets out detailed guidance on the matter and outlines the duties on education authorities and the time frame within which these duties should be carried out.[110] Furthermore, the Scottish Government trough the Project '16+ Learning Choices' supports young people to stay in learning after 16 years for ensuring their long term employability.[111]

Also the transition to adult life presents difficulties, therefore the Scottish Strategy recalls that Education (Additional Support for Learning ASL) (Scotland) Act (2004 and 2009) requires education authorities to plan in advance when a young person with additional support needs is preparing to leave school. Under the Act, the education authorities have the duty to identify, meet and keep under review the additional support needs of all pupils, including those with ASD.[112] Furthermore, the Act extended the jurisdiction of the Additional Support Needs Tribunal for Scotland to include complaints in relation to an alleged failure of an authority to comply with any of its duties in relation to post school transitions.

The Scottish Strategy also mentions a series of specific Government's initiatives to support inclusion in education, such as the National Framework for Inclusion which promotes the principle that achieving inclusion is the responsibility of all teachers in all schools. Also learning and teaching materials have been developed to allow teachers make their learning in the classroom more inclusive for pupils.[113]

---

which sets out detailed guidance of the Act 2004. The Education (Additional Support for Learning) (Scotland) Act 2009 emended the Act 2004, reinforcing the rights of parents, including increased parental rights in respect of access to the Additional Support Needs Tribunals for Scotland (ASNTS). See Meikle and Watt (2013), pp. 107–111.

[110] This recommendation is consistent with other key national policies developments such as *Getting it Right For Every Child* (GIRFEC, 2010) which is the Scottish Government's child-centred approach to children's services, including those supporting children with disabilities.

[111] The Government appointed a national transitions officer to work with local authorities and partners to support transition pathways for young people who are most at risk of missing out on education and training opportunities, including those with autism.

[112] See Alexander and Inch (2013), pp. 37–46.

[113] See also the Inclusive Practice Project at the University of Aberdeen to develop inclusive education principles within teacher training and the Autism Toolbox commissioned by the Scottish Government and published in 2009 with the aim to support education authorities in their planning of services for children and young people with ASD and practice in the classroom (see Scottish Strategy, p. 63).

6.6 Northern Ireland

In the *NI Autism Strategy* (2013–2020) the issue of education is one of the 11 key themes and one of the 16 strategic priorities.[114] This aligns with the Autism Act (Northern Ireland) 2011 which prescribed, among others, that the Strategy had to 'set out how the needs of people with autism are to be addressed throughout their lives including (but not limited to) their *educational*, health and social needs'.[115]

In the Theme 5 entitled 'Education', it is affirmed: 'There is one strategic priority within this themed area aiming to ensure that children and young people with autism are provided with high quality education services which meets their needs appropriately'. In the field of education the Strategy identifies the following cross governmental actions: (1) continue to build capacity in schools to effectively meet the needs of children and young people with autism; (2) provide effective support to parents and carers of children and young people with autism to ensure they are involved and informed regarding their children's education; (3) formalise collaboration between health and social care and education sector to help improve support, including specialist support; and (4) expand trans-disciplinary assessments, interventions and support for children and young people with complex needs.

The Strategic Priority 8 entitled 'education' has the objective to 'ensure that children and young people with autism receive a high quality education that prepares them for life and work and enables them to fulfil their potential'. It is important to underline that this Strategic Priority is consistent with the Article 24 of the CRPD expressly recalled in the Strategy where it is pointed out that this norm provides access to an inclusive education system at all levels and to lifelong learning. This is a further confirmation of the role that the CRPD can play at the domestic level to reinforce the rights of persons with autism and their inclusion in the society. Also the UN Convention on Rights of the Child of 1989 is recalled in order to conform the Strategic Priority on education with the rights and obligations enshrined in this treaty.

The Strategic Priority 8 must be assessed in the context of the NI educational legislative framework. In particular, the Disability Discrimination Act (1995) (DDA) enshrines disabled people's rights to participate in civil society by placing duties on employers, service providers, landlords, schools and colleges, while Part IV contains some provisions on special educational needs.[116] This Act has been completed by the Special Educational Needs and Disability (Northern Ireland) Order 2005, which has amended the existing legislation contained in the Education (Northern Ireland) Order 1996, and the Education (Northern Ireland) Order

[114] For each of the 11 key themes, the Strategy sets out cross governmental actions to be implemented. These latter form the basis for the Action Plan (2013–2016).

[115] Italic added.

[116] The Act was amended by the Disability Discrimination (NI) Order 2006 and by Autism Act (NI) 2011. See Sect. 2 in this chapter.

2006.[117] As for children's services, under the Health and Social Care (Reform) Act (Northern Ireland) 2009, they are commissioned by Health and Social Care Board and provided by five Health and Social Care (HSC) Trusts: Belfast, South Eastern, Southern, Northern and Western.[118]

Education provision for children and young people with ASD is made under the special educational needs legislative framework and the statutory Code of Practice (and Supplement) on the Identification and Assessment of Special Educational Needs (SEN) of September 2005.[119] In this context, it is also relevant the 'Strategy to improve the lives of people with disabilities 2012-2015' which sets out a framework to improve the health, well-being and life opportunities of all children and young people and their families particularly those who are most in need.

As for the institutional level, the Department of Education's (DE) has the primary statutory duty to promote the education and ensure effective implementation of education policy. The DE main statutory areas of responsibility are: age 0–4, primary, post-primary, special education and the youth service.

With regard to the education support to children with ASD, the Strategy highlights that many schools have tailored the classroom environment and educational programmes to meet their individual strengths and needs and the DE promoted the publication of materials to be used by school staff in supporting pupils with SEN. Another good practice in the field of education support mentioned in the Strategy is the Middletown Centre for Autism, established in 2007 and funded jointly by the DE and the Department of Education and Skills in the Republic of Ireland (RoI), to work with children and young people whose needs are more persistent, challenging and complex and to provide training to professionals and parents, and research services.

[117] The Special Educational Needs and Disability (Northern Ireland) Order 2005 regulates, in Part II, the 'Education in ordinary schools of children with special educational needs' ('Duty to educate children with special educational needs in ordinary schools') and the 'Education otherwise than in ordinary schools'. See also the Children (NI) Order 1995 which is the primary piece of legislation in respect of children.

[118] The Strategy lists the series of services for 'children in need' and their families. In particular, the Understanding the Needs of Children in NI (UNOCINI) framework is the primary service pathway for children's services within the HSC and for key agencies involved with children and young people; the Children and Young People's Strategic Partnership (CYPSP) leads integrated planning and commissioning of support and services aimed at improving outcomes for children and young people across the province. The CYPSP includes a number of regional sub-groups which aim to improve outcomes for specific groups of children and young people at a particular disadvantage, and their families, across NI.

[119] On May 2012 the Education Minister presented to the Education Committee a Policy Memorandum Paper on the Review of Special Educational Needs (SEN) and Inclusion. One of the proposals is 'to introduce a new inclusive model based on the concept of Additional Educational Needs (AEN), which promotes a whole school ethos of inclusion and responsibility for children who face barriers to learning'. http://www.deni.gov.uk/summary_of_key_proposals_july_2012.pdf. All documents are available at the DE website http://www.deni.gov.uk/review_of_special_educational_needs_and_inclusion.htm.

In line with the Strategic Priority 8 and the above-described legislative framework, the DE has identified the following key aspects for 'education': (1) schools, in partnership with parents, and supported by the ELBs/ESA[120] and other agencies, should improve identification, assessment and appropriate early intervention to support pupils who may have autism; ELBs/ESA, in collaboration with health and other agencies, should provide support to schools (including the continuing professional development of staff providing autism support) to identify good practice in meeting the needs of their pupils with autism; the Middletown Centre for Autism should continue to provide a range of support and intervention to professionals, parents and children with autism; schools, supported by ELBs/ESA, working in collaboration with health and other agencies, should help parents and carers in supporting their child's education and providing appropriate autism interventions; and ELB youth services should provide a wide range of youth activities for groups with specific and general disabilities as well as training to assist youth workers in providing services for them.

Further Education (FE) and Higher Education (HE) are treated under 'Employment and Learning' section because the Department for Employment and Learning (DEL) is responsible for FE and HE, training and skills, and employment programmes. DEL and its key delivery partners such as colleges, universities and training providers, offer a range of programmes and services to support people with autism. With regard to FE, the Strategy recalls that colleges are responsible for responding to the educational and vocational needs of the local population. Moreover, under the Special Educational Needs and Disability (NI) Order 2005, further education colleges have a duty to make reasonable adjustments to enable students with autism to access the mainstream curriculum (Article 37). All students with autism enrolling in colleges undergo an assessment of needs in order to help identify appropriate additional levels of support.[121] As for HE, DEL's strategic goal is widening participation for students with learning difficulties and disabilities, and to this end a specific Regional Strategy called 'Access To Success' was published in 2012.

As for the implementation of the cross governmental actions in the field of education, the Action Plan (2013–2016) attached to the Strategy (Section 5) sets out actions, outcome required/performance indicator, responsibility, and timescale.[122]

---

[120] Following the education reform, the Education and Skills Authority (ESA) is the single authority for the administration of education, subsuming the functions, assets and liabilities of the five Education and Library Boards (ELBs), and other organs (http://www.deni.gov.uk/index/about-the-department/8-admin-of-education-pg/education-and-skills-authority.htm).

[121] Colleges can access annual funds to help meet the cost of any additional support required.

[122] See Action Plan (2013–2016), pp. 97–98.

6.7 France

The Third Autism Plan adopted in France, covering the period 2013–2017, is build on five main strands: (1) earliest detection and diagnosis; (2) strengthening and adaptation of support on a lifelong basis; (3) support for families; (4) continued research; and (5) awareness raising and training for all professionals involved in caring for and supporting people with autism.[123] For each strand, the Autism Plan identifies measures and actions to be implemented through a cooperation among different sectors, such as research, health, medico-social and educational fields, and with the involvement of persons with autism and their families.[124]

The role of education is first of all recognized under the issue 'early interventions'. The Autism Plan recalls that in 2012 the National Higher Authority for Health has recommended tailored, comprehensive and coordinated interventions which are considered to be more effective if provided at early stage.[125] The same Authority has also recognized the relevance of the educational, behavioral and developmental approach to support children diagnosed with autism since the age of 18 months. Indeed, this support helps children with autism to improve a set of sensory, motor, linguistic, and cognitive capacities, facilitating their integration in primary schools and, then, in ordinary secondary schools. The Autism Plan recognizes that this kind of support is also relevant for the transition into adulthood in so far as it helps to gain more autonomy.

In order to develop early diagnosis, the Autism Plan, among other measures, recommends the creation of a national network for detection and diagnosis since the age of 18 months, with the involvement of physicians, professionals of early childhood (such as pediatricians, nursery schools' assistants) and tutors (Action Sheet no. 1). The national network should be completed by regional poles of early intervention and teaching units established at nursery schools. These latter are composed of teachers and socio-medical professionals and provide educational and healthy interventions with the purpose to increase the capacities of inclusion and learning of children with PDDs.[126] Strictly linked with these measures, it is the training on cognitive and behavioral problems that the Autism Plan extends to all people involved in the educational field (teachers, psychiatrics, physicians and nurses of the National Education).

---

[123] In the Autism Plan training is considered a tool for changing professionals' practices and improve the quality of the taking care of people with autism. For these reasons, the Plan extends training to all stakeholders, see Troisième Plan Autisme (2013–2017), pp. 26 ff.

[124] At central level the Secretary General of the Interdepartmental Disability Committee is charged with the Plan's implementation with the involvement of all the stakeholders represented in the National Autism Committee (CAN).

[125] See Haute Autorité de Santé/ANESM (2012).

[126] The Autism Plan provides the development of the research in human and social sciences and the carrying out of research projects concerning specific pedagogical and educational approaches or the assessment of intervention practices on persons with autism, both children and adults.

With regard to the education of children with autism in France, it is important to recall that according to government data only 15–20 % of school-aged children with PDDs have access to school.[127] These data contrast with the Law no. 2005-102 which provides an express obligation on the State to ensure education of all disabled children in mainstream school and parallel rights of children with disabilities to access to local mainstream schools and to a personalized educational project.[128] The Autism Plan tries to reverse this negative trend providing additional 550 places in special education and home care services (SESSADs) in order to support the mainstream schooling for children with autism and other PDDs and their transition to young people.[129] To this purpose, the Autism Plan provides for a better organization between the educational and socio-medical sectors which are required to work jointly to achieve a series of objectives listed in the Action Sheet no. 5 entitled 'Schooling of children and adolescents with PDDs'. Among these objectives, the Autism Plan mentions the following: support to adapted education through the development of SESSADs, in continuity with the French Second Autism Plan; strengthening of the territorial network of support to mainstreaming schooling, with pupils notably at 'Classes d'intégration scolaire (CLIS)' in primary schools and at 'Unités Pédagogiques d'Intégration (UPI)' in secondary schools; reinforcement of SESSADs to support the transition from adolescence to adulthood (16–25 years of age).

The Third Autism Plan seems to make some improvements to the French methods of care of children with autism whose inappropriateness was emphasized by the ECSR in the decision on the complaint *Action européenne des handicapés* (AEH) v. *France*. In condemning France for the violation of the European Social Charter the Committee affirmed the following: '...France is not fulfilling its obligation, under Article 15(1), to ensure that, in the context of care provision for children and adolescents suffering from autism within specialised institutions such as IMEs or day-hospital units, the work done by these institutions and the working methods they utilize are predominantly of an educational nature. In this respect, the Law (Article L112-1, §7) only foresees educational provision within these institutions as a subsidiary element amongst a number of other activities (pedagogical, psychological, social, medical and paramedical)'.[130]

---

[127] See Plan Autisme 2013–2015. Diversification des parcours d'inclusion et de scolarisation des enfants avec troubles du spectre autistique (TSA). Note technique. http://www.autismefrance.fr/offres/file_inline_src/577/577_A_16315_1.pdf.

[128] See also Code of Education, article L112-4. The legal system allows parents to place their child also in a special school.

[129] The Autism Plan also provides an increase of 100 teachers in nursery schools with a cost of 6 million euro a year.

[130] See Resolution CM/ResChS(2014)2, *Action européenne des handicapés* (AEH) v. France, Complaint No. 81/2012, adopted by the Committee of Ministers on 5 February 2014. In France autism is considered a mental illness, or a psychosis, to be treated with the methods of psychiatry; this approach is criticized by parents and associations. In May 2013, the Minister Marie-Arlette Carlotti delegate for disabled people and the fight against exclusion in a interview said that 'in the

The ECSR also criticized the lack of action to consolidate the applied behavior analysis (ABA) method employed in about 30 new institutions on an experimental basis.[131] The Third Autism Plan in Action sheets no. 7 and no. 8 (Cross-sectoral external review of experimental facilities) makes provision for such method in 28 experimental facilities which are under evaluation.

7 National Autism Plans and Strategies in the EU Member States: Actions and Services in the Field of Employment

As for education, also in the field of employment each national autism plan and strategy follows its own approach based on the domestic legislative background and the existing services.

7.1 *Denmark*

The *Danish NAP* (2008) deals with employment, in particular, under the sections 'adult life' and 'old age' affirming that adults with ASD should have the possibility of choosing occupation or daily activity based on their needs and abilities, that access to education and continuous learning should be ensured and the person should have the right to try out his or her possibilities on the regular labour market.[132]

To this end, the NAP recommends to develop meaningful daily activities, ranging from day centres with no requirement of productivity to actual jobs, mentor and support schemes for people with ASD in regular jobs. It is also recommended that large firms should employ or make use of job consultants with autism specific knowledge to guide and structure the work for people with ASD, including the ordinary working conditions and cooperation with colleagues. Also mentors to strengthen the introduction to a workplace and personal assistants are highly recommended. In this context, the NAP recognizes the role of relatives that in the field of employment may collaborate with professionals, if adults with ASD so desire and under a clear agreement on what is included in this collaboration.

upcoming years, ranging from 2014-2017, France would be rolling out new methods of treatment and no longer consider autism a mental illness. The plan includes more Americanized models of treatment such as behavioral modifications and teachings'. http://www.autismdailynewscast.com/documentary-influences-a-change-in-frances-autisim-policy/77/richardjames/.

[131] ABA is recognized an essential and scientifically valid method of educating and managing children and youth with ASD, but around this method a debate is open concerning diverse aspects, see Simpson (2001) and Foxx (2008).

[132] The Danish Law on Equal Treatment in the Labour Market (LBK no. 1349 of 16 December 2008) forbids employers and labour market agreements to discriminate on the basis, among others, of disability.

The NAP also suggests occupation for elderly people with ASD in order to avoid passivity, stereotypical activities and depression. For this group of people, practical employment similar to light employment with pension is recommended. The NAP specifies that elderly people with ASD are not trained in structural environment as children, for this reason they have a more individual need for structure and predictability than other age groups with ASD.

7.2 Hungary

The *Hungarian National Autism Strategy* (2008–2013) dedicates the Chapter 8 to 'Ensuring Autism-specific Employment' with the goal to improve the employment of people with autism matching their specific situation, special needs, individual abilities and skills. The Strategy recognizes that employment for people with autism is a basic human right that can be ensured only through a close co-operation with the social services. At the same time, the entire spectrum of employment must be supported and each segment of employment must be passable according to the individual needs and labour market policies must be involved.

The Strategy also requires to establish 'Standards for the Employment of People with Autism' in order to define the special tools required to facilitate the employment of the person with autism for each labour market service. These Standards should be compulsory for all public and private labour market service providers who take on the employment and support of people with autism and receive Hungarian and EU funding. Moreover, they should be the basis of the 'Autism-specific Employment and Operating a Labour Market Services Model Program' that according to the Strategy should be prepared in cooperation with the organizations employing or offering labour market services to people with autism and should ensure individualized forms of employment and autism-specific work orientation and assistance. The Strategy also suggests the contents of the Model Program such as: elements that prepare the employers for receiving people with autism (adapting the workplace to the individual's skills and needs, e.g.: info-communication accessibility, mentoring, offering information and/or internal training, follow-up, indication system); actions and publications to spread information connected with employment; co-operation of an autism expert and an appropriate assessment tool in order to assess the individual map of competencies; sharing experiences gained from the projects and dissemination; be market-oriented. The Strategy also foresees the opportunity for organizations, such as NGOs, to offer alternative labour market services to people with ASD.

7.3 Wales

The *Autistic Spectrum Disorder Strategic Action Plan for Wales* (2008–2018) provides that all young people leaving school at 16 plus should have the opportunity to engage in employment or training. Careers Wales has a key role in ensuring that unemployed young people up to the age of 18 receive timely and effective help to secure and retain suitable placements in education, training and employment.[133]

As for adults, the Action Plan outlines that only 11 % of adults with ASD are in full time employment; it is therefore necessary to help and support them to find work and stay in work. In this context, Job Centre Plus Disability Employment Advisers have a key role in providing specialist support, such as the Employment Assessment, which can help people with ASD to find out how their condition might affect the type of work or training they like.[134] With regard to training and employment for adults, the Action Plan outlines that 'people with ASD should have equal access to the full range of government funded programmes including education and life-long learning services and other training opportunities. The principle is that all people with ASD should be able to use services that are likely to assist them in their personal development, or provide career opportunities or secure their employment and which should be based on an understanding of their learning patterns'. The Action Plan suggests the 'supported employment' for adults who do not achieve the criteria for entry to training or educational services. In such cases, the Action Plan recommends a co-operation among local employers, supported employment services, social services and mainstream Wales employment services. Of paramount importance is the ASD awareness training for all professionals who may come into contact with people with autism, such as professionals of Job Centres, Careers Offices and Employment Training Agencies.[135] Finally, the Action Plan recognizes the key role of specialist employment training programmes such as those offered by specialized agencies outside Wales: ASPIRE (Autism West Midlands) and for adults with Asperger syndrome, PROSPECTS (NAS).

---

[133] Careers Wales works with partners as part of the transition planning process from the age of 14, draws together relevant professional information and assessments to produce a Learning and Skills Plan which sets out the post 16 educational needs of the client and the provision required to meet them.

[134] In Wales, there are over 100 different employment support services that young people with autism could use, the problem is that not all young people with autism know about these services, or use them. http://www.asdinfowales.co.uk/resource/140602-employment-young-people-autism-easy-read-summary2-en.pdf.

[135] In Wales the partnership with the Institute of Directors (IOD) led to the appointment in 2010 of Robert Lloyd Griffiths, IOD's Director in Wales, as *Wales Autism Employment Ambassador* charged with raising awareness of how people with ASD can bring benefits from the talents, skills and knowledge, to enterprises across Wales http://www.asdinfowales.co.uk/home.php?page_id=5997.

7.4 England

As for England, in the Ministerial Forward to the 2014 Strategy it is affirmed: 'we must do more to ensure that people with autism have the opportunity to achieve their aspirations in employment' because many persons have skills to offer but they are not being put to good use. Employment is considered of paramount importance to social inclusion of people with autism and to be part of their communities,[136] for this reason under the key area 'Promoting Innovation and Awareness' the 2014 Strategy recommends to promote innovative local ideas, services or projects which can help people in their communities, including those aimed at finding employment, and to make proposals in the field of employment, particularly involving the use of apprenticeships. The 2014 Strategy suggests some characteristics of these proposals, such as: (a) involvement of people with autism; (b) innovation, including either technology or innovative service design or provision; and (c) partnership, that is an integrated approach to local services and/or partnership with local businesses, employers or other services.[137]

In conformity with these indications, in the Priority Challenge for Action no. 11 it is affirmed that Government sees apprenticeships as an important tool for social mobility and a great opportunity for people with autism of all ages and backgrounds to secure a job with excellent training and real career prospects (para 11.8). Following a practical approach, the 2014 Strategy gives a series of information concerning apprenticeship such as national initiatives and funds, websites where it is possible to get information or ask for support. In this context, the Strategy mentions the 'supported internships' which are study programmes for young people aged 16–24 with a statement of SEN, a Learning Difficulty Assessment or an EHC plan who want to move into employment and need extra support. These internships enable young people with complex learning difficulties to achieve sustainable paid employment by equipping them with the skills they need for work, through learning in the workplace.[138]

The 2014 Strategy develops the field of employment under the Priority Challenge for Action no. 15 entitled 'I want support to get a job and support from my employer to help me keep it', starting from these considerations: 'Most people with

---

[136] The Equality Act 2010 sets out the rights of disabled people in workplaces and wider society, and states a legal duty on employers to make reasonable adjustments with regard to most aspects of the employment process and working conditions.

[137] For 2014/2015 a revenue and capital funding of £4.5 million are available to support the delivery of some of the key priorities set out in the 2014 Strategy, including local innovation and awareness (para 3.5). An Autism Innovation Fund was established to fund projects in four areas, including employment (para 3.6) https://www.gov.uk/government/uploads/system/uploads/attachment_data/file/338199/autisminnovationfundfinaljuly__3_.pdf.

[138] DfE's supported internship trial in 2012/2013 allowed young people with the most complex needs to show employers what they can do. It resulted in an employment rate of 36 %, against a national average employment rate of 7 % for people with complex learning difficulties (para 11.11 of the 2014 Strategy).

autism want to work and have skills and talents that would be useful in the workplace. With support, people with autism can both get and keep a job'. Currently, adults with autism are significantly underrepresented in the labour market with negative consequences on social inclusion and personal financial situations. In this regard, the 2014 Strategy recalls all relevant measures adopted by the Department for Work and Pensions (DWP) in implementation of the 2010 Strategy to increase the number of people with autism in work, such as: the 'Work Programme' and the 'Work Choice and Access to Work' introduced with the purpose to help people with disabilities, including persons with autism, to find employment and stay in work; the Disability Employment Advisers (DEAs) who are specialists working with people facing complex employment situations because of their disability or health condition, including persons with autism, and who receive training in awareness of autism; training for DWP staff; the Hidden Impairment Toolkit designed to offer practical guidance to Customer Care Officers (security staff) on how best to support individuals with hidden impairments, including reasonable adjustment solutions; 'One Stop Shop' service to support employers in employing disabled people; 'Untapped Talent', a guide for employers to help them to practice autism-friendly recruitment and to better support the people with autism in their workforce; the 'Think Autism awareness programme' in partnership with DH to promote autism-friendly practice in working.

Another relevant initiative that may be considered a good practice in the field of inclusion of people with ASD in the employment is 'The Disability and Health Employment Strategy: the Discussion so far' of December 2013 which sets out a more personalised and tailored approach to employment support for disabled people, including persons with autism. This strategy provides for a national network of specialist advisers who will be responsible for pre-employment support, job matching, work entry and sustained in work support, ensuring that people with disabilities, including those with autism, make a smoother transition into work and receive adequate in-work support. Further improvements to better access to job opportunities for people with autism will rise from the Action plan that DWP will present to the Autism Programme Board by the end of 2014.[139]

In supporting adults with autism to gain employment, local authorities play a key role. The 2010 Autism Strategy and the statutory guidance (2010) recommended to establish an Autism Partnership Board (APB) in every local area with the involvement of all relevant stakeholders, people with autism and their families and senior commissioners of health and care services, with the task to help identify local need and develop local plan of appropriate services and support. The 2014 Strategy reaffirms the role of local authorities and recommends as good practice that they should take into account the employment support needs of the local population of adults with autism, and that representatives from Jobcentre Plus as well as

[139] On the Board see Sect. 8 in this chapter. The Action Plan will be based how the outcomes of the workshop of 3 March 2014 — held by DWP, DH and NAS together with stakeholders and people with autism — to hear about their experiences in the labour.

employers join the local Autism Partnership Board.[140] In this context, the Care Act 2014 is particularly relevant because it provides new duties for local authorities, including to prevent, delay or reduce adults needs for care and support. In conformity with the Care Act, the 2014 Strategy recommends to local authorities the development of employment support services as a tool to meet the prevention duties.

Finally, the 2014 Strategy recommends key actions to local authorities to support increased employment such as: (1) ensuring that transition plans for young people with autism include employment as a key outcome, in conformity with the Children and Families Act 2014 requiring employment to be part of the new SEN local offer (Article 30); (2) assuring that the work of the local authority in relation to promoting employment effectively addresses the needs of people with autism and promoting apprenticeship schemes; (3) guaranteeing that the care planning process for adult social care needs considers employment as a key outcome, as appropriate, and looks particularly at whether personal budgets can be used to support adults with autism to become work ready;[141] (4) ensuring that the assessment process for adult social care includes signposting, as appropriate to Access to Work for interview support,[142] other appropriate benefits and agencies that can help people with autism to find and keep a job; and (5) setting the example locally and becoming an autism friendly place to work.

7.5 Scotland

The *Scottish Strategy for Autism* of 2011 recognizes that 'there are many people with autism who would like to work but who face significant barriers to getting and sustaining a job. We will support them through training, creating opportunities and improving access to the workplace'. Consequently, 'it is recommended that the supported employment framework for Scotland is evaluated in terms of its impact on employment and employability for people with autism' (recommendation no. 26).

The sixth aim of the Strategy concerning 'Wider opportunities' outlines that the Scottish Government is committed to removing barriers which prevent an effective transitions into employment and has developed, together with the Convention of Scottish Local Authorities (COSLA), a Supported Employment Framework for Scotland with the aim to provide the necessary mechanisms to support a disabled

[140] Jobcentre Plus manages a national network of local Job Centres charged to assist unemployed people to find jobs, including disabled people, and also deal with welfare benefit applications.

[141] Personal budget is money from the local authority that a person of 18 years or over, eligible for social care support, may spend for services and support. Personal budgets can be used to buy support from both the council and other providers such as domiciliary care agencies.

[142] See the website 'Access to Work' of the United Kingdom government. https://www.gov.uk/access-to-work/overview.

person's move to paid employment in the open labour market. In order to ensure that the needs of people with autism are taken into account an ASD representative is member of the Employment working group which focuses on employment for people with learning disability and ASD. Also a Scottish Autism Services Network (SASN) Employability Network is active, while the Employability team has funded a national project at the Scottish Consortium for Learning Disability (SCLD) to consider the job opportunities available to people with ASD.

It is interesting to observe that in the Scottish Strategy a link is made between the economic cost of autism and work of people with ASD. In fact, 'it is recommended that Knapp's work on the economic costs of autism is analysed and applied to the Scottish context to inform strategy and planning on what interventions lead to positive impacts both for individuals and for the economy as a whole.[143] Particular attention should be paid to his 'invest to save' assertion that if 4 % of those with Asperger's were given appropriate support into work this would ultimately mean that those individuals may not require services and could contribute to the economy' (recommendation no. 5).

In the explanation of this recommendation, the Scottish Strategy outlines that work for people with ASD is a tool to realize their inclusion in society. In particular, the Strategy recognizes that 'people with ASD have a right to the information, equipment, assistance and support services necessary to live a fully productive life with dignity and independence of choice, and to feel included in society'.[144]

7.6 Northern Ireland

In the *NI Autism Strategy* (2013–2020) to the issue of employment one of the 11 key themes and two of the 16 strategic priorities are dedicated. The Theme 7 'Employability' affirms 'There are two strategic priorities within this themed area aiming to increase opportunities for people with autism to access employment, training, lifelong learning and to attain skills'. Consequently, the Strategic Priority 10 requires to 'increase the number of people with autism entering all levels of employment and safeguard the rights of those people with autism already in work', while Strategic Priority 11 requires to 'increase the opportunities for people with autism to attain skills and qualifications through access to appropriate training and lifelong learning opportunities'.

The contents of these priorities conform respectively with Article 27 of the CRPD on the right to work and employment of persons with disabilities on an equal basis with others, and Article 24 of the CRPD on education of persons with

[143] Knapp et al. (2009), pp. 317–336. The study focuses on individuals across the autism spectrum, and a prevalence rate of 1 % was used (100/10,000). On the basis of these elements and a wider range of other factors the annual cost of autism in the UK was estimated to be £28 billion. Cf. MacKay et al. (2013), pp. 101–106.

[144] See the Scottish Strategy, p. 27.

disabilities which provides for access to an inclusive education system at all levels and lifelong learning. Indeed, the Strategy expressly refers to these provisions in relation to the two priorities.

Employment and employability are issues which require a number of government departments to work together to support people with autism to gain and retain employment. Under theme 7, the Strategy identifies the following cross departmental actions: (1) increase awareness about the support available to people with autism to help access opportunities for employment, training, and life-long learning; and (2) promote opportunities to access and attain employment, training and life-long learning for people with autism.

As already mentioned, at the institutional level the Department for Employment and Learning (DEL) is responsible of the field of employment and through its partners (colleges, universities and training providers) offers services to assist individuals with ASD to obtain and sustain work, move towards employment, or develop new/existing skills. For people with autism DEL's services cover four main areas: (1) Employment Support with a range of vocational and pre-vocational programmes to meet the needs of people with autism and services;[145] (2) Careers Advice and Guidance which provides careers information through a network of professionally qualified advisers trained to work with clients with autism;[146] (3) Further and Higher Education;[147] and (4) Professional/Technical Training, including Apprenticeships.[148] Moreover, DEL has developed a range of strategies which guide the delivery of its services across these key areas and the DEL's Disability Employment Service helps to raise awareness with employers on the benefits of employing people with autism and provide tailored support for them.

In line with the two strategic priorities and building on existing employment policies and programmes, DEL has identified the following key aspects for the 'employment' theme: increase awareness of DEL's services amongst people with

---

[145] They include: employment assessments carried out by a team of occupational psychologists; specialist support to find and keep suitable employment; residential training for those disabled people who are not ready to access mainstream training; and menu-based employment support to better target individuals' barriers to employment via 'Steps to Work' and new 'Work Connect' programmes.

[146] The Careers Service has arrangements in place with 99 % of post-primary schools to support the schools' careers education programmes. Through the partnership agreements the schools' careers advisers are invited to attend transition planning meetings at year-10 and subsequent annual reviews until a young person leaves post-primary education.

[147] See Sect. 6 in this chapter.

[148] DEL's Training for Success (TfS) Programme provides training for young people with autism up to the age of 22 who have not yet found full time employment. The TfS Programme provides training to address personal and social development needs, develop occupational and employability skills and, where necessary, essential skills. It is delivered through two components: (1) 'Skills for Your Life' to address the personal and development needs of young people who have disengaged from learning and/or have significant obstacles; and (2) 'Skills for Work' to help young people gain skills and a vocational related qualification at Level 1 to be able to gain employment or to progress to higher level training.

autism, their parents and carers; provide effective support in higher education for people with autism through the delivery of the Access to Success Strategy; improve employment prospects of people with autism through the delivery of an Economic Inactivity Strategy; deliver the Pathways to Success Strategy to improve participation in employment, education and training by young people with autism; and provide individual support for students with autism in further education. These aspects are then listed in the Autism Action Plan (2013–2016) under the column 'Outcome Required/Performance Indicator' with the indication of the timescale and the lead responsibility of LED as for implementation.[149]

7.7 *France*

In the Third Autism Plan, the field of the employment is treated with reference to the condition of adults with autism and other PDDs. In the Action Sheet no. 10 entitled 'Scheme of actions for adults' the Autism Plan underlines that, actually, inadequate care pathways are offered to adults with autism in France, as reported by a study carried out in three regions in implementation of the Second Autism Plan.[150] Indeed, in France most adults with autism are institutionalized with low self-care skills as a result of failed educational policies and lack of access to work.[151]

The Third Autism Plan foresees the improvement of pathways and quality of life of adults with autism through adapted interventions and a multifaceted offer, and the involvement of families. In this context, it is recognized that access to work contributes to the autonomy and to the improvement of life of adults with autism and other PDDs and that measures to be developed are the same of those required for disable people, but with the necessary adaptations.[152]

In order to achieve the objectives concerning the improvement of the pathways and quality of life of adults with autism and other PDDs and to create the necessary conditions to support them in employment, the Autism Plan also lists a set of interrelated actions to be implemented (Action Sheet no. 10). Among these

[149] See Autism Action Plan (2013–2016), pp. 99–100.

[150] See Baghdadli et al. (2011).

[151] http://www.thinkingautismguide.com/2012/01/culture-of-abuse-autism-care-in-france.html.

[152] As for the French legal framework in the field of employment of persons with disabilities see the following acts: the Law no. 90-602 of 12 July 1990 regarding the protection of persons against discriminations because of their health state or disability, the Law 2005-102 of 11 February 2005 which extended the principle of non-discrimination according to the EU Council Directive 2000/78/EC framework for equal treatment in employment and occupation. In parallel with anti-discrimination legislation, a 6 % quota of employees with disabilities within the workforce should be respected by employers of at least 20 employees in both the private and public sectors. Furthermore, in 2009 France adopted a National Employment Pact for People with Disabilities ('Pacte national pour l'emploi des personnes handicapées').

measures, the Plan mentions the following: raising awareness and training for staff in the field of employment dealing with adults with autism or PDDS, autism specific training programmes for professionals of 'Cap Emploi' and 'Services d'Appui au Maintien dans l'Emploi des Travailleurs Handicapés (SAMETH)', and pooling socio-medical and employment interventions. It should be noted that vocational training and lifelong learning are not included in the actions, and even a reference to tertiary education is lacking.

8 National Autism Plans and Strategies: Implementation, Monitoring and Revision

Implementation, monitoring and revision are distinguishing aspects of all autism national plans and strategies that have been examined. These phases are interrelated and involve central and local organs, together with *ad hoc* organisms often set up for these purposes and stakeholders. Just to highlight some aspects of these phases we can refer to the Strategy for adults with autism in England (2010, updated in 2014) and NI Autism Strategy (2013–2020). Both have a legal foundation in primary legislation and their implementation, monitoring and revision are regulated respectively in the Autism Act 2009 and the Autism Act (Northern Ireland) 2011.

Concerning England, under Section 1 of the Autism Act (2009) the Secretary of State must keep the autism strategy under review, may revise it, and must publish it as revised. Moreover, the Secretary of State must consult and seek the participation of such persons considered appropriate in revising it. Under Section 2, the Secretary of State is required to issue a guidance to local authorities, NHS bodies and NHS to implement the Strategy and to keep the guidance under review.[153] Subsection (5) contains a non-exhaustive list of matters that must be addressed in the guidance, while Subsection (6) requires the Secretary of State to consult and seek the participation of local authorities, NHS bodies and NHS foundation trusts before issuing guidance and before making substantial changes to the guidance once issued. A relevant legal aspect which is worth mentioning concerns the remedies that English legal order offers in case of failure to comply with the guidance. Under Section 3 of the Autism Act (2009) local authorities and NHS bodies have a 'duty to act under guidance', if they fail to comply and have 'no reasonable excuse',[154] they are subject to judicial review or default action by the Secretary of State.[155]

---

[153] For the Guidance see Sect. 4 in this chapter.

[154] To have a reasonable excuse local authorities can prove they are providing an equivalent or better alternative service.

[155] Under Section 7D of the Local Authority Social Services Act 1970 the Secretary of State for Health has the power to step in when a local authority fails to comply with its statutory community care duties and has 'no reasonable excuse' for this failure. Moreover, each local authority in England, Northern Ireland, Scotland and Wales has a complaints procedure and a citizen may

Under the 2010 Adults Autism Strategy the Autism Programme Board was charged with the duty to oversee the progress on delivering the Strategy and provide overall direction and governance at national level (para 1.8). The Board, currently chaired by the Minister of State for Care and Support, has been confirmed in its role by the 2014 Strategy and carries out the following activities: monitoring general progress in implementing the Strategy; providing challenge and support to government departments, the NHS and local authorities on their contributions to the adult autism agenda; considering and acting upon issues raised by key stakeholders. Moreover, the 2010 Adults Autism Strategy recognised that 'effective local leadership is essential to ensuring the needs of adults with autism are met in each area', and, consequently, recommended a range of measures to ensure local leadership, among which, to set up local Autism Partnership Board bringing together different organisations, services and stakeholders locally (para 6.12).[156] The 2014 Strategy reaffirms the role of local planning and leadership in the provision of services, taking into account the progress made at local level in implementing the 2010 Strategy.

With regard to Northern Ireland, under Section 2 of the Autism Act (NI) 2011 the Department of Health, Social Services and Public Safety (Department) has the following duties: to keep the autism strategy under review and publish a revised version at intervals of not more than 7 years; to monitor the implementation of the autism strategy by the Northern Ireland departments;[157] to implement that part of the autism Strategy which falls within its responsibilities; to prepare a report on implementation of the autism strategy by the Northern Ireland departments and the same Department not more than 3 years after the publication of the autism strategy, and at intervals of no more than 3 years thereafter. Under the same Section, the Northern Ireland departments must co-operate with the Department in relation to the preparation, review and implementation of the autism strategy and effectively implement the parts of the autism strategy that fall within their areas of responsibility.

The NI Autism Strategy (2013–2020) completes the provisions of the Act in Section 4 entitled, 'Implementing Approach' where the implementation structures, monitoring and reporting arrangements to ensure the delivery of the initial Action Plan (2013–2016) are set out. In particular, the Strategy underlines the role of the Regional Autism Co-ordinator and establishes the tasks and responsibilities of the various organs.

The implementation of the autism plans and strategies and its monitoring are two relevant steps which are necessary to identify new priories and actions to meet the

lodge a complaint if a service hasn't been delivered. After the local council's complaints another remedy is to complaint to local ombudsman.

[156] As set out in the Strategy, in each local authority local lead commissioner/senior manager has been appointed. They have a key role in developing local commissioning plans and in making sure that adults with autism and parents/carers are involved in the development of local services (through working with autism partnership boards).

[157] Section 4 of the Act lists the NI Departments.

needs of people with ASD as well as gaps in the delivery of services that must be filled. The revision of autism plans and strategies passes through an in-depth evaluation of the outcomes obtained[158] and the objectivities achieved with the involvement of all stakeholders and, in particular, of autism representative organizations. The case of the Autistic Spectrum Disorder Strategic Action Plan for Wales (2008–2018) whose refreshing is currently underway shows the key role that autism associations may play in this context. In order to update the Strategic Action Plan a public consultation took place in November 2012 in partnership with the voluntary sector organizations and a set of priorities has been identified for the final refreshed Strategic Action Plan and the Delivery Plan, whose implantation should start in 2015.[159] It is interesting to observe that an ASD Stakeholder Advisory Group[160] has been established to provide expert advice and guidance, and small consultation workshops have been organized to discuss directly with stakeholders and ASD leads at local level.[161]

Feedbacks from all stakeholders and public consultations are relevant elements in all processes of revision and are one of the strengths of autism plans and strategies.

9 National Autism Plans and Strategies: An Appraisal

The number of national autism plans and strategies adopted in the last few years, both in the EU countries and outside Europe, shows a growing awareness of public institutions towards the challenges that confront people with ASD and their families. Governments are slowly becoming aware of their key role in safeguarding and protecting the rights of the individuals with ASD, and in guaranteeing their inclusion and participation in society. In this perspective, national autism plans and strategies are instruments through which States provide tailored services in key

[158] The Scottish Autism Strategy has identified ten indicators to be used to identify outcome-focused actions 'that may be achieved over the two, five and ten year timeline of the autism strategy, as agreed locally' (pp. 11–13).

[159] The Welsh Government has allocated additional £2.1 m over the 3 years 2014/2015–2016/2017 to support the refresh of the Strategic Action Plan. http://wales.gov.uk/about/cabinet/decisions/dl2014/aprjun1/health/gt0837/?lang=en.

[160] Membership includes a parent carer representative, a person with Asperger Syndrome, senior representatives from the statutory services and the voluntary sector working to support people with autism.

[161] Wales has developed a solid infrastructures to implement the Strategic Action Plan. At a national level there is an ASD Implementation Manager based in the Welsh Assembly Government. At a regional level there is a small ASD Regional Support Team, based in the Welsh Local Government Association (WLGA), which supports local areas to work together and develop regional initiatives. At a local level each Local Authority area has an ASD Lead and has developed an ASD Local Action Plan to be implemented and reviewed via a Local Stakeholder Group. http://www.asdinfowales.co.uk/home.php?page_id=5998.

areas having a great impact on the life of people with ASD, such as health, education and employment. Furthermore, these plans and strategies are consistent with the recent indications of the World Health Assembly that, as already mentioned, has recommended to develop national policies, legislation, and *multi-sectoral plans*, supported by sufficient human, financial and technical resources to address issues related to ASD.

Autism plans and strategies could be therefore the proper way to support and improve the quality of life for people with ASD and their families. Indeed, practice shows that in general they have positive impacts at domestic level even if the objectives envisaged in a plan may not always be fully achieved[162] and the adoption of these instruments does not guarantee that the rights of people with ASD will be effectively protected by the State concerned. The case of France is emblematic in this regard. Notwithstanding three autism plans, the ECSR condemned twice the State for the violation of the right to education of children with autism as guaranteed by the European Social Charter (revised) and a petition against France was presented to the competent Committee of the European Parliament in 2013.[163] In the above-mentioned case *Action européenne des handicapés* (AEH) v. France, the ECSR reached the conclusions that France violated the European Social Charter concerning the right to education of children and adolescents with autism also considering the ground of the limited funds in the State's social budget for this field as emerged from the second Autism Plan (2008–2010) whose measures were not fully implemented.

However, it should be noted that the analysis of the national autism plans and strategies has revealed that these instruments are characterized by some distinguishing aspects. First, they follow a practical approach that allows to identify the real needs of the people to whom the plan addresses (children, young people, adults with ASD, but also families and carers) and, accordingly, the key areas of intervention and the necessary services. In this context, it is important to underline that all national autism plans and strategies adopted by the EU Member States have been outlined in partnership with autism associations and, in most cases, after a public consultation. The information gathered from consultations, the involvement of autism representative organizations and families demonstrate that the plans are developed with the contribution of those who have a direct knowledge and experience of the ASD. In some cases, autism representative organizations lobby Governments to have an autism plan as a way to coordinate national efforts to meet the complex needs of people with ASD (as for the case of Canada). The active involvement of autism associations in developing autism plans and strategies is a very positive aspect and a substantial added value for these instruments.

---

162 See, for example, the evaluation concerning the implementation of the Adult Autism Strategy for England in the field of employment, cf. López and Keenan (2014).

163 See petition 0031/2013 to the Committee on Petitions of the European Parliament by Marie Bradot (French), on behalf of the 'Diamant association' on the right to education of persons with autism in France (Commission reply of 28 February 2014). On these cases see the chapter by G. Palmisano, in this volume.

Second, autism plans and strategies have a flexible nature that allows their revision without recurring to formal procedures. This flexibility is strictly linked with their implementation and monitoring which are fundamental elements for all autism plans and strategies.[164] Competent Ministries or Departments are usually charged with the task of autism plans' implementation and updating, often with the collaboration of specific organs or networks at national and local levels, and autism associations. For the autism plans and strategies adopted in the EU Member States having a legal basis in primary legislation, such as the above-mentioned cases of England and Northern Ireland, the relevant Acts contain both the broad legal framework of the strategy and 'the enabling clause' that confers the power to an administrative branch to issue and revise it.[165] In this way, it is possible to reformulate objectives and priorities, and identify new actions and challenges to include in a updated plan.

Third, autism plans set out strategic direction and co-ordination of services at national and local levels, mapping out the existing services, identifying the priority areas of intervention and the organs responsible to provide the services and carry out the actions. In some cases, they have also recommended a rationalization of services thus ensuring saving of public money.

The last common aspect concerns public funding. All autism plans and strategies adopted in the EU Member States have the support of Governments that should assure the necessary resources to implement these instruments. France allocated 205.5 million euros to fund the third autism plan (2013–2017), additional 18 million euros than the second autism plan.[166] At the launch of the Scottish Strategy for Autism on 2 November 2011, the Minister for Public Health announced that the Scottish Government would provide £13.4 million over four years, until March 2015, to support implementation of the Strategy.[167] Moreover, the Scottish Strategy (2011–2021) recommends that existing studies on the economic costs of autism should be applied to inform the Strategy leading to positive impacts both for individuals and for the economy as a whole (recommendation 5). In Northern Ireland, before the adoption of the Autism Strategy (2013–2020) and its Action Plan (2013–2016), the Government commissioned a report concerning the costs of ASD in order to provide policymakers and public representatives with background financial information on public expenses for ASD.[168] As already mentioned, also in Canada individual members of the Senate requested an inquiry on funding for ASD, an issue linked with the proposal of a national autism strategy.[169]

---

[164] On the implementation of autism plans and strategies see Sect. 8 in this chapter.

[165] See Sect. 8 in this chapter.

[166] http://www.social-sante.gouv.fr/actualite-presse,42/breves,2325/presentation-du-3eme-plan-autisme,15797.html.

[167] http://www.autismstrategyscotland.org.uk/development-fund/autism-development-fund.html.

[168] See Autism NI-PAPA (2007).

[169] See Sect. 5 in this chapter.

Having a clear picture of autism costs is of paramount importance in the current world economic situation where every public sector is facing budget restrictions and the austerity measures introduced by many European Governments have impacted above all on disabled people and their families. A recent study led by the London School of Economics and Political Science (LSE) published in June 2014 has estimated that autism costs in the United States and United Kingdom. Its results are the following: the cost of supporting an individual with ASD and intellectual disability during his or her lifespan was $2.4 million in the United States and £1.5 million (US$2.2 million) in the United Kingdom. The cost of supporting an individual with an ASD without intellectual disability was $1.4 million in the United States and £0.92 million (US$1.4 million) in the United Kingdom. The largest cost components for children were special education services and parental productivity loss. During adulthood, residential care or supportive living accommodation and individual productivity loss contributed the highest costs. Medical costs were much higher for adults than for children.[170] The conclusions reached through this study are worth mentioning. Researchers have emphasized 'the need to continue to search for effective interventions that make best use of scarce societal resources. The distribution of economic effect across many different service systems raises questions about coordination of services and sectors. The enormous effect on families also warrants policy attention'.

These are relevant aspects to be considered by States in developing autism plans and strategies. A better coordination of services at national and local level is of paramount importance in order to have more efficient delivery of services for people with ASD and avoid the waste of public money.

10 Conclusions

In the Resolution 67/82 of 19 March 2013, the UNGA recommended to Member States 'to enhance access to appropriate support services and equal opportunities for inclusion and participation in society by providing, as appropriate, training to public administrators, service providers, carers, caregivers, families and non-professionals on the needs and rights of persons with autism spectrum disorders, developmental disorders and associated disabilities' (para 1).

At the same time, the UNGA recognized that, in order to develop and implement feasible, effective and sustainable intervention programmes for addressing ASD, developmental disorders and associated disabilities, an innovative, integrated approach would benefit from a focus, *inter alia*, on: (1) increasing public and

[170] See Buescher et al. (2014). The objective of the research was to update estimates of age-specific, direct, indirect, and lifetime societal economic costs, including new findings on indirect costs, such as individual and parental productivity costs, associated with ASD. A synthesis of the results are available at http://archpedi.jamanetwork.com/article.aspx?articleid=1879723.

professional awareness of ASD; (2) enhancing and increasing research expertise and service delivery, including through international collaboration, by training researchers, service providers, as well as non-professionals, in early diagnosis and interventions within health and other relevant sectors; (3) enhancing inclusive educational programmes suited to infants, children and adults, with autism; (4) emphasizing the unique needs of each person with autism across a spectrum of different characteristics and experiences; and (5) increasing awareness of the advantages of the inclusion of individuals with ASD in society through occupational and leisure activities.

These recommendations aim at addressing the conducts of Member States towards the inclusion of people with ASD in the different fields of society, with particular emphasize on education and employment, and at improving services to meet their needs. In this perspective, the UNGA's Resolution completes the principles enshrined in the CRPD having regard to the specific needs of people with autism. It is interesting to observe that national autism plans and strategies adopted by the UE Member States that have been examined, in most cases, are consistent with the UNGA's recommendations. Indeed, within these instruments the lifelong needs of people with ASD are met through the recognition of the role of early diagnosis, tailored services and support for individuals with ASD, parents and carers (advice, guidance, information, training, and others); autism awareness; inclusive education, employment and training.

National autism plans and strategies are flexible instruments that address the needs of people with ASD setting out adapted, life-long support and services to enable them to enjoy full inclusion and participation in relevant social fields. In particular, the national autism plans and strategies developed in the United Kingdom which take into account the needs of people with autism from childhood to adulthood are more respondent to the international recommendations and to the rights enshrined in the CRPD whose overall aim is the inclusion and full participation of persons with disabilities in all aspects of life. In this framework, a good practice is the Northern Ireland Autism Strategy (2013–2020) and its Action Plan (2013–2016) modeled on the CRPD which is expressly recalled as a legal source to which the strategic priorities are conformed and an instrument to reinforce the human rights of persons with autism in the domestic legal order.

References

Alexander M, Inch W (2013) Transition: preparing secondary school leavers on the autism spectrum for life beyond school. In: Jones G, MacKay T (eds) Good autism practice: the Scottish perspective. Good autism practice, vol. 14, Supplement 1. Build, Birmingham, pp 37–46

American Psychiatric Association (2013) Autism spectrum disorders. http://www.psych.org/practice/dsm/dsm5. Accessed 31 Oct 2014

ANED (Academic Network of European Disability Experts) (2009) Country Report on the implementation of policies supporting independent living for disabled people, France. http://www.disabilityeurope.net/content/aned/media/ANED%20Independent%20Living%20report%20-%20France.pdf. Accessed 31 Oct 2014

Asperger H (1944) Die Autistischen Psychopathen im Kindesalter [Autistic Psychopaths in Childhood]. Archiv für Psychiatrie und Nervenkrankheiten 117:76–136. doi:10.1007/BF01837709

Autism-Europe (2009) The right to healthcare and habilitation for persons with ASD. A toolkit for parents, self-advocates and advocacy organizations. http://www.autismeurope.org/files/files/autism-right-rehabilitation-and-health.pdf?phpMyAdmin=6b5bf7f8d78e834db66115fb8a480868. Accessed 31 Oct 2014

Autism NI-PAPA (2007) Autism: the costs. Autism NI (PAPA), Belfast

Baghdadli A, Rattaz C, Ledésert B (2011) Etude des modalités d'accompagnement des personnes avec troubles envahissants du développement (TED) dans trois régions françaises. http://www.sante.gouv.fr/IMG/pdf/Synthese_Etude_des_modalites_d_accompagnement_des_avec_troubles_envahissants_du_developpement_TED_dans_trois_regions_francaises_mars_2011.pdf. Accessed 31 Oct 2014

Buescher AVS, Cidav Z, Knapp M, Mandell DS (2014) Costs of autism spectrum disorders in the United Kingdom and the United States. JAMA Pediatr 168(8):721–728. doi:10.1001/jamapediatrics.2014.210

Caruso D (2010) Autism in the US: social movement and legal change. Am J Law Med 36(4):483–539

Danish National Centre for Autism, the National Board of Social Services (2008) National autism plan-a summary. Danish National Centre for Autism, Kongevejen

Della Fina V (2010) Articolo 1. In: Marchisio S, Cera R, Della Fina V (eds) La Convenzione delle Nazioni Unite sui diritti delle persone con disabilità. Commentario. Aracne, Roma, pp 17–34

Foxx RM (2008) Applied behavior analysis treatment of autism: the state of the art. Child Adolesc Psychiatr Clin N Am 17(4):821–834

Frith U (ed) (1991) Autism and Asperger syndrome. Cambridge University Press, New York

Haute Autorité de Santé/ANESM (2012) Autisme ou autres TED: interventions éducatives et thérapeutiques coordonnées chez l'enfant et l'adolescent. http://www.has-sante.fr/portail/upload/docs/application/pdf/2012-03/recommandations_autisme_ted_enfant_adolescent_interventions.pdf. Accessed 31 Oct 2014

Kanner L (1943) Autistic disturbances of affective contact. Nerv Child 2:217–250

Kelly G, McConkey R, Casey K (2007) A strategy for the delivery of autism services in Northern Ireland. University of Ulster, Londonderry

Knapp M, Romeo R, Beecham J (2009) Economic cost of autism in the UK. Autism 13(3):317–36. doi:10.1177/1362361309104246

López B, Keenan L (2014) Barriers to employment in autism: future challenges to implementing the adult autism strategy. University of Portsmouth, Portsmouth

MacKay T, Boyle J, Knapp M, Connolly M (2013) A multi-strand investigation of micro-segmentation of the autism spectrum to enhance the data on the economic costs and benefits of provision. In: Jones G, MacKay T (eds) Good autism practice: the Scottish perspective. Good autism practice, vol 14, Supplement 1. Build, Birmingham, pp 101–106

Maginnis K (2008) Independent review of autism services. http://www.dhsspsni.gov.uk/independent_review_of_autism_services_final_report.pdf. Accessed 31 Oct 2014

Meikle L, Watt D (2013) Autism and Scottish education: information from data. In: Jones G, MacKay T (eds) Good autism practice: the Scottish perspective. Good autism practice, vol 14, Supplement 1. Build, Birmingham, pp 107–111

National Autistic Society for National Initiative for Autism: Screening and Assessment (NIASA) (2003) National Autism Plan for Children (NAPC). Newnorth Print Ltd, London

O'Reilly B, Wicks K (2013) The Australian autism handbook: the essential resource guide for autism spectrum disorder. Jane Carry Publishing, Edgecliff
Roth L (2013) Autism spectrum disorder, Briefing Paper No. 5/2013. https://www.parliament.nsw.gov.au/prod/parlment/publications.nsf/0/B2142391F94516FECA257B78001FB961/$File/Autism%20Spectrum%20Disorder.briefing%20paper.pdf. Accessed 31 Oct 2014
Simpson RL (2001) ABA and students with autism spectrum disorders issues and considerations for effective practice. Focus Autism Other Dev Disabl 16:68–71. doi:10.1177/108835760101600202
Standing Senate Committee on Social Affairs, Science and Technology (2007) Pay now or pay later. Autism families in crisis, final report. http://www.parl.gc.ca/Content/SEN/Committee/391/soci/rep/repfinmar07-e.htm#_Toc162403116. Accessed 31 Oct 2014
Thomas G (Deputy Minister for Social Services) (2010) The implementation of the autistic spectrum disorder (ASD) strategic action plan for Wales. http://wales.gov.uk/about/cabinet/cabinetstatements/2010/100122asd/?lang=en
Welsh Assembly Government (2007) The autistic spectrum disorder (ASD) strategic action plan for Wales, Consultation Document
Welsh Assembly Government (2011) The ASD strategic action plan for Wales (2008). Evaluating the foundation phase. http://www.asdinfowales.co.uk/resource/k_m_ASD_SAP_Evaluation_Report_Final_18_3_2011__2_.pdf. Accessed 31 Oct 2014
Wing L, Gould J (1979) Severe impairment of social interactions and associate abnormalities in children: epidemiology and classification. J Autism Dev Disord 9(1):11–29

Valentina Della Fina is Senior Researcher at the Institute for International Legal Studies of the Italian Research Council (ISGI-CNR), Rome, Italy.

National Legislations on Inclusive Education and Special Educational Needs of People with Autism in the Perspective of Article 24 of the CRPD

Rachele Cera

1 Introduction

Education is vital not only in itself, but also for participating in all areas of social activity. In poet, the right to education works as a multiplier by enabling people to exercise other human rights. It enhances both economic, social and cultural rights, such as the right to work and the right to food, and civil and political rights, like the right to vote and the freedom of expression. Being its realization a precondition for socio-economic inclusion and full participation in society, the right to education has, therefore, been recognized as an example of the indivisibility and interdependence of all human rights on account of its key role in the full and effective realization of other rights.[1]

Historically people with disabilities have often suffered, and in most parts of the world are still suffering, from a pervasive and disproportionate denial of the right to education. In many countries, children with disabilities are sent away to institutions where they receive no education and are isolated from society for their entire lives. In other countries, children with disabilities are forced to attend separate schools instead of general schools in the community. The vast barriers children with disabilities face in accessing education in most societies has led to a low employment rate for persons with disabilities and a disproportionately high rate of poverty.

In such context, international law plays as a facilitator for the realization of the right to education of people with disabilities throughout the world. As the most

[1] UN Committee on Economic, Social and Cultural Rights (CESCR) *General Comment No. 11: Plans of Action for Primary Education* (E/1992/23), 10.5.1999, and *General Comment No. 13: The Right to Education* (E/C.12/1999/10), 8.12.1999.

R. Cera (✉)
Institute for International Legal Studies, National Research Council (CNR), Rome, Italy
e-mail: rachele.cera@cnr.it

V. Della Fina, R. Cera (eds.), *Protecting the Rights of People with Autism in the Fields of Education and Employment*, DOI 10.1007/978-3-319-13791-9_4

recent, integral and legally binding international instrument to protect the rights of persons with disabilities, the Convention on the Rights of Persons with Disabilities (CRPD) put steps forwards for the protection of their right to education.

The normative impetus behind the CRPD is inclusive equality of disabled people in all socio-economic sectors. In this vein, Article 24 of the CRPD specifically responds to the legacy of exclusion and marginalization of disabled learners in the education sector by guaranteeing the right to equality and non-discrimination in State provision of education. More significantly, Article 24 breaks new ground by recognizing 'inclusive education' as a human right. The recognition of inclusive education as a human right is largely a culmination of global advocacy for an education system that is inclusive as to accommodate diverse learning needs and capacities.[2]

2 Definitions of Inclusive Education and Special Educational Needs: The ASD Perspective

From a legal point of view, there is no consensus on the definition of the concept of 'inclusive education'. Neither the CRPD provides for such a definition.

What is clear, however, is what it is not. Inclusive education is obviously not equal to education in special schools, especially when no choice is given to people with disabilities to refuse their enrolment in such schools.[3] But neither is inclusive education equal to integration, which would simply provide access to regular schools for children with disabilities without allowing them to be educated there in a way that takes account of their special needs. This interpretation is confirmed in the Concluding observations of the Committee on the Rights of Persons with Disabilities (CRPD Committee) to Austria's initial report, noting that 'there is some confusion between "inclusive" education and "integrated" education' in that State.

Inclusive education recognizes that all children are different and acknowledges that children with disabilities should be able to participate in the general education system. By taking into account the diversity among learners, it seeks to combat discriminatory attitudes, create welcoming communities, achieve education for all as well as improve the quality and effectiveness of education of mainstream learners.[4]

---

[2] See Arnardóttir (2011), pp. 219–221.

[3] The terms 'mainstream schools', 'general education', 'regular schools' and 'ordinary schools' are commonly used to refer to schools systems that receive students with or without impairments as opposed to 'special schools' that only receive students with impairments.

[4] OHCHR-Office of the United Nations High Commissioner for Human Rights *The right to education of persons with disabilities. Report of the Special Rapporteur on the Right to Education* (UN Doc A/HRC/4/29), 19.2.2007, para. 9.

According to the Office of the UN High Commissioner for Human Rights (OHCHR), inclusion is 'a process that recognizes: (a) the *obligation to eliminate barriers* that restrict or ban participation, and (b) the *need to change culture, policy and practice* of the mainstream schools to accommodate the needs of all students, including those with impairments'.[5] It requires 'accommodating both different styles and rates of learning and ensuring quality education to all through appropriate curricula, organizational arrangements, teaching strategies, resource use and partnerships with their communities'.

The idea underlying inclusive education is that some children, because of their impairments or other circumstances, have special needs in education which prevent them to benefit from the school education made generally available for children of the same age without additional support or adaptations in the content of studies.

Defining Special Educational Needs (SEN) has an administrative function whereby a group of students is identified for different or additional educational provision. No universally accepted system of SEN classification exists. Definitions of SEN vary widely across countries as they are specific to each domestic legislation. Some countries define SEN using a general definition covering a wide range of needs including a wide range of physical, mental, cognition or educational impairments. Others categorize SEN according to a disability classification system with a different number and types of disabilities.[6]

Education is the primary form of treatment in autism, as it fosters the acquisition of skills or knowledge—including not only academic learning, but also socialization, adaptive skills, language and communication, and reduction of behavior problems—and it assists a child to develop independence and personal responsibility.[7]

Because of the very nature of the disorder, students with Autism Spectrum Disorder (ASD) are commonly recognized as having special educational needs.[8] In some countries, autism appears in a specific normative category within SEN classification (such as in Czech Republic,[9] Hungary,[10] USA[11]); in others, where classification does not pursue to disabilities but to type of difficulties, autism falls within other categories and professional judgment plays a larger part in identification.

---

[5] OHCHR-Office of the United Nations High Commissioner for Human Rights *Thematic study on the right of persons with disabilities to education* (UN Doc A/HRC/25/29), 18.12.2013, para. 7.

[6] See Reindal (2008). Disability classification systems have been criticised for categorising impairments and special needs into disabilities, through classification systems grounded in a medical understanding of disability.

[7] See Lord and McGee (2001).

[8] See King (2006).

[9] Act No. 561 on Pre-school, Basic, Secondary, Tertiary Professional and Other Education (the Education Act) of 2004, Section 16.

[10] Act CXC on National Public Education of 2011, Section 4.

[11] Individuals with Disabilities Education Act (IDEA) of 2004, Sec. 300.8.

It is argued if, given their specific learning needs, students with ASD would require an alternative educational approach than that applied for students without ASD and specialized instructional techniques and learning environments would be recommended for them.[12]

The challenge of inclusive education is to fulfill the right to education by providing access for persons with disabilities to a high-quality and meaningful place in education system. This objective can be reached by adapting education to the needs of persons with disabilities. Excluding people with autism from the inclusive education process would increase stereotypes and negative attitudes towards them. In fact, the UN General Assembly Resolution 67/82 of 19 March 2013 stressed on the importance of enhancing inclusive educational programmes suited to infants, children and adults with autism as part of an integrated approach for addressing ASD. Furthermore, in its message on the World Autism Awareness Day of 2 April 2014, the UN General Secretary emphasized the key value of education for people with autism since ‘schools connect children to their communities. By including children with different learning abilities in mainstream and specialized schools, we can change attitudes and promote respect’.

3 The Right to Inclusive Education: The International Policy Framework

While the CRPD is the first legally binding instrument to protect the right to inclusive education, the idea was already expressed in previously adopted international instruments.

The shift towards an inclusive approach to education was reflected at the 1990 World Conference on Education for All, by which the problem of the exclusion of students with disabilities from school systems was acknowledged. Following the Conference, the *World Declaration on Education For All: Meeting Basic Learning Needs* (Jomtien Declaration) declared that ‘steps need to be taken to provide equal access to education to every category of disabled persons as an integral part of the education system’.[13]

The adoption in 1993 of the *Standard Rules on the Equalization of Opportunities for Persons with Disabilities* provided for integration in mainstream schools affirming that ‘education for persons with disabilities should form an integral part of national educational planning, curriculum development and school organisation’[14] and that ‘education in mainstream schools presupposes the provision of

[12] See Renty and Roeyers (2005).

[13] UNESCO (1990) World Declaration on Education For All: Meeting Basic Learning Needs, Article 3 (5).

[14] UNGA Resolution 48/96 *Standard Rules on the Equalization of Opportunities for Persons with Disabilities* (A/RES/48/96), 20.12.1993, Rule 6 (1).

interpreter and other appropriate support services' and 'adequate accessibility and support services, designed to meet the needs of persons with different disabilities'.[15] However, it also recognised that 'in situations where the general school system does not yet adequately meet the needs of all persons with disabilities, special education may be considered' but 'should be aimed at preparing students for education in the general school system'.[16]

It was not until the *UNESCO World Conference on Special Needs Education: Access and Equality* in 1994 that, for the first time, specific attention was paid to the right to inclusive education in particular. Signed by 92 Governments, the resulting *Salamanca Statement* required mainstream schools to provide quality education to all students, including students with disabilities, without discriminating on the basis of the higher requirements of support that they may need. The Salamanca Statement proclaimed that every child has unique characteristics, interests, abilities, and learning needs and provided that 'those with special educational needs must have access to regular schools which should accommodate them within a child-centred pedagogy capable of meeting these needs'. It also asserted that 'regular schools with this inclusive orientation are the most effective means of combating discriminatory attitudes, creating welcoming communities, building an inclusive society and achieving education for all'.[17]

Subsequently, the Dakar Framework for Action on Education for All adopted in 2000 a *World Declaration on Education for All* affirming the notion of education as a fundamental right and establishing the new millennium goal to provide every girl and boy with primary school education by 2015. To this end, the Declaration stressed that education systems must be inclusive and respond flexibly to the circumstances and needs of all learners. Children with disabilities were not explicitly mentioned in this framework but implicitly included in references to most vulnerable and disadvantaged children. However, it has been noted that the lack of reference to particular minority groups by name, without consequently articulating strategies most appropriate for their inclusion, may have led to a lesser response by governments than has been the case when addressing the needs of more clearly stated groups.[18]

The above-mentioned international legal instruments are not legally binding on Member States.[19] Neither they provide for monitoring of their implementation. Conventions, instead, do constitute binding international law on the States that ratify them.

---

[15] Standard Rules, Rule 6 (2).

[16] Standard Rules, Rule 6 (3).

[17] World Conference on Special Needs Education: Access and Equality, *Salamanca Statement and Framework for Action on Special Needs Education*, Salamanca, 7–10.6.1994, paras. 2 and 3, http://unesdoc.unesco.org/images/0009/000984/098427eo.pdf, accessed 17 Sep 2014.

[18] UNESCO (2009).

[19] According to some commentators, the Standard Rules have achieved "customary law" law status through legislation conforming to these rules in a significant number of States.

Until the CRPD, the Convention on the Rights of the Child (CRC) was the only treaty containing provisions on inclusive education for children and youth with disabilities. Recognizing the special needs of disabled children, Article 23 of the CRC requires State to provide assistance designed to ensure that the disabled child has effective access to and receives education. However, Article 23 has been strongly challenged by Disabled People Organizations (DPOs) because its wording makes rights contingent on 'available resources', allowing States a large degree of discretion concerning allocation of resources to special needs education.

In 2006, building on these precedents, the CRPD gave legally binding status to the concept of 'inclusive education', which is recognized as the only mean to ensure the right to education to all students, including persons with disabilities, without discrimination and on equal terms with others. In other words, in the Convention it is underscored that the right to education is in fact the right to inclusive education.

4 The Action of the European Union

Disability as a social aspect lies within the so-called supporting competency of the European Union (EU) and this is also true when talking about education—especially inclusive education—because there is no explicit EU competence on children with disabilities. In fact, Article 165 of the Treaty on the Functioning of the European Union (TFEU) confers only a supporting competence upon the EU in the field of education. Hence, the European Union can only encourage cooperation between Member States by supporting and supplementing their action, where necessary, and must respect their responsibility for the content of teaching and the organization of education systems and their cultural and linguistic diversity.

Within such a limited competence, the EU has adopted some acts addressing and promoting inclusive education.

By its *Resolution on equal opportunities for pupils and students with disabilities in education and training* of 5 May 2003, the EU Council invites Member States and the Commission, within their respective competencies, 'to encourage and support the full integration of children and young people with special needs in society through their appropriate education and training, and their insertion in a school system which is adapted to their needs'.[20] It specifically recommends measures as regards assistance, information, training, and exchanges of good practices.

The *Communication on Improving Competences for the 21st Century: An Agenda for European Cooperation on Schools* of the Commission, of 3 July

[20] Council *Resolution on equal opportunities for pupils and students with disabilities in education and training*, 5.5.2003.

2008,[21] recognizes that achieving inclusion while supporting those with specific needs involves re-thinking policies for organizing learning support, improving collaboration between schools and other services, and implementing personalized learning. The Communication proposes to focus future cooperation on 'providing more timely support and personalized learning approaches within mainstream schooling for students with special needs, among other things'.

'Education and training' is one of the eight priority areas under the *Disability Strategy 2010–2020*.[22] The specific goal is to promote inclusive education and lifelong learning for pupils and students with disabilities. The Strategy lists a series of actions to ensure that people with disabilities receive the support required within the general education system to facilitate their education, and that effective individualized support measures are provided in environments that maximize academic and social development, consistent with the goal of full inclusion.

The goal of inclusive education and training is supported within the framework of the *Youth and Move Initiative* which promotes actions for the exchange of good practices on inclusive education and dissemination of guidance materials on the principle of reasonable accommodation in education. The initiative, which includes a commitment to reducing school drop-out rates and increasing participation in tertiary education, is expected to have an impact on inclusive education and job placement schemes for young people with disabilities.

Furthermore, the Strategy provides for the EU supports to national efforts through the *Education and Training 2020* (ET 2020) framework, which establishes common strategic objectives for Member States. One of its four strategic objectives is promoting equity, social cohesion and active citizenship. In the context of ET2020, the 2013 report 'Supporting Teachers' Competence Development for Better Learning Outcomes' acknowledged the need for teachers to possess the knowledge, skills and attitudes to deal with diversity and inclusion.

A stronger EU action can be found in the field of non-discrimination based on disability.

The Treaty on the Functioning of the European Union established the legal basis for the EU action to combat discrimination (Article 19), providing that the Council may take appropriate action to combat discrimination based on disability.

Currently, the EU anti-discrimination law covers to the educational field at least to a limited extent. The *Employment Equality Directive*[23] includes within its

[21] Communication from the Commission to the European Parliament, the Council, the European Economic and Social Committee and the Committee of the Regions *Improving competences for the 21st Century: an Agenda for European Cooperation on Schools* (COM/2008/0425 final), 3.7.2008.

[22] Communication for the Commission to the European Parliament, the Council, the European Economic and Social Committee and the Committee of the Regions *European Disability Strategy 2010–2020: A Renewed Commitment to a Barrier-Free Europe* (COM(2010) 636 final), 15.11.2010.

[23] Council *Directive establishing a general framework for equal treatment in employment and occupation* (2000/78/EC), 27.11.2000.

material scope the field of vocational training, which has been defined by the EU Court of Justice as 'any form of education which prepares for a qualification for a particular profession, trade or employment or which provides the necessary training and skills for such a profession, trade or employment [...] even if the training programme includes an element of general education'.

In 2008, the Commission adopted a proposal for a *Multi-Ground Beyond-Employment Directive* aimed at extending the protection against discrimination on the grounds of religion or belief, disability, age or sexual orientation to areas outside employment, including education.[24]

A large majority of delegations welcomed the proposal in principle, many endorsing the fact that it complements the existing EU legal framework by addressing all four grounds of discrimination through a horizontal approach and underlining the significance of the proposal in the context of the implementation of the CRPD.

The genuine novelty in the definition of discrimination in Article 2 (2) (5) is the proposal to create a fifth limb to the concept of discrimination which would be the 'denial of reasonable accommodation'. This is an advancement with respect to the Employment Directive which does not clearly include such a failure within its definition of 'discrimination'. It can be only presumed by the preface of the duty reading 'in order to guarantee compliance with the principle of equal treatment in relation to persons with disabilities'. By stating that the denial of reasonable accommodation is a specific form of unlawful discrimination, the proposed Directive endorses the approach of the CRPD.

Another positive aspect is the establishment in Article 4 (1) (a) of an anticipatory duty to provide 'effective non-discriminatory access to social protection, social advantages, health care, education and access to and supply of goods and services which are available to the public, including housing and transport'. The Directive does not spell out on whom this duty falls, but it implies that Member States and service-providers have a positive obligation to take measures to ensure equal access for disabled persons.

However, in the field of disability, some delegations would have preferred more ambitious provisions within the proposed Directive.

One of the most debated provisions concerns the restrictions to the application of the Directive under Article 3. This article concerns the material scope of the Directive, therefore strictly speaking, these provisions are not exceptions to the prohibition of discrimination, but simply limitations on the scope of application of the Directive. In particular, such provision provides that the Directive is 'without prejudice' to the content of teaching, organization of the educational system, including *special needs education.*

[24] Proposal for a Council *Directive on implementing the principle of equal treatment between persons irrespective of religion or belief, disability, age or sexual orientation* (COM/2008/0426 final—CNS 2008/0140), 2.7.2008.

Such provision raised many criticisms. First, 'special needs education' are not defined and therefore it appears unclear whether the proposal only intends to reserve this concept for specialized schools, or whether it also includes mainstream schools that provide reasonable accommodations (such as an adapted curriculum, or provision of tuition in alternative communication means) for children with special educational needs.

Secondly, it is unclear if the restriction excludes all aspects of 'special needs education' from the scope of the Directive, or only those aspects which relate to 'the content of teaching, activities and organization' of special needs education. If all aspects of 'special needs education' fall outside the scope of the Directive then, for example, a child who experiences discrimination on one of the prohibited grounds at a mainstream school would be protected, whilst a child who is victim of a similar discriminatory treatment in a 'special needs' setting would not be.

The EU Parliament tackled such concerns in its resolution of 2 April 2009 on the proposal Directive, by introducing an amendment to Article 3.[25] While it confirms that the Directive shall not apply to the content of teaching, activities and organization of national educational systems, the amendment obliges Member States to ensure the right of persons with disabilities to education without discrimination and on the basis of equal opportunities. In addition, it requires Member States to ensure that, in determining which type of education or training is appropriate, the views of the person with disabilities are respected.

While emphasizing the importance of such new Directive for the fight against discrimination, certain delegations have general reservations, questioning the need for the Commission's proposal, which they see as infringing on national competence for certain issues and as conflicting with the principles of subsidiarity and proportionality.

The European Union formally ratified the UN Convention on the Rights of Persons with Disabilities on 23 December 2010. The commitments deriving from the Convention argue for the EU to take an active role on education, hopefully moving forward the process for adopting the proposal Directive.

5 Article 24 of the CRPD

The normative construction under the CRPD is a ringing rejection of conceiving disability as individual impairment and equality as formal equality. It sees disability through the lens of a human rights model of disability whose ultimate focus is not on identifying intrinsic impairment, but on the interaction between impairment and

[25] European Parliament legislative *resolution on the proposal for a Council directive on implementing the principle of equal treatment between persons irrespective of religion or belief, disability, age or sexual orientation* (COM(2008)0426—C6-0291/2008—2008/0140(CNS)), 2.4.2009.

the environment and on overcoming systemic barriers in order to accommodate different disabilities.

Article 24 of the CRPD provides even in the most straightforward way for inclusion in the entire Convention and increases the chances of people with disabilities to enjoy equal treatment. As the other UN thematic human rights treaties, the CRPD does not establish a new right, but rather it clarifies the specific implications for persons with disabilities of enjoying the right to education without discrimination and sets out the obligations for Contracting Parties to ensure education systems are inclusive for persons with disabilities.

5.1 The Right to Inclusive Education

The drafters of the CRPD did not immediately agree on the right to inclusive education. There was a lot of discussion in this regard, where among others the question arose whether or not special education still had to be made available. The Ad Hoc Committee, charged with elaborating the Convention, initially left persons with disabilities the right to choose between inclusive and special education. Draft Article 17 (3) of the CRPD provided that 'where the general education system does not adequately meet the needs of persons with disabilities special and alternative forms of learning should be made available'. Any such forms should:

a) reflect the same standards and objectives provided in the general education system;
b) be provided in such a manner to allow children with disabilities to participate in the general education system to the maximum extent possible;
c) allow a free and informed choice between general and special systems;
d) in no way limit the duty of States Parties to continue to strive to meet the needs of students with disabilities in the general education system.[26]

The intent of this draft Article was to provide the right to choose inclusive and accessible education. There is no intention to create an obligation on students with disabilities to attend general schools where their needs may not be adequately met.

This provision reflected the different opinions among the drafters regarding the right to education of persons with disabilities. While some delegations considered that choice was an important element of this Article, some others considered that the right to education was more important. Other members would have liked greater emphasis on the best interests of the child in this choice. In this regard, different

[26] Ad Hoc Committee on a Comprehensive and Integral International Convention on the Protection and Promotion of the Rights and Dignity of Persons with Disabilities Working Group *Report of the Working Group to the Ad Hoc Committee. Annex I: Draft articles for a Comprehensive and Integral International Convention on the Protection and Promotion of the Rights and Dignity of Persons with Disabilities* (A/AC.265/2004/WG.1), 27.1.2004. http://www.un.org/esa/socdev/enable/rights/ahcwgreportax1.htm. Accessed 17 Sep 2014.

approaches were also identified to setting out the relationship between the provision of specialist education services and the general education system. While some drafters considered that both mainstream and special schools should exist in parallel, others thought that inclusive education should be the norm and special education the exception.

In the meanwhile, the Committee on the Rights of the Child adopted General Comment No. 9 on the rights of children with disabilities, which likewise provided that inclusive education must be the objective of education for children with disabilities. However, it also recognized that 'the measure in which the inclusion occurs may vary' and that 'a continuum of services and programme options must be maintained in circumstances where fully inclusive education is not feasible to achieve in the immediate future'.[27]

The drafters of the CRPD laid down the principle that inclusive education has to be guaranteed for all persons with disabilities. Article 24 (1) of the CRPD establishes that 'States Parties shall ensure an inclusive education system at all levels and lifelong learning'.

Article 24 (2) (a) and (b), of the CRPD further stipulates that the States Parties shall ensure that 'children with disabilities are not excluded from free and compulsory primary education on the basis of disability' and that 'persons with disabilities can access an inclusive, quality and free primary education and secondary education on an equal basis with others in the communities in which they live'. Consequently, children with disabilities may not be denied education because of their impairments and must, together with their parents, be able to opt for regular schools in their neighborhood.

The right to education of persons with disabilities may be achieved over a certain period of time. In fact, Article 4 (2), of the CRPD provides that economic, social and cultural rights have to be progressively realized within the maximum available resources. The progressive realization of the right to education of persons with disabilities does not mean that inclusive education can just be postponed. Contracting Parties should make greater efforts to comply with the obligation to progressively realize the right to inclusive education within the maximum available resources. States Parties must take steps to this end, even though the objective does not have to be reached right away, and put in place their resources with a view to fully realize the right to education by providing reasonable accommodations and adopting support measures. As a best practice of fulfilling the purpose of Article 24, in conformity with Article 4 (2) of the Convention, in its Concluding observations on the initial report of Spain, the CRPD Committee commended the State Party for the high percentage (78.35 %) of enrolment of children with disabilities in

[27] UN Committee on the Rights of the Child *General Comment No. 9 (2006): The rights of children with disabilities* (CRC/C/GC/9), 27.2.2007, para. 66.

the regular education system, and for 'the efforts made to maintain the funding for programmes for persons with disabilities in times of economic crisis.'[28]

In this regard, it must be said that an inclusive education system is not more expensive than a segregated education system. According to UNICEF, 'countries are now increasingly realizing the inefficiency of multiple systems of administration, organizational structures and services, and that it is the option of special schools which is financially unrealistic'.[29] Inclusive education could bring additional costs in the short term and only become profitable in the long term.

The question is what must be done about special schools.

Special education is specifically provided in Article 24 (3) (c) of the CRPD for persons with sensory or communication impairments in order to reflects the opinions expressed during the negotiations by their representative organizations fearing that inclusive education would neglect the identity of deaf and blind children and would in practice mean exclusion. The result is that persons with sensory or communication impairments should be allowed to be educated in special schools, although this option should not prevent them from asking to be able to participate in the general education system.

Beyond the exception for blind, deaf or deaf-blind children contained in Article 24 (3) (c), there is still ambiguity on special schools.

The proposal made by the Centre for Studies on Inclusive Education (CSIE) to prohibit providing special education for children with disabilities was rejected.[30] Even though any reference to special education has been deleted, it is still debated to what extent special schools are allowed under the Convention. Article 24 (2) (e), in fact, seems to make room for special education, stating that 'effective individualized support measures are provided in *environments that maximize academic and social development*, consistent with the goal of full inclusion'.

It cannot be ruled out that for a limited number of children with serious and multiple disabilities reasonable accommodations are not possible or support measures not desired. Consequently, it could be that mainstream education is not achievable for these children. Article 24 does not prevent States from establishing special schools for these children. Nor, however, does it compel them to be equipped with special schools, as was confirmed during the negotiations.[31] In other words, while such schools can be established for some children with disabilities, there is no requirement to have them. States, thus, have a certain leeway, although they should provide a strong CRPD-based justification if they keep a (partially) segregated education system.

However, the problem remains for those States that have strongly segregated education systems. In these States special schools cannot be suddenly closed,

---

[28] CRPD Committee *Concluding observations on the initial report of Spain* (CRPD/C/ESP/CO/1), 19.10.2011, para. 9.

[29] See UNICEF (2012).

[30] See Shaw (2014).

[31] See Arnardóttir (2011), pp. 214–215.

because to do so would lead to discrimination against children with disabilities, if these children could no longer receive education. They must instead start immediately with building an inclusive education system, while at the same time the special schools must continue to function. There should be a gradual move from segregated to inclusive education systems, starting from transferring resources from the special schools to the mainstream schools.

Many States, in fact, allocate substantial resources to special education instead to provide mainstream school with the financial means necessary to accommodate special needs. The CRPD Committee has requested that States use these resources for the purpose of inclusive education.[32]

In such countries, the transition towards an inclusive education system can encounter resistance resulting from the legacy of policies and prejudices surrounding children with disabilities, who are considered not to fit in the general education system. There is sometimes a fear that children with disabilities would push the level of education downward and schools are usually not willing to adapt their curricula in order to make them accessible to children with intellectual disabilities in particular. Difficult to remove in historically segregated structures, social barriers are the real obstacles to inclusive education.

5.2 The Duty to Provide a Reasonable Accommodation

Article 24 of the CRPD provides for instruments to concretely realize inclusive education systems. One of them, and the most important, is the provision of reasonable accommodation.

According to Article 24 (2) (c) of the CRPD, States shall ensure that 'reasonable accommodation of the individual's requirements is provided'. While this obligation is already foreseen in Article 5 (3), it is repeated in relation to education, which shows its importance for inclusive education. Article 2 of the CRPD defines the concept of 'reasonable accommodation' as follows: 'necessary and appropriate modifications and adjustments not imposing a disproportionate or undue burden, where needed in a particular case, to ensure to persons with disabilities the enjoyment or exercise on an equal basis with others of all human rights and fundamental freedoms'. It furthermore provides that 'denial of reasonable accommodation' is a form of discrimination. Consequently, the provision of reasonable accommodation is an obligation which has to be fulfilled immediately.

Reasonable accommodations are individualized measures meeting the special needs of children with disabilities. They aim at moving beyond formal equality and

---

[32] The Committee recommended to China to 'reallocate resources from the special education system to promote the inclusive education in mainstream schools, so as to ensure that more children with disabilities can attend mainstream education'. CRPD Committee *Concluding observations on the initial report of China* (CRPD/C/CHN/CO/1), 15.10.2012, para. 36.

achieving substantive equality by ensuring that persons with disabilities can reach the same level of opportunities as other persons. In the field of education, the duty to provide reasonable accommodation means, for example, that buildings and classrooms must be accessible, transportation to schools is available and communication technology is used, as also provided for in Article 9 (1) of the CRPD. Such duty also applies to higher education, as well as to pre-school and adult education, since Article 24 (1) of the CRPD, guarantees 'an inclusive education system at all levels and lifelong learning'. Reasonable accommodations should be provided by public, but also private schools which are prohibited to discriminate since they provide a public service.

The way in which a reasonable accommodation is determined must be decided in consultation with all involved parties, including the applicant(s).

Since education has to be free, reasonable accommodation should likewise be provided by the State, which is responsible for the achievement of inclusive education. In this regard, Article 24 of the CRPD must be read in combination with Article 13 (2) of the International Covenant on Economic, Social and Cultural Rights (ICESCR) providing for free education.[33] In its Concluding observations to the initial report of Spain the CRPD Committee asked the State to 'ensure that the parents of children with disabilities are not obliged to pay [...] for the measures of reasonable accommodation in mainstream schools'.[34]

The question is of course when accommodation is considered 'reasonable'.

This question will never have a definite answer and has to be examined on a case-by-case basis.

It can be considered that accommodations are reasonable if they do not create an undue burden.[35] There may be a burden, which means that efforts are required, but this burden may not be undue. This involves a comparison between costs, which should be calculated taking into account compensations that can be obtained, and benefits, which includes advantages for parties other than those for whom the measures are taken.

The OHCHR defines 'reasonableness' as 'the result of an objective test that involves an analysis of the availability of resources, as well as the relevance of the accommodation, and the expected goal of countering discrimination'. The OHCHR, however, acknowledges that 'testing standards are yet to be developed in jurisprudence by the Committee on the Rights of Persons with Disabilities'.[36]

---

[33] Article 13 (2) of the ICESCR provides that 'a. primary education must be compulsory and free for everybody; b. secondary education ... in particular through the gradual introduction of free education, must be made generally available and accessible for everybody; [and] c. higher education ... in particular through the gradual introduction of free education, must be made equally accessible based on each person's competence'.

[34] CRPD Committee *Concluding observations on the initial report of Spain* (CRPD/C/ESP/CO/1), 19.10.2011, para. 44.

[35] See de Campos Velho Martel (2011).

[36] See OHCHR (2013), para. 43.

Significant factors to decide whether hardships are excessive or 'undue' in a school, college or university setting, are indicated in a conference document prepared for the Ad Hoc Committee, such as the financial resources required to provide an accommodation; the degree and kinds of effects that accommodations will have on other students; the impact of accommodations on the educational program itself; unusual risks, if any, that accommodations may pose for staff or other students, including other students who have a disability.[37]

Even though the reasonable character of an accommodation for the purpose of inclusive education is difficult to determine, several sources point out that their cost is often over-estimated and that most of the time they are available. The Handbook for Parliamentarians underlies that experience has shown that as many as 80–90 % of children with specific education needs, including children with intellectual disabilities, can easily be integrated into regular schools and classrooms, as long as there is basic support for their inclusion.[38]

5.3 *Support Measures*

In addition, the CRPD prescribes a number of support measures in order to enable children with disabilities to access the general education system.

According to Article 24 (2) (d) of the CRPD, States Parties guarantee that 'persons with disabilities receive the support required, within the general education system, to facilitate their effective education'. It is worth recalling that the draft proposal mentioned 'effective alternative support measures' to be provided by States Parties in exceptional circumstances of failure of general school, but such expression was to be understood as special education or a mixed form of education.[39] The obligation to 'ensure that effective alternative support measures are provided' was subsequently replaced by the obligation to 'ensure that effective individualized support measures are provided in environments that maximize academic and social development', which eventually became Article 24 (2) (e). While there remains ambiguity concerning the interpretation of the term 'environments that maximize academic and social development' as special schools, Article 24 (2) (e), provides that the support measures have to be provided 'consistent with the goal of full inclusion'. It could therefore refer more to a mixed form of education than special education.

The support measures supplement reasonable accommodations and differ from them. The support measures are subject to the obligation to progressively realize the

[37] The Concept of Reasonable Accommodation in Selected National Disability Legislation. Background conference document by the Department of Economic and Social Affairs, http://www.un.org/esa/socdev/enable/rights/ahc7bkgrndra.htm.

[38] See UNDESA et al. (2007), p. 85.

[39] See Arnardóttir (2011), p. 217.

right to inclusive education within the maximum available resources (contrary to the duty to provide reasonable accommodation). Support measures are general measures which must gradually achieve inclusive education. Consequently, these measures do not have to be adopted all at once, provided that the available resources are used to achieve inclusive education and that immediate action is undertaken by States in this regard.

Differently from reasonable accommodations which target individuals, support measures aims at adapting the general education system with a view to making it accessible to persons with disabilities. They do not aim at providing for particular adjustments, but to adapt the general education system in order to include all children. It has been noted that while the two overlap to certain extent, the more support measures are taken, fewer reasonable accommodations would be needed since through support measures the general education system would take account of special needs from the outset.[40]

The general measures include providing personal assistance, including medical assistance, as well as the necessary equipment and material, including Braille and sign language, as established in Article 24 (3) of the CRPD. According to the Special Rapporteur on the Right to Education, both external and personal factors should be addressed in order to create inclusive education systems. The former include 'altering the physical environment, such as the design of hallways and classrooms, desks, widening entrances, building ramps, installation of elevators, altering or reconsidering geographical locations, adapting rules and admission standards', whereas the latter entail 'the provision of supplementary classes, alternative/additional forms of communication, special tutors or support staff, and nutritious meals'.[41] Furthermore, inclusive education requires States Parties to adapt not only teaching methods and curricula but also evaluation tools for children with intellectual disabilities.

As a good example of support measures consistent with Article 24 (2) (d) of the Convention, the OHCHR report indicates the Individual Educational Programme (IEP).[42] Such programme plays a major role for inclusive special needs education. This document present information on how mainstream curriculum is adapted, and what are the necessary additional resources, goals and evaluation of the educational approach. There is a growing consensus that the provision and implementation of an appropriate IEP is the most effective form of inclusion of pupils with autism. In fact, such programmes affect a child's participation in education, the community, and family life by providing educational objectives aimed at developing social skills, expressive verbal and non-verbal language, cognitive skills, independent organizational skills and so on.[43]

[40] See de Beco (2014), pp. 283–284.

[41] See OHCHR (2007), para. 14.

[42] See OHCHR (2013), paras. 46–47.

[43] See Lord and McGee (2001).

A crucial aspect for realizing inclusive education systems is the support given to teaching staff and the quality of its training. Article 24 (4) of the CRPD requires that teachers are trained in how to deal with persons with disabilities and to use alternative or facilitating forms of communication and other methods to support persons with disabilities. Training in disability rights should not only be included in specialization courses but also in general courses which must pay attention to diversity. There are often special teaching curricula for those interested in working with children with disabilities (in special schools), but rarely are those courses integrated into the mainstream teaching curricula. It is also important that teachers continue to be supported and trained during their teaching career.

6 National Approaches to Inclusive Education of EU Member States

Different patterns emerge among EU Member States in how they approach their policies for children with SEN. The report of the NESSE network of experts commissioned by the EU Commission in 2012 identifies three distinctive approaches adopted by EU countries.[44]

The first category (called *one-track* approach) includes States (such as Italy, Greece, Sweden) that develop policy and practices geared towards inclusion of almost all pupils within mainstream education. Generally speaking, this type of integration is supported by a wide range of services focusing on the mainstream school. The percentage of pupils attending special schools or classes is less than 1 %.

States belonging to the second category (*multi-track* approach) have a multiplicity of approaches to inclusion. They do not offer one single solution (inclusion in mainstream education with the support of many different services) or a choice between two options (mainstream or special education). They range from special multiple classes (full-time or part-time) to different forms of inter-school cooperation including exchange categories (with teacher and pupils from mainstream and special schools arranging temporary or part-time exchange). States like Denmark, France, United Kingdom fall into this category.

In the third category (*two-track* approach), there are two distinct education systems. Pupils with SEN are usually placed in special schools or special classes. Generally, a vast majority of pupils officially as having special educational needs do not follow the mainstream curriculum among their non-disabled peers. In this way, mainstream and special schools run in parallel. Switzerland and the Flemish Community of Belgium belongs to this category.

However, the NESSE report highlights that at times it can be difficult to classify a country according to the type if inclusion policy, because of policy changes.

---

[44] See NESSE (2012).

For instance, Germany and the Netherlands are positioned within the two-track system but they are recently moving towards the multi-track system. There is, in fact, a common trend in Europe consisting in transforming special schools and institutes into resource centres. These centres are given different names and different tasks are assigned to them, such as provision for training and course for teachers and other professionals, development and dissemination of materials and methods, support for mainstreams schools and parents, short-time or part-time help for individual students. Special education resources can support mainstream schools in the integration process.

7 EU Member States' Implementation of Article 24

In its Concluding observations, the CRPD Committee has stressed the importance of enabling children with disabilities to obtain education, and preferably inclusive education where children with disabilities are alongside other children in the classroom.[45]

Implementing inclusive education is high on the agenda of many EU Member States, though the policy is approached from differing historical and structural perspectives.

For instance, there are EU Member States with selective rather than comprehensive school systems where special schools are still numerous. Germany and both the French and Flemish communities of Belgium may be cited as examples in this regard.

In Germany, special schooling has a tradition in the field of child education. The country has a highly differentiated (segregated) system that is based on a division between regular schooling and special schooling. When the CRPD came into force in 2009, 85 % of persons with recognized special needs attended special schools.[46]

The right to education is stated in the Basic Law (Grundgesetz, Art. 3—R1) and in Book Twelve of the Social Code (Sozialgesetzbuch XII—Sozialhilfe). However, in such country education is a matter for the Länder and therefore the right of disabled pupils to education and training appropriate to their needs is stated in the Länder constitutions and more detailed provisions are set out in their educational legislations. So far, only some States have adopted a co-education system of disabled and non-disabled children in school.

In its Report on the CRPD implementation, the German Federal Government referred about its endeavours in ensuring that inclusive learning becomes the norm in Germany, by harmonizing the development and the organization of special education in the Länder through the resolutions adopted by the Standing Conference of the Ministers of Education and Cultural Affairs of the Länder. In this vein,

[45] See OHCHR (2013), paras. 26 ff., 56 ff., 68 ff.

[46] See German Institute for Human Rights (2014), p. 17.

the Recommendations of the Conference of Ministers of Culture and Education are being revised in order to address some specific issues such as the teaching of children with autism. The current situation is documented in the Recommendations on Special Needs Education in the Schools of the Federal Republic of Germany (*Empfehlungen zur sonderpädagogischen Förderung in den Schulen in der Bundesrepublik Deutschland*, Resolution of May 1994), which form the basis for the development at Land level in the field of special education. In 2000, the Standing Conference has also made Recommendations on the Education and Teaching of Children and Young People with Autistic Behaviour (*Erziehung und Unterricht von Kindern und Jugendlichen mit autistischem Verhalten*).

The CRPD Committee has not yet adopted its Concluding observations on the initial report of Germany and therefore its views on the German education system and the action undertaken for increasing inclusive education are not known.

However, it is worth to mention that the Committee on the Rights of the Child expressed its concerns about the non-inclusive nature of education in Germany, particularly at the secondary school level. In that context, the Committee also noted with concern that in certain Länder, children at the primary level are assigned to special schools against their parents' will, the vast majority of pupils with disabilities attend special schools, and a high number of children with disabilities leave school without a diploma. Furthermore, the need for individual support and reasonable accommodation in the area of education is not recognized.[47] Consequently, the CRC Committee urged Germany to take 'all necessary legislative and structural reforms to ensure that the right to inclusive education is guaranteed to children with disabilities and provide for it to encompass the right to individual support and reasonable accommodation in the area of education'.

Discrepancies in education organization exist also in Belgium, where each community (Dutch speaking community, French speaking community and German speaking community) has its own education system. Special needs education is spread over the different communities and types of educational institution take the form of special schools or integrated education.

In Flanders, special schools have been established by the 1970 Special Education Law whereby special schools are organized on the basis of the type of disabilities (primary level)[48] and pedagogical programme of education (secondary level).[49] The establishment of this categorical approach led to a proliferation of

[47] CRC Committee *Concluding observations on the combined third and fourth periodic reports of Germany* (CRC/C/DEU/CO/3-4), 31.1.2014, paras. 50–55.

[48] At primary level, special education is organized for type of disabilities, such as Type 1: children with mild intellectual disabilities; Type 2: children with moderate or severe intellectual disabilities; Type 3: children with serious emotional and/or behavioural problems; Type 4: children with physical disabilities; Type 5: children admitted to hospital or in quarantine for medical reasons; Type 6: children with visual impairments; Type 7: children with hearing impairments; Type 8: children with serious learning difficulties.

[49] At secondary level, special needs education is subdivided in training forms (TF), namely TF1: offering social training with the aim of integration into a protected environment (for students of

new-built special schools and the closure of existing special classrooms in regular schools, creating a problematic structural legacy in subsequent moves towards an 'inclusion agenda'. In order to address such problem, in 1986 the Law was amended to give students with disabilities the opportunity to receive a supported education in a mainstream school. Accordingly, children with disabilities may be to a certain degree educated within mainstream education according to the system of integrated education or the inclusive education project.

Integrated education can be organized on all educational levels. It aims at children with (a) minor mental disabilities, (b) serious emotional and/or behavioral problems, (c) physical disabilities, (d) visual disabilities, (e) auditory disabilities or (f) serious learning disabilities. Such kind of education comprises attendance in mainstream education classes mixed with additional teaching periods and/or additional resources provided by a school for special education.

Children with a moderate or severe mental disability are not covered, but may be qualified for participating in the mainstream school through the *Inclusive Education Project* (*Inclusief Onderwijs*) or ION, by which students receive individual learning-pathway support.

However, the Law limited the program to 100 students and no special type of class for children with ASD was provided, so children with ASD who choose to attend a special education school, as a result, were scattered over different types of special schools where ASD adaptations and teaching expertise are inappropriate.

In order to increase inclusive education, a Decree adopted in 2002 on equal education opportunities (GOK Decree) established that mainstream primary and secondary education may enroll a pupil with SEN, but it is allowed to refuse the enrolment if the school does not have sufficient means to provide for the pupil's specific needs in terms of teaching. In this case, the pupil is referred to special needs education.

The education system in Belgium is not consistent with Article 24 of the CRPD that establishes the right to mainstream education for all people with disabilities. In fact, the CRPD Committee in its Concluding observations on the Belgium initial report expressed its concern on the segregate education system in Belgium, underlying the high number of students of disabilities obliged to be enrolled in special schools in reason of the missing of reasonable accommodations in the ordinary education system.[50]

In March 2014, the Flemish Parliament passed the Decree concerning measure for pupils with specific educational needs, known as the 'M-decree', aimed at

types T2, T3, T4, T6, T7); TF2: offering general and social training with the aim of integration into a protected environment and work situation (T2, T3, T4, T6, T7); TF3: offering social and vocational training with the aim of integration into a regular environment and work situation (T1, T3, T4, T6, T7); TF4: offering preparation for study in higher education and integration into active life (T3, T4, T5, T6, T7).

[50] CRPD Committee *Concluding observations on the initial report of Belgium* (CRPD/C/BEL/CO/1), 28.10.2014, paras. 36–37.

ensuring greater access to mainstream education for children with disabilities.[51] Such Decree introduces a new Type 9 for 'children with autism without intellectual disabilities' within the system of disability typologies under which is assessed if a students have special needs.

Providing the right for reasonable accommodation, the M-decree establishes that students can be referred to special education only if schools can prove that they have tried all 'reasonable adjustments'. In particular, it states that every child with disability has the right to be enrolled in regular school if it is possible to follow the regular curriculum with reasonable adaptations, such as extra-time to make tests.

As for the children with disabilities who need an individual curriculum, the M-decree points out that they can go to regular school if the student support service and the teaching staff concludes that it is possible with reasonable adaptations. When adaptations are too extreme, the child will be referred to special education.

Being the entry into force of the Decree, originally scheduled in September 2014, delayed until September 2015, the effect of the new law once it is in force is unknown.

However, the M-decree has raised several criticisms from DPOs. As underlined in the complaint submitted by the MDAC to the European Committee of Social Rights in 2014,[52] the Decree appears to be discriminatory since it does not even apply to children who cannot follow the regular curriculum, thereby excluding children with more significant intellectual or learning disabilities. Furthermore, no new funding mechanisms have been introduced in order to increase the number or range of supports that schools or local authorities can provide to students who require accommodations. Therefore, it seems that the M-decree will not change the current practices by which schools refuse admission to students claiming that they cannot provide the needed supports if considered disproportionate and an undue burden.

In contrast with clearly separated systems, some EU Member States, such as the UK and Spain, have some provisions on special education while a comprehensive school system has been established.

As far as the United Kingdom is concerned, mainstream school system co-exists with special schools. In this regards, it must be recalled that the State made a reservation on Article 24 of the CRPD stating that 'the general education system in the United Kingdom includes mainstream, and special schools, which the UK Government understands is allowed under the Convention'. Such reservation is aimed at enabling parents to continue to have access to places for their children at mainstream and special schools.[53]

---

[51] The entry into force of the decree which was originally scheduled for September 2014, was delayed until September 2015.

[52] European Committee of Social Rights *Mental Disability Advocacy Center (MDAC) v. Belgium*, Complaint No. 109/2014. https://www.coe.int/t/dghl/monitoring/socialcharter/Complaints/CC109CaseDoc1_en.pdf. Accessed 17 Sep 2014.

[53] The UK reservation reads as follow: 'The United Kingdom reserves the right for disabled children to be educated outside their local community where more appropriate education provision

Discrimination against people in education is prohibited in Great Britain by the 2010 Equality Act and in Northern Ireland by the 2005 Special Educational Needs and Disability Order. Both acts provides that schools must take reasonable accommodation ('steps' in the 2010 Equality Act, 'adjustment' in the 2005 Order) to ensure equal access to all areas of school life.

In England, the education system for children and young people with SEN or disability, under the terms of the 1996 Education Act, has been reformed following the Children and Families Act entered into force in September 2014.

The Act is committed to inclusive education of disabled children and young people and to progressively remove the barriers to their learning and participation in mainstream education. The Children and Families Act secures the general presumption in law of mainstream education in relation to decisions about where children and young people with SEN should be educated.

It places duties on local authorities and other services in relation to both disabled children and young people and those with SEN, although not all the sections of the Act apply to both groups. The strategic planning duties generally apply to all disabled children and young people and those with SEN. The specific duties, in particular those contained in Part 3 of the Act, apply only to children and young people with SEN, while duties to disabled people are contained in the 2010 Equality Act.

The Act incorporates the definition of SEN contained in the 1996 Education Act. A child or young person has special educational needs if they have a learning difficulty or disability which calls for special educational provision to be made for them (Section 20). Special educational provision is additional to or different from that which would normally be provided for children or young people of the same age in a mainstream education setting (Section 21).

Statements of special educational needs for children in schools are replaced with a combined Education, Health and Care plan (EHC plan), which includes health and social care support that is required as well as education provisions. In the field of education the plan specifies, *inter alia*, the child's or young person's special educational needs, the outcomes sought for him or her and the special educational provision required by him or her. Many of the legal requirements for EHC plans are the same or similar to those required for SEN statements, but significant differences exist as far as their duration. EHC plans covers the age range 0–25 years. Therefore, such plans do not necessarily cease when a young person leaves school and can be maintained when a young person is in college, undertaking an apprenticeship, or not in education, employment or training.

Section 33 of the Act places a duty on the local authority to ensure that a child or young person with an EHC plan is educated in a mainstream setting. The only

---

is available elsewhere. Nevertheless, parents of disabled children have the same opportunity as other parents to state a preference for the school at which they wish their child to be educated. The United Kingdom Government is committed to continuing to develop an inclusive system where parents of disabled children have increasing access to mainstream schools and staff, which have the capacity to meet the needs of disabled children'.

exceptions to this rule are if this goes against the wishes of the young person or the child's parent, or would impact on the efficient education of others and there are no reasonable steps that could be taken to overcome this incompatibility.

Within the UK, the educational provisions for students with SEN broadly operates under similar legislative framework. Nonetheless, it is worth to mention some main innovations introduced outside England.

In Scotland, the legal framework substantially changed with the 2004 Education Additional Support for Learning Scotland Act, by which the term SEN has been replaced by the broader definition of 'additional support need', referring to all children who would benefit from extra-help for overcoming barriers to their learning.

In Wales, where the legal framework for the provision of special education is governed by the 2002 Education (SEN) Welsh Regulation, in June 2014 the Government has published a White Paper which proposed to change the law. The reform, which will apply to learners aged 0–25, will replace the existing statutory definition of SEN with a more flexible and inclusive legal concept of Additional Learning Needs (ALN) and substitute statements of SEN with Individual Development Plans (IDPs) as the basis for meeting a child or young person's ALN.

The organization of special educational provision and the definition of SEN in Northern Ireland are similar to those employed in England. Special education is governed by the 1996 Education (Northern Ireland) Order as amended by the 2005 Special Educational Needs and Disability (Northern Ireland) Order, by which special educational needs are addressed in special schools, special units attached to mainstream schools, or in mainstream classes.

In Spain, the concept of special education has been introduced by the 1990 Organic Law of General Arrangement of the Educational System (LOGSE), which asserted the incorporation of special education into mainstream system and stated that SEN pupils can attend mainstream or special education establishments. This Act established that pupils with special educational needs should attend mainstream setting, by adapting regular programmes to the individual capacities of each pupil. Their schooling in special education units or establishments, or a combined schooling, only took place when pupils' needs cannot be met in mainstream establishments.

Following LOGSE, Spain progressed in its efforts to promote inclusive education adopting new provisions for students with special needs.

The current 2006 Organic Law of Education (LOE) is based on the principle that the same quality of education has to be provided for all pupils, regardless of their condition or circumstances, on the assumption that guaranteeing equality of opportunities, educational inclusion and non-discrimination serves as an element for compensating personal, cultural, economic and social inequalities, with special emphasis on inequalities arising from disability.

Part II of the Law deals with students with special educational needs who require certain support and specific educational attention due to disability or serious behavioral disorders, either for a period or throughout the whole of their schooling.

The schooling of students with SEN will be governed by principles of normalization and inclusion and will ensure non-discrimination and real equality in the access to the education system and continued attendance, allowing flexibility in the different stages of their education when necessary. Schooling in special education centres or units, which may be extended to the age of 21, will only take place when their needs cannot be met by the special needs provisions available in normal schools.

In pursuance of the LOE, royal decrees have been issued laying down minimum educational content in the three stages of schooling—pre-primary, primary and secondary. Such decrees envisage the provision of necessary support for students with SEN from the beginning of their schooling or as soon as they are identified as having special needs. In principle, schools have to guarantee appropriate scholastic organization in order to enable every pupil to attain the educational goals, as well as they have to ensure available the personnel and material resources needed to provide appropriate care for pupils with educational needs deriving from disabilities. The schools develop the curriculum through Individual Educational Plans (IEP), which have to take into account the student's needs and characteristics.

Following such legal instruments, significant results have been achieved in Spain. Most children with disabilities follow regular education system and the overall number of special schools in Spain has tended to decrease. While some special institutions have been transformed into resources centres, others have been dismantled as a result of inclusive policies, but still exist.[54]

In spite of such evolution, the CRPD Committee raised concerns on the implementation of Spanish laws in practice. In particular, in its Concluding observations on Spain's report the Committee stressed on the reported cases of failure to provide reasonable accommodations or of enrollment in special schools, even against parents' will. In this regard, the Committee noted with concern that parents challenging the placement of their children with disabilities in special education have no possibility of appeal and their only alternative is to educate them at their own expense or pay for the reasonable accommodation of their child in the regular education system.[55]

Finally, there are EU countries that in the absence of any historical tradition of special schooling, educate almost all children in mainstream schools.

Italy is boosting an advanced regulatory framework regarding the inclusion of pupils with disabilities in mainstream classes. In Italy the movement supporting inclusion in mainstream education dates back to the end of the 1960s and has led to a widespread and broadly discussed experience.

---

[54] See Rotatori et al. (2014).

[55] CRPD Committee *Concluding observations on the initial report of Spain* (CRPD/C/ESP/CO/1), 19.10.2011, para. 43.

Inclusion for pupils with disabilities began with Law 118/1971, which granted all children the right to be educated in common classes, and with Law 517/1977,[56] which abolished special schools. In 1992, the whole process led to Law 104, a general legislative framework, which tries to meet the complex needs of disabled people more systematically over the different stages of their life.

With regards to education, Article 12 of Law 104/1992 states that all persons with disabilities, 'regardless of their type and degree of disability', attend mainstream education from kindergarten to the level of education that they are able to attain according to their personal capacities (Article 12). In this perspective, the Law provides for the removal of barriers (architectural or sensorial) and the introduction of appropriate aids and tools to support pupils with disabilities in education and training. In particular, this Framework Law ensures coordinated planning of educational, health, social, cultural, leisure and sport services for students with disabilities and it requires that schools are provided with technical equipment and educational materials as well as any other kind of technical help (Article 13).

In compliance with Law 104/92, school inclusion of children with disability is organized on the basis of *Individualized Educational Plans* (PEI), taking into account the necessary adjustments for students with disabilities. Following the identification of student's capabilities and potentialities, a PEI is drawn up by including the general lines of the didactic project of scholastic and social inclusion. The individualized educational plan is jointly worked out by specialized teachers, health and education professionals and parents.[57]

---

[56] Law 517/1977 provided a series of service delivery parameters to support inclusive education such as: (a) specially trained support teachers (*insegnante di sostegno*) were to be paired with classroom teachers with the intention that they would work together to improve educational opportunities for all students, thus mitigating stigma for students with disabilities; (b) no more than 20 students were to be in classes that included a student with a disability, and (c) extracurricular activities must provide access for all students.

[57] Such plan results from the other tools provided by Law 104/1992 for challenging the functions and the potentials of the disabled child as much as possible: the functional diagnosis and the dynamic-functional profile.

The *functional diagnosis* aims at identifying a child as an individual with a disability and to gather information about the child's history and his\her family. It is filled in by a team of specialists in different fields of disability. It specifies the kind and the level of disability and the functioning profile of the child on the basis of: affective-emotional (identity and relations with other persons), cognitive, motor-sensorial, communicative and linguistic features, neuropsychological competences (attention memory and space-time organization), self-help and autonomy capabilities. It is filled in according to the ICF model (International Classification of Functioning 2001).

The *dynamic-functional profile* is an educational tool to sketch a global profile of the disabled child, aiming to answer the question: what are the best objectives for "this" child, on the basis of his\her diagnosis, his\her actual performance, the life skills and the life project that child, family, and professionals foresee for himself\herself? The dynamic-functional profile is the link between the developmental level of the child and the methodology of the individualized educational programme.

Further legal instruments focused on the special needs of students with learning disabilities, namely Law 170/2010 *New rules on Specific Learning Disabilities in School*[58]—and Ministerial Directive of 27 December 2012 *Intervention tools for children with special educational needs and territorial organization for inclusion in schools*.

By endorsing the concept of special educational needs, the 2012 Ministerial Directive converged the Italian school system on the point of view that not only disabled students, but also students with special needs, namely due to specific language or learning impairments or to social-cultural disadvantages, need particular attention from the school. Such Directive responds, in fact, to the practice of not labeling high disabilities as such as learning disabilities, with the result that only 2 % of students are certified (or identified) as having special needs in Italy.[59]

The Directive deals with the initiatives to be taken for different types of pupils with SEN: pupils with assessed disabilities, with specific developmental disorders or with socio-economic, linguistic and cultural disadvantages. It provides for the personalization of learning paths for all SEN students through the adoption of an Individualized Didactic Program, identifying learning abilities and methodological strategies. It also extends tools and measures provided by Law 170/2010 for the SLD students to further include all students with special educational needs. Therefore, SEN students are entitled to receive compensative measures, namely facilitative and technological tools, and dispensatory measures, i.e. exoneration from some performances, extra-time, reduction of school works.

In order to strengthen the inclusion policy, the Ministerial Directive stresses on the need to make all the scholastic community, not only some teachers, responsible for the inclusion for all kind of special needs. In this vein, it foresees the training of all teachers in the field of disability, also by the institution of a Master's degree dedicated to didactics and psycho-pedagogy for the various forms of disturbance or disability and the enhancement of territorial centres (CTS) with specialized teachers that can support schools in the inclusive policy and promote good practices.

Notwithstanding Italy is continuing to refine its model of inclusion, many challenges to inclusive education remains mainly reflecting gaps in implementation of the law. Such challenges varies from the lack of accessible schools and transportation systems to the shortage of trained teachers and precariousness of support

[58] Law 170/2010 recognises dyslexia, dysgraphia, dysorthographia and dyscalculia as specific learning disorders (SLD). This Law states that pupils with learning disorders do not need special teachers, but rather a new way of teaching, according to their way of learning. Amongst the measures provided by the Law, students can use speech synthesis tools, which allow them to learn by listening rather than reading, tape recorders which let them listen to lessons, word-processing programmes with spelling checkers and many more. University students with SLD have the right to these compensatory and dispensatory measures from the moment of the admission test.

[59] See Giangreco et al. (2012).

teachers for students with disabilities, to cases of micro exclusion perpetuated in ordinary settings.[60]

In order to improve the quality of inclusive education in Italy, a Bill have been presented to the Italian Parliament in 2014. Such Bill provides for the continuity of support teachers by establishing specific figures for the didactic support in each educational level and proposes the replacement of the functional diagnosis and the dynamic-functional profile with the functioning profile to be elaborated not only by medical specialists but also by families and teachers. Furthermore, in order to fully comply with Article 24 of the CRPD, the Bill introduces the specific duty to provide reasonable accommodations.

8 Conclusions

The inclusion concept entails that everyone is equal and should stand in the same position at the starting point with the others even if the achievement of such goal requires the provision of individualized measures. Giving a legally binding status to the right to inclusive education, the CRPD has stimulated an important discussion throughout the world about inclusion in education of children with disabilities.

There is no best practice model of inclusive education. Inclusion is, indeed, a difficult path, and it is undoubtedly impossible to state that 'all has been done' since inclusion is a process that must continually be reviewed and revised. So, there is a great deal of progress to be made in fulfilling the obligation of inclusive education for children with disabilities.

Improving inclusive education means to fully comply with Article 24 of the CRPD looking at the authoritative interpretation of such provision made by the CRPD Committee. In fact, a number of key themes emerged from the UN Committee's Concluding observations, such as the need to develop a comprehensive State education policy that guarantees the right to inclusive education; the prohibition of forced enrolment in special education settings and the provision of effective and swift appeal against decisions on student's placement; the immediate applicability of the duty to provide reasonable accommodation, the allocation of sufficient financial and human resources to implement the right to inclusive education; the quality training of teachers and all other educational staff to enable them to work in inclusive educational settings.

The current tendency in EU Member States is to develop a policy towards inclusion of pupils with special educational needs. In some countries, there is still a selective rather than an inclusive education system, but some advancements have been put in place. For instance, in European countries with a relatively two-track

[60] See D'Alessio (2011). The author reports that some schools in Italy are establishing new separate support room (known as *aule del sostegno*), where support teachers take students out of regular supports or services in segregated settings.

system of special needs education there is a trend to developing a continuum of services between the two systems or transforming special schools as resources centres for mainstream schools.[61]

On the contrary, some EU Member States, such as Italy or UK, have long been leaders in protecting the right to inclusive education of children with disabilities and their legal systems have much to offer as implementing practice of Article 24 of the CRPD.

However, many challenges to realizing the goal of full inclusion remain reflecting, in many cases, gaps in implementation of the law, due also to economic constraints. Even in more advanced inclusive system, most laws have yet to be fully implemented. While it is considered perhaps the most inclusive education system in the world,[62] Italy serves as an important reminder about the many challenges of translating the language and values of law into practice.

Article 24 of the CRPD calls for an inclusive education system which should be flexible to meet the special needs of people with disabilities. Adjustments are especially needed to address ASD pupils' needs, for whom education cannot rely on centrally-determined curricula and teaching methodologies and, therefore, an individually tailored educational plan based on a set of individualized objectives should be provided. Qualified by the OHCHR has a good example of support measures consistent with Article 24 (2) (d) of the CRPD, the Individual Educational Plans (IEPs) take into account the needs of the individual child and his/her family, and require to adapt the child's schedule and educational environment, both in and out of the classroom. In order to meet the needs of pupils with ASD, such plans should be intended as a global plan including didactic, rehabilitative, social and welfare aspects, like the PEI in Italy and the EHC plans in England.

There will be some pupils with ASD whose autism is so severe that they will need a specialist support, but it does not need to be in a segregated setting. The best model is where the child with autism belongs to his peer group teacher but has the support of staff with expertise and a 'haven' in which to recover when needed.[63]

There is still a role for specialist schools, but to be consistent with Article 24 of the CRPD they must have a better reason for their existence than that they pick up those who 'fail' in mainstream schooling. As it is occurring in Europe, specialist schools should be centres of excellence, pioneering new ways of working with ASD and dealing with the most extreme cases. They should be centres of research as well as teaching and have a role in working alongside mainstream schools to bring about more effective inclusion. However, special schools must be seen more as supports for an inclusive system rather than an alternative to it.

[61] See Meijer (2010).

[62] See Kanter et al. (2014), p. 29.

[63] See Jordan (2008), p. 13.

References

Arnardóttir O (2011) The right to inclusive education for children with disabilities – innovations in the CRPD. In: Eide A, Möller J, Ziemele I (eds) Making peoples heard. Essays on human rights in honour of Gudmundur Alfredsson. Martinus Nijhoff Publishers, Leiden/Boston, pp 219–221

D'Alessio S (2011) Inclusive education in Italy. A critical analysis of the policy of *Integrazione Scolastica*. Sense Publishers, Rotterdam

de Beco G (2014) The right to inclusive education according to Article 24 of the UN Convention on the rights of persons with disabilities: background, requirements and (remaining) questions. Netherland Q Hum Rights 3:263–287

de Campos Velho Martel L (2011) Reasonable accommodation: the new concept from an inclusive constitutional perspective. Int J Hum Rights 8(14):85–103

German Institute for Human Rights (2014) Submission of the National CRPD monitoring body of Germany to the CRPD Committee on the rights of persons with disabilities on the occasion of the preparation of a list of issues by the Committee in the review of Germany's initial report in 2014. http://www.institut-fuer-menschenrechte.de/uploads/tx_commerce/Submission_of_the_National_CRPD_Monitoring_Body_of_Germany_to_the_CRPD_Committee_on_the_occasion_of_the_preparation_of_a_list_of_issues_by_the_Committee_in_the_review_of_Germanys_Initial_Report_2014.pdf. Accessed 17 Sep 2014

Giangreco MF, Doyle MB, Suter JC (2012) Demographic and personnel service delivery data: implication for including students with disabilities in Italian schools. Life Span Disabil 15 (1):97–123

Jordan R (2008) Autistic spectrum disorders: a challenge and model for inclusion in education. Br J Spec Educ 35(1):11–15

Kanter AS, Damiani ML, Ferri BA (2014) The right to inclusive education under international law: following Italy's lead. J Int Spec Needs Educ 17(1):21–32

King M (2006) How law defines the special educational needs of autistic children. Child Fam Law Q 18(1):23–42

Lord C, McGee JP (eds) (2001) Educating children with autism. National Research Council, Committee on Educational Interventions for children with autism. National Academy Press, Washington, DC

Meijer JW (2010) special needs education in Europe: inclusive policies and practices. Zeitschrift für Inklusion-online.net. http://www.inklusion-online.net/index.php/inklusion-online/article/view/136/136. Accessed 17 Sep 2014

NESSE-Network of Experts in Social Sciences of Education and Training (2012) Education and disability/special needs. Policies and practices in education, training and employment for students with disabilities and special educational needs in the EU. http://www.nesse.fr/nesse/activities/reports/activities/reports/disability-special-needs-1. Accessed 17 Sep 2014

Reindal SM (2008) A social relational model of disability: a theoretical framework for special education? Eur J Spec Needs Educ 23(2):135–146

Renty J, Roeyers H (2005) Students with autism spectrum disorder in special and general education school in Flanders. Br J Dev Disabil 1(100):27–39

Rotatori AF, Bakken JP, Burkhardt S, Obiakor FE, Sharma U (eds) (2014) Special education international perspectives: practices across the globe. Emerald Group Publishing Limited, Bingley

Shaw B (2014) Inclusion or choice? Securing the right to inclusive education for all. In: Sabatello M, Schulze M (eds) Human rights & disability advocacy. University of Pennsylvania Press, Philadelphia, pp 58–63
UNDESA-Department of Economic and Social Affairs, OHCHR-Office of the United Nations High Commissioner for Human Rights, IPU-Inter-Parliamentary Union (2007) From exclusion to equality. Realizing the rights of persons with disabilities. Handbook for parliamentarians on the Convention on the rights of persons with disabilities and its optional protocol. United Nations, Geneva. http://www.un.org/disabilities/documents/toolaction/ipuhb.pdf. Accessed 17 Sep 2014
UNESCO (2009) Towards inclusive education for children with disabilities: a guideline. UNESCO Bangkok, Bangkok
UNICEF (2012) The right of children with disabilities to education: a rights-based approach to inclusive education. Position Paper. http://www.unicef.org/ceecis/IEPositionPaper_ENGLISH.pdf. Accessed 17 Sep 2014

Rachele Cera is Researcher at the Institute for International Legal Studies of the Italian Researcher Council (ISGI-CNR), Rome, Italy.

Tertiary Education, Vocational Training and Lifelong Learning for Adults with Autism: Comparing Domestic Laws and Best Practices

Lucia Chiappetta Cajola

1 Introduction

This paper is inspired by the need to disseminate and share knowledge on the status of adults with Autism Spectrum Disorders (ASD) with regard to higher education,[1] vocational training and lifelong learning, whether as a result of national legislations and the more accredited scientific research or due to the multiple operational approaches proposed in different regional and local contexts, as well as through good practices.

The overall picture will be enhanced by a look at the international situation, providing a kind of survey of the laws and regulations that govern these areas, the situation in Italy and that of some European countries. Although Italy is productive in protecting the rights of persons with disabilities (Law no. 104/1992, Presidential Decree, 24 February 1994, Law no. 17/1999, Law no. 68 of 23 March 1999, Law no. 328/2000, Law no. 53/2003, and the Prime Ministerial Decree of 29 November 2001), where persons with autism are concerned, legislation is lacking.

The situation regarding the general rights of the disabled which also relate to autism will be covered (in the United Kingdom, France and Germany) as well as those which refer specifically to autism (Poland and Hungary). In this context, the significant contribution by Autism-Europe[2] to international literature in relation to

[1] Not only in the case of autism, but also in other types of disability, there is a need for access to knowledge, information and data. These are, in fact, very difficult to acquire, both nationally and internationally. See Chiappetta Cajola (2014).

[2] This is a European network which brings together some 80 associations of parents of persons with autism in 31 countries, including EU Member States, with the aim of promoting the defence of the rights of people with autism and their families, as well as improving their quality of life. Autism-Europe is a founder member of the Platform of European Social NGOs and the European Disability Forum.

L. Chiappetta Cajola (✉)
University Roma Tre, Rome, Italy
e-mail: lucia.chiappettacajola@uniroma3.it

V. Della Fina, R. Cera (eds.), *Protecting the Rights of People with Autism in the Fields of Education and Employment*, DOI 10.1007/978-3-319-13791-9_5

adults with autism is also considered, their having produced, amongst other things, the 'Charter of Rights for Persons with Autism', adopted by the European Parliament. Autism-Europe is committed to collecting national legal cases to allow them to make an analysis of the state of the rights to education for persons with autism.[3]

Particular attention is also paid to proposals for regional Italian laws, among which are highlighted no. 427 of 21 July 2014, *Disposizioni in Materia di Disturbi dello Spettro Autistico* (Provisions on Autism Spectrum Disorders), issued by the Marche region and approved on October 7 2014, following the various draft laws put forward by some other regions (Abruzzo, Campania, Emilia Romagna, Lazio, Liguria, Marche, Piedmont, Sardinia, Tuscany, the Autonomous Province of Trento, Umbria, Valle d'Aosta, and Veneto) which were collected in the unified text adopted by the committee for draft laws.[4] During this research, the initiatives taken by the foundations (e.g., Marino, Serono, *Sacra Famiglia*, *Oltre il Labirinto*) and associations (e.g., ANGSA, *Gruppo Asperger*, *Associazione Genitori Autismo* non-profit organization) were particularly interesting. By carrying out a prominent role in social and welfare activities, they engage in policy guidance for training and integrating adults with autism in the workplace which, in Italy, give rise to best practices. Among these activities, those promoted on a regional or local level provide important relevant information relating, in particular, to tertiary education. They give accounts of some of the main groups (*Insettopia*, a social network, the 'Job Trainer Disability' project; *Autismo e lavoro agricolo* [Autism and agricultural work], the *Sotto-Progetto per l'Istituzione di Servizi per Adolescenti ed Adulti con Disturbi Autistici* [Sub-Project for the Establishment of Services for Adolescents and Adults with Autistic Disorders], etc.) and describe implements for innovations and their application, which may be true operational models for further regional and local projects to improve vocational training and lifelong learning for people with autism.

2 The Evolution of Autism in Adulthood and Diverse Measures

Once his schooling is finished, the person with autism and his family very often run the risk of being 'forgotten' by society and find themselves isolated or forced to refer to services that are not always adequately and properly organized to take responsibility and manage their needs.[5] The difficulties of personal and

[3] The law is an important source of jurisdiction; in fact, a court decision is binding, and takes the value of a precedent, which may be invoked in further legal cases. In this context, a legal appeal against non-observance of fundamental rights represents an essential process towards the defence of these rights and allows the texts concerning integration or social integration to become a reality.

[4] Summary no. 109 of 3 April 2014.

[5] Cottini (2010), p. 196.

interpersonal communication, in addition to cognitive-behavioral problems, make the path towards social autonomy very difficult for individuals with autism and, therefore, there is a very high risk of being cared for exclusively by the family or being placed in institutions which, for various reasons, do not specifically aim to integrate them into community life in a concrete way.

At present, the necessary sensitivity for the problems of adults with autism still does not exist. Although attention to the study of autism in childhood is relevant; sensitivity towards family members is completely lacking, for whom the end of school signifies the most critical moment.[6] The parents themselves, in fact, are faced with the complexity determined by the disorder which, over time, becomes increasingly difficult to manage: the lack of independence, more frequent and intense aggressive actions towards self and others, autistic symptoms in general occurring ever more clearly, without further improvements after those achieved during childhood and adolescence.[7] Therefore, it is urgent that measures and effective procedures are developed from a careful survey of the currently available and reliable scientific data; in this respect, the synthesis proposed by some scholars is interesting:

> At the present state of knowledge it is possible to indicate some 'almost certainties':
>
> 1. The vast majority of autistic people will never be independent. Many will make even significant progress in mental and social functioning, but very few will become autonomous. Almost all adults with autism will therefore need a safe living environment.
> 2. It is difficult to establish a relationship between types of treatment and outcomes. The type of measure affects the appearance of the skills and competencies facilitated. In any case, the handicap should never be treated as a statistic, under the banner of 'all or nothing', but as a set of functions in which, however, traces are to be found, so one can try to stimulate where and how it is possible.[8]

The basic global line would appear to be related, not so much with individual types of measures (there is still not enough evidence for this) as to the constancy, systematicity, the length of the treatments, their internal consistency, their ability to create and maintain, however, a climate of constant investment and emotional support around the autistic. It is necessary to consider what to do next.

The evolutions of autism in adulthood are very diverse. Even the type of treatment should be differentiated. As far as the types of measures are concerned, it is evident that an adult with autism who has developed strong social skills could usefully form part of a non-residential community support network, and maybe enjoy supported employment and in some cases live independently or in partly-

---

[6] 'The network of services, which at this stage is critical to the family of the person with autism should provide greater support, in reality extend its links; once adolescence has passed, the autistic is progressively 'abandoned' by the services of paediatrics and infant neuropsychiatry, as well as the educational and rehabilitative function of school placement. Therefore, an assessment of the autistic adult plays a role of the utmost importance for his inclusion in the most suitable rehabilitative context'. Alessandroni (2010), p. 196.

[7] Howlin et al. (2004).

[8] Uccelli di Nemi and Barale (2010), pp. 196–197.

independent assisted facilities. But this concerns, however, a small minority of adult autistics. The others should also be considered.

In Europe and the USA there are three types of more protected measures: communities for autistics, apartments for autistic groups and mixed apartments for communities or groups. Each of these choices has its problems, advantages and specific difficulties. This paper focuses on agricultural and residential communities. The movement towards farm communities for autistics started at the end of the 1960s and spread throughout the Western world, the communities generally being promoted by organizations or groups of parents. Their fortune and the interest they have aroused are due to the fact that their characteristics are particularly suited to the following requirements:

a) they create places to live and work and they provide treatment; they are secure, pleasant, orderly, consistent and at the same time full of stimuli, offering the chance for significant work experience;
b) they are places to live, therefore, in which the need for stability, consistency, and predictability, etc. can be respected;
c) they are places where various psychoeducational, therapeutic or rehabilitative treatments do not take place in an abstract, fragmented and demotivating environment, but in 'natural settings', which are closely linked to one another, together with the experiences of having both a working life and leisure time;
d) moreover, these are sites for adults, i.e. 'places to live and work' which, although protected, are not a repetition of infantile patterns, but areas of adult life.

In fact, in all the communities for which documentation is available, a significant clinical improvement has been obtained in their living conditions, with a reduction in behavioural problems and the use of drugs. It is here that learning skills and rehabilitation are an active and valued synergy, since they establish an improvement in the abilities of communication and expression in adolescent and adult autistics. There are numerous studies[9] that have demonstrated through empirical research and the use of assessment tools, that the diagnosis of autism remains almost stable throughout life. In adulthood, in particular, symptoms which characterize autistic syndromes are more evident, especially in the context of difficulties in social interaction and communication.[10] Not only that, but the abnormalities in processing sensory stimuli encountered in children with autism are present in 94.4 % of the sample of adults examined in a study by Crane, Goddard and Pring using the AASP (Adult/Adolescent Sensory Profile, 2009).[11] These findings regarding the persistence and severity of symptoms are significant of the poor quality of life of adults with autism, both with respect to cognitive abilities as well as social ones, without prejudice towards the better outcome for high-functioning than for

[9] Seltzer et al. (2004).

[10] Matson and Smith (2008).

[11] Raffin (2010), p. 1.

low-functioning adults.[12] Nevertheless, there are few high-functioning autistic individuals who lead an independent life and who have permanent employment. Most of them remain dependent on family and support services.[13]

2.1 Measures in Italy Compared to Europe in General

As far as job opportunities in Italy are concerned, there are three types of 'employment' for autistics: sheltered workshops, supported employment or prevocational training for competitive employment.

Sheltered workshops welcome people with autism, who perform an occupational activity whose main objective is not to give them a working activity in itself, but rather to 'keep them busy' to market products or services resulting from such activities. 'In this way, the value of work as a vehicle for self-assertion and self-esteem has been seriously compromised and the lack of a real economic value (workshops do not finance themselves with what they produce, but are subsidized by the public services) permits exemption from many duties such as responsibility, quality, punctuality, productivity, etc. which are at the base of the individual and social growth represented by work'.[14]

Job placement in Italy is regulated by the Law no. 68, 12 March 1999, *Norme per il diritto al lavoro dei disabili* (Standards for the right to work of persons with disabilities),[15] which has the aim of promoting the inclusion and integration of people with disabilities into the labour market through support services and targeted employment (Article 2). The latter puts the right person in the appropriate workplace, supporting him with appropriate incentives and facilities, as most recently reaffirmed by the Presidential Decree of 4 October 2013: *Adozione del programma di azione biennale per la promozione dei diritti e l'integrazione delle persone con disabilità* (Adoption of the biennial programme of action for the promotion of the rights and inclusion of people with disabilities). The Decree proposes, as a first step, a definition of the guidelines to operate services for targeted placements and then to disseminate all available data digitally.

Law no. 68/1999 introduces several critical points, particularly for people with severe mental disabilities and with autism.[16] In fact, according to the *Diario di transizione/3* (Diary of transition/3) by Censis (in which more important issues

[12] McGovern and Sigman (2005).

[13] Billstedt et al. (2010).

[14] Ibid.

[15] The Law is published in Official Gazette no. 68, 23 March 1999—Ordinary Supplement no. 57.

[16] According to a study conducted in 1999 by the *Osservatorio Autismo* (Autism Observatory) in the Lombardy Region, even though the autistic adults identified in that region (approximately 145) were in a protected type of employment, none was active either at a higher level or in productive competition on the market.

were identified and described on the agenda for the spring-summer period 2014), by 2020, there will be about 4.8 million people with disabilities (7.9 % of the European population), and currently, only 10 % of autistic individuals over 20 years old work, although the age range is wider: 15–44 years, equal to 66 %. It is well understood, therefore, that the main reason our welfare system is based on an informal model is that response to the needs of adults with autism, is represented by families,[17] whose access to institutional support is very limited, being exclusively of an economic nature. By making a comparison with other European countries it can be seen that spending on social protection benefits for disability amounts to 437 euros *per capita* per year, higher only than the figure in Spain (404 euros), and significantly lower than the European average (535 euros). The percentage of the service charge, which is only 5.8 % of the total (25 euros *per capita* per year) is particularly significant: it is less than a fifth of the EU average and even lower than the figure for Spain.[18] In Italy, among people with autism aged 21 years and older, 50 % attend a daycare centre, but 21.7 % of them do not do any kind of working activity.[19] From the statistical data, then, it emerges that care management of people with autism is almost totally borne by the family. The controversy, however, does not concern only Italy, to the point that Autism-Europe has strongly emphasized the need for adequate training in specific needs in the field of continuing education and vocational training, adapted not only to develop job skills, but also the social and personal skills necessary to access, really and effectively, a job or profession. As far as this is concerned, in the years 2001–2002, Autism-Europe had already launched a survey[20] among its members and those of relevant European organizations, by means of a questionnaire, translated into eight languages, focusing on the problems of working-age people with autism and their families. The most important point emerging from this survey is that, in the vast majority of cases, autistic people 'do not want to or cannot work' (61.5 %). Speaking of which, there remains the fact that only 37 % of autistic individuals receive professional and/or continuous training. The consequence is, of course, a lack of participation in social life.

---

[17] The families become, in most cases, the central subjects of care who, despite their efforts, suffer from emargination and isolation in turn, especially when the children reach adulthood and complete their path of studies. Throughout childhood, in fact, the parents of children and adolescents with autism may enjoy the integration and inclusion that occurs in schools, the pride of the Italian institutions. Suffice it to say that, according to a survey by Censis, it was recorded that up to 19 years old, 93.4 % of subjects with autism spectrum disorders attend school, but the figure drops considerably to 61.4 % between 14 and 20 years, and goes even lower, to exactly 6.7 %, for those over 20 years old.

[18] Censis (2014).

[19] 'Between the hours available for support and those of mere supervision, parents of people with autism and Down syndrome spend 17 hours a day together. The economic value of this time [. . .] comes to a truly substantial annual amount [. . .]: approximately 51,000 Euros for people with Autism Spectrum Disorders' (Ibid).

[20] The data pertaining thereto are available from the Secretariat of Autism-Europe and on their Web pages.

The initiatives promoted by the European Union in the field of combating discrimination, in particular the directive in favour of 'equal opportunities in employment and occupation',[21] adopted by the Council in November 2000, have not yet received adequate responses in favour from those with autism and their families.

In Italy, too, the efforts to include such adults socially and in the labour market are rather weak. Although the context of the needs and difficulties has been defined as a result of the *Tavolo nazionale di lavoro sull'autismo* (National Working Table on Autism), effective and sufficient measures and funding have not followed. Currently, there is not available, in fact, an organized network of public services responsible for people with autism and, for most situations, there is a no homogeneous reality able to respond effectively to the growing request by family members and the institutions themselves for help in the management of their everyday life.

Given, therefore, the decades of copious Italian legislation in the field of education and school and the social integration[22] of students with disabilities, an analysis by Autism-Europe notes that both national laws and international standards allow, in general, an effective guarantee of the right to education of persons with disabilities, also recognized in court proceedings. However, the legislative path concerning access to employment for people with disabilities is different, as stated above.

3 Continuous Training and Job Placement in the Context of the UN Convention and the European Disability Strategy 2010–2020

The 'UN Convention on the Rights of Persons with Disabilities' is the 'first legally-binding instrument in the field of human rights' to which the European Union has adhered.[23] The Convention requires the states to protect and safeguard all human rights and the fundamental freedom of persons with disabilities.[24] Among the topics

[21] European Union Council Directive no. 2000/78/EC, 27 November 2000, *Establishing a general framework for equal treatment in employment and occupation.*

[22] See Article 3 of the Constitution; Law no. 118/1971, Law no. 517 (1977), Law no. 104 (1992), Presidential Decree, 24 February 1994. Note of the 4 August 2009, protocol no. 4274.

[23] Communication from the Commission to the European Parliament, the Council, the European Economic and Social Committee and the European Committee and the Committee of the Regions (2010). *European Disability Strategy 2010–2020: A Renewed Commitment to a Europe without Barriers. Brussels*, 15 November 2010.

[24] 'That which characterizes the UN Convention in question is that it has definitely exceeded an approach focused solely on the deficit of the disabled person, by accepting the 'social model' of disability and introducing the principles of non-discrimination, equal opportunities, autonomy and independence with the aim of achieving full social inclusion through the involvement of people with disabilities themselves who, in less favoured contextual conditions, are difficult to reach. [...] For this purpose it is necessary that the context (environment, procedures, educational tools and aids) fits the specific needs of people with disabilities, through what the Convention defines 'reasonable accommodation' [...].' (Note 4 August 2009, protocol 4274—Policy guidelines on inclusion in education of disabled students, Part I, Item 2).

of this paper, those of specific relevance are Articles 24 and 27 dedicated to education, and labour and employment, respectively. In detail, Article 24(5) states: 'Party states shall ensure that persons with disabilities are able to access general tertiary education, vocational training, adult education and lifelong learning without discrimination and on the basis of equality with others. To this end, party states shall ensure that proper accommodation is provided for persons with disabilities'. Article 27(1) strongly states that, 'member states recognize the right of persons with disabilities to work, on an equal basis with others; this includes the right to the opportunity to support oneself through work, freely chosen or accepted in a labour market and work environment that is open, inclusive and accessible to persons with disabilities. Party states shall safeguard and promote the exercise of their right to work, including those who acquire a disability during employment, by taking appropriate steps—including through legislation'. In order to place people with disabilities in an optimal condition to exercise their rights and enjoy full and active participation in social life the 'European Disability Strategy 2010–2020' has identified eight main areas for action: accessibility, participation, equality, employment, education and training, social protection, health and external actions.[25] In terms of occupation, the aforementioned European Strategy states that 'to achieve the goals of growth in the EU, it is necessary that people with disabilities in paid employment are more numerous on the open labour market. The Commission will use the full potential of the Europe 2020 strategy and its programme for the renewal of skills and labour, making available to member states: analyses, policy guidance, information and other forms of aid. It will improve information on the employment situation of men and women with disabilities, identify problems and propose solutions, with particular attention to young people with disabilities in their transition from education to the world of work'.[26] Within the outlines concerning tertiary education, vocational training and lifelong learning, the following pages on the state of the art related to these issues, with reference to adults with autism, is analysed in Italy and in Europe, also in order to verify consistent application of the existing rules.

[25] These sectors have been identified by virtue of their potential contribution to achieving the objectives of the strategy itself: the UN Convention, documents of the institutions of the European Union and the Council of Europe, the EU action plan for disabled people 2003–2010, and public consultations with member states and stakeholders.

[26] European Disability Strategy 2010–2020 (2010). Section 4. Employment.

3.1 *The Effectiveness and Protection of Rights in Some European Countries*

In the international arena, relating to the effectiveness of rights and their protection at a jurisdictional level,[27] interesting decisions have been made in which the court has recognized the state's responsibility for the fulfilment of the rights enshrined in the UN Convention.[28] For the purposes of this paper, it is useful to underline that the European Committee of Social Rights, in commenting on the specific case of Autism-Europe v France, Complaint no. 13/2002, defined that the task of the State is to take concrete measures to ensure the effective protection of the rights referred to in the aforementioned 'Charter for autistic people'.[29] This case is presented here as an example to understand how, even in an international context, the scarcity of resources does not constitute an element of legitimacy, but is rather a determining factor for measures aimed to protect and ensure the effective fulfilment of rights, including those of education, social inclusion, and integration into the labour market of people with disabilities. The example shows that the French government continued to adopt a restrictive definition of autism compared to that adopted by the World Health Organization, without considering the scarcity of statistical data related to progress in the right to education.[30] The Committee therefore, held that France had not made any progress towards the full guarantee of education for people with autism. This decision is of great importance regarding tutelage and focuses on the issue of recognition as a form of state responsibility, as a key to ensure a guarantee of the right to education. Due to this, the French judges made the decision to compensate the families of people with autism spectrum disorders, recognizing the responsibility of the state; nevertheless, by virtue of the legal framework, the courts have not found concrete solutions.[31]

[27] This is the concept of *giustiziabilità* (the ability to make a judicial decision) and the possibility to have recourse to an independent and impartial body that can guarantee the fulfilment of the infringed right.

[28] See the case People's Union For Civil Liberties v Union of India and Others, Supreme Court of India-HCJ 2599/00, 14 August 2002.

[29] The committee also pointed out that, in the event that such a guarantee is complex and costly, the state may use measures to ensure a progressive and real pursuit of the right (in the case of France, it was the right to education), considering the effect that such a choice would mean for the community as a whole.

[30] This narrow definition of autism has produced such severe consequences that a very small number of children with autism has been able to take advantage of special services for education.

[31] 'In a decision on 13 October 2005, the administrative tribunal of Lyon ordered the state to pay 36,000 euros, by way of compensation, to the parents of a teenager with autism who had not 'received educational support for more than three years'. More specifically, the courts recognized the responsibility of the state for the period during which the boy had not received any education. However, because of 'the efforts made by the state to respond to the needs of the boy', the judges considered that the state, though responsible, did not err'. Giofrè (2010), p. 57.

In 1998, Ireland promulgated an anti-discrimination law, the Employment Equality Act, which declared discrimination in employment unlawful, consenting action in favour of all persons with disabilities, and with the intention of securing their social and professional integration. In Germany, the principle of non-discrimination is governed by the Disability Discrimination Act, and in 1993, in England and Wales, a special and independent court was set up (SENDIST, Special Educational Needs and Disability Service Tribunal) with the task of deciding on the specific needs of people with disabilities in the educational field.[32]

Among the European countries that have given significant and specific attention to the plight of people with autism, it should be noted that England boasts the first law on Autism Spectrum Disorders, the 'Autism Act',[33] which outlines expected standards of care practices and establishes the legal obligation to provide services and adequate support for adults with autism. It is, by far, the first law dedicated to a specific disability and establishes the duty, on the part of the Minister of Health, to develop and publish a document setting out a strategy to meet the needs of adults with Autism Spectrum Disorders in England and Wales.[34]

Hungary is the first country in Europe to have ratified the UN Convention on the Rights of Persons with Disabilities and the government adopted in 2008 a 'National Strategy for Autism' which specifies the actions to be taken by Hungarian ministers for the years 2008–2013. The development of the Strategy was coordinated by the Hungarian Autistic Society and the national network of Magyar non-profit organizations active in the field of Autism Spectrum Disorders.[35] Moreover, the Act CXXXIX of 2005 on Higher Education expressly applies to students with autism.[36]

In Poland, legislation on the subject of education is very precise and targeted, and takes into account the rights of people with disabilities, specifically people with autism. However, as can be seen from a study by Autism-Europe, notwithstanding the fact that appropriate regulatory acts and financial loans have been promulgated,

---

[32] 'And in one particular case that body acknowledged that in practice the only way for [...] the teenager to receive a sufficient and appropriate education in terms of academic and social learning, which could lead to a more independent life, consisted of taking specific responsibility for autism and placing him in a residential centre, regardless of the cost, which in reality had represented the obstacle that the local authorities had found in guaranteeing the adolescent the right to receive a suitable education for his state'. Ibid, p. 57.

[33] The Act received Royal Assent on 12 November 2009.

[34] On this Strategy see the chapter by V. Della Fina, in this volume.

[35] This process was carried out to implement a coherent plan of social and educational policies and, in parallel, to plan the development of the institutional system. The strategy was inserted into section IV/3 of the Hungarian Government Decree 1062/2007 on the fulfillment of the national programme for issues of disability for the period 2007–2010.

[36] Section 147 (8) of the Act states: 'Student (applicant) with disability means a student (applicant) who suffers from physical, sense, speech disorders, autism, and disorders in cognitive and behavioural development' (http://www.nefmi.gov.hu/letolt/nemzet/naric/act_cxxxix_2005.pdf). For all websites, last access 31 October 2014.

the educational services offered are quantitatively and qualitatively insufficient to meet their demands and needs.[37]

4 People with Autism in European Legislation

The 'Charter of Rights for Persons with Autism' is a paper, presented at the fourth Autism-Europe Congress held in The Hague on 10 May 1992, which was adopted by the European Parliament in May 1996 in the form of a written declaration. It emphasizes the importance for people with autism to enjoy the same rights as all people in Europe, as far as they can, taking into account their best interests. It is also stated that these rights should be highlighted, protected and made operational through appropriate legislation in each state, taking into account the UN Declaration on the Rights of the Mentally Retarded (1971) and the UN Declaration on the Rights of Disabled Persons (1975). In more detail, the recommendations for people with autism are:

1. the right to lead an independent life, to be carried out according to their means
2. the right to a diagnosis and an accurate clinical assessment, comprehensible and free from preconceptions
3. the right to receive an appropriate education, freely accessible to all
4. the right for them (or their representatives) to participate in all decisions about their future
5. the right to accessible and adequate housing
6. the right to have all appropriate means, help and the responsibility necessary to lead a fully productive life with dignity and independence
7. the right to receive a pension or a salary sufficient to provide food, clothing, shelter and all other vital necessities
8. the right to participate, as much as possible, in the development and management of services that take care of their welfare
9. the right to benefit from the advice and care appropriate to their mental and physical health and for their spiritual life
10. the right to an education corresponding to their desires and meaningful employment without discrimination and without preconceived ideas
11. the right to benefit from means of transport and freedom of movement
12. the right of access to culture, recreation and leisure activities.

5 Italian Legislation Concerning People with Autism

The *Legge quadro n. 104 per l'assistenza, l'integrazione sociale e i diritti delle persone handicappate* of 1992 (Framework law no. 104 for the assistance, social integration and rights of persons with disabilities of 5 February 1992) includes 'full

[37] The families who are not receiving adequate services do not engage in any legal action, as Autism-Europe pointed out, as Poland admits the presentation of a judicial appeal against the administration only in the event that friendly appeals to the same administration have failed.

respect of human dignity and human rights concerning the freedom and independence of the handicapped person' among its aims[38] and it promotes their full integration in the family, at work and in society, and is an extremely important reference point for the purposes of recognition and the basic legislation for the theme of this paper. In fact, as it is a framework law, it does not recommend particular action with reference to specific diseases, but general principles to apply to all people with disabilities who need to find timely implementation for the particular circumstances of individual cases. The exceptional reach of the law, in fact, constitutes, *inter alia*, the legitimacy of the principle of social integration.[39]

This framework legislation was subsequently recalled and further recognized in the Act no. 67 of 1 March 2006, *Misure per la tutela giudiziaria delle persone con disabilità vittime di discriminazioni* (Measures for the judicial tutelage of persons with disabilities who are victims of discrimination). This promotes the full implementation of the principle of equal treatment and equal opportunities for people with disabilities (referred to in Article 3 of the Law of 5 February 1992, no. 104), so as to ensure the full enjoyment of their civil, political, economic and social rights.[40] Between May 2007 and January 2008, the aforementioned *Tavolo nazionale di lavoro sull'autismo* (National Working Table on Autism)[41] was established on the recommendation of the Minister of Health, who, with the help of a special scientific committee and specific study groups, addressed issues that concerned, in particular, the spread of autism and its causes, as well as problems at intake, structural services, the effectiveness of treatments, the training of workers and the need for scientific research.

In this forum,[42] full convergence of the opinions of the scientific committee was expressed regarding some aspects concerning people with autism in adulthood. It was stated, *inter alia*, that 'programmes for the care and protection of persons with autistic disorders require a paradigm shift in the approach to disability by pivoting on the person, their rights, their needs and their potential. This approach entails a general policy of services respecting the wholeness of the person with autism and his plans for life and those of his family; this overall policy must be developed throughout the whole lives of people with autism. In addition, the protection of health, access to learning and social inclusion must be guaranteed to every person regardless of the nature and severity of their disability or age'. Still more relevant to the purposes of this research, as will be underlined in the following, is namely: 'The need to spread the awareness that autism is a problem that affects the entire life

[38] Article 1, para a.

[39] Affirms and protects *subjective right* to the full development of the human potential of people with disabilities, a right which cannot be limited by obstacles or impediments of any kind, which may be removed at the initiative of the State.

[40] Law no. 67 of 1 March 2006, Article 1.

[41] It was composed of members of the most representative associations in the country, experts, technicians from the regions, the *Istituto Superiore di Sanità* (National Institute of Health), scientific societies and professional associations for rehabilitation.

[42] This refers to the final report of the *Tavolo nazionale di lavoro sull'autismo* (National Working Table on Autism), January 2008.

cycle. More than one research project, conducted in various regions, signal the numerical collapse of the diagnoses of autism after the age of 18. The situation of adults with autism is strongly affected by the severe shortage of services, planning and programming for the future which too often produce an exorbitant burden for families, with the risk of loss of autonomy and skills laboriously achieved, pharmacological abuse to overcome the lack of appropriate treatment techniques or the proper organization of contexts and habitats due to strongly segregating, purely custodial and restrictive institutionalization. There is therefore a need to take responsibility for the whole lifecycle of people with autism, from childhood to adulthood and old age'.[43]

The considerations outlined by the *Tavolo nazionale di lavoro sull'autismo* (National Working Table on Autism) demonstrate that Autism Spectrum Disorders are more common than previously thought and, above all, that there is an urgent need and priority for an appropriate integrated therapeutic and rehabilitative training plan, able to provide assistance to adults, with a view to inclusion in society and the world of work. One very interesting proposal originating from the work of the National working party is to design and test a plan of measures for a 'national action system', defined as the *Progetto Nazionale Autismo* (National Autism Project).[44] The Ministry of Health accompanied the activities of the working party with initiatives for making connections, which have already led to very positive results, indicating the importance of stabilizing links of dialogue with the *Coordinamento delle Regioni* (Regional Coordination) and the *Istituto Superiore di Sanità* (National Institute of Health).[45]

---

[43] Ibid.

[44] Among their goals, the main ones are summarized as: '[...] the Ministry of Health will develop, in collaboration with the Regional Authorities, a working plan to address providing operating instructions for the homogeneous programming, implementation and monitoring of activities for children and adults with autism, to improve the performance of network services, to promote links and coordination between all the areas affected; [...] To provide a concrete answer for the whole lifecycle of patients, directing the integration of health, educational and social services in their mutual relations and connections with initiatives from Family Associations, private groups and private social groups'. See *Relazione finale del Tavolo nazionale di lavoro sulle problematiche dell'autismo* (Final Report of the National Working Table on Autism), January 2008.

[45] 'As far as relationships with the Regional Administrations are concerned, it should be noted that firstly the link was activated through the request forwarded to the *Gruppo Interregionale sulla Salute Mentale e Assistenza Psichiatrica Interregionale* (Inter-regional Group on Mental Health and Inter-regional Psychiatric Care) to join with their two representatives in the National working party on autism. Please note that the Interregional Group had indicated two child psychiatrists appointed by the Piedmont Region and the Region of Sicily. [...]. Moreover, work is being carried out to insert needs for programming in the field of autism in the *Piano Strategico Salute Mentale* (Strategic Mental Health Plan), which is being developed through integration between the Ministry and the Interregional Group. In the context of these activities of linking and joint programming, between the Ministry and Regional Co-ordination it was asserted that each region draw up a working plan for autism and that these plans be envisaged as connecting and sharing some basic programming principles. For this purpose, particular significance could be given to the dissemination and application of the *Linee Guida sull'Autismo elaborate dalla Società Italiana di Neuropsichiatria dell'Infanzia e dell'Adolescenza SINPIA (*Guidelines developed by the Autism Society of Italian Childhood and Adolescence) which, in some regions have already been implemented and used in their programme planning' (Ibid).

In the *Linee di indirizzo per la promozione ed il miglioramento della qualità e dell'appropriatezza degli interventi assistenziali nei disturbi pervasivi dello sviluppo* (DPS), *con particolare riferimento ai disturbi dello spettro autistico* (Guidelines for the promotion and improvement of the quality and appropriateness of care measures in Pervasive Developmental Disorders (PDDs), with particular reference to autism spectrum disorders)[46] there is a very strong awareness of the complexity of the phenomenon of autism and its implications within the family and society. It is equally important to recall that they underline urgent and concrete commitment on the part of national institutions and central and regional authorities in close cooperation with family associations, which in Italy are an essential and tangible reality, for the protection of the rights of people with autism at all stages of life.[47] The document urges making essential levels of assistance (the so called *Livelli essenziali di assistenza* 'LEA') accessible and homogeneously diffuse in all regions, so that they are part of a network of coordinated measures 'ensuring a specific interdisciplinary multi-professional approach, essential for dealing with the complexity and heterogeneity of autistic syndromes'.[48] Thus, the stress is on the importance of activating health-planning initiatives as well as achieving inclusive education and social development at a regional level.

At present, there is a small number of experiments in this direction, limited to a quarter of the country, and the overall picture shows a lack of consistency of approach to the management of the different conditions of persons with autism. However, for the purposes of this paper, it is important to note that, in the guidelines mentioned above, the areas of Health, Social, Education and Labour are encouraged to link up across policy areas and to promote, among other things:

[46] Document approved as an agreement in Joint Conference, 22 November 2012.

[47] Consider that in a recent British study (2007), Ganz calculated that each individual with autism cost about $3.2 million to society and for families throughout their life. A cost which includes the loss of productivity and necessary assistance (approximately 59.3 % of resources is due to lost productivity and other indirect costs). Similar findings are to be seen in the early results of a study currently underway at ISS (National Institute of Health), as part of the *Primo programma nazionale di ricerca strategica in età evolutiva* (First National Programme for Strategic Research in developmental age), in order to quantify and characterize the burden of suffering and the needs of families with a child with an autism spectrum disorder and the demographic, socio-economic and welfare factors associated with it. A recent view on the needs of families with a member with autism is also offered by the first results of the research *Centralità della persona e della famiglia* (The centrality of the person and the family), Serono Foundation and Angsa performed by Censis, tabled in Parliament, 22 November 2011'. *Linee di indirizzo per la promozione ed il miglioramento della qualità e dell'appropriatezza degli interventi assistenziali nei Disturbi pervasivi dello sviluppo (DPS), con particolare riferimento ai Disturbi dello spettro autistico* (Guidelines for the promotion and improvement of the quality and appropriateness of care interventions in Pervasive Developmental Disorders (PDDs), with particular reference to Autism Spectrum Disorders), Ministry of Health, 22 November 2012.

[48] Ibid.

a) multidimensional assessment combining health, education and social aspects operating as a Multidimensional Assessment Unit of skills and needs and the identification of an operational profile;
b) activation, even after school age, of a case manager who is responsible for the execution of the PAI (Patient Assessment Instrument);
c) liaison and coordination of different measures and different services in order to ensure adequate continuity for the entire life cycle of the person;
d) enhancement of daycare facilities and activities for social inclusion, and inclusion in the world of work for adults with autism
e) expansion of residential facilities for people with pervasive developmental disorders in adulthood, aimed at the acquisition of a greater autonomy and/or assistance to the family.

By means of the 'Ratification and implementation of the UN Convention on the Rights of Persons with Disabilities', (Act no. 18, 3 March 2009), Italy ratified the 'UN Convention on the Rights of Persons with Disabilities' and also its Optional Protocol, signed in New York on December 13 2006. In addition, the Act established the *Osservatorio nazionale sulla condizione delle persone con disabilità* (National Observatory on the Status of persons with Disabilities) (Article 3), chaired by the Minister of Labour, Health and Social Policy. The Observatory was given tasks intended to ensure the promotion of the implementation of the Convention; it was also entrusted with collecting statistics relating to the situation of people with disabilities, together with reference to different situations in the country (Article 3, para 5, letter c), the preparation of a biennial programme of action for the promotion of rights to integration (Article 3, para 5, letter b), and the preparation of a report on the implementation of policies on disability, pursuant to Article 4 of Law no. 104/1992 (Article 3, para 5, d).

6 Protection of the Rights of People with Autism in Italian Regional Laws

On 7 October 2014, the Marche region was the first among the Italian regions to have approved an organic law[49] on autism, whose purpose, as explained in the explanatory report, is to 'promote the well-being and social inclusion of people with autism spectrum disorders. In detail, through an integrated network of services it would guarantee diagnostic, therapeutic, and rehabilitative care for children and adults with autism spectrum disorders. In addition, the social integration, education and employment of these individuals will be pursued, recognizing the crucial role

[49] Referring to Draft Law no. 427 of 21 July 2014, *Disposizioni in materia di disturbi dello spettro autistico* (Provisions for autism spectrum disorders).

of the family as an active part in processing and implementing the overall project for life'.

In Italy, there are other regions which have demonstrated their sensitivity towards the problem of higher education and professional training for individuals with autism, in particular, and who have developed guidelines that have sometimes anticipated the content of the results of the *Tavolo tecnico di lavoro nazionale* (Technical board of national labour), such as, for example, Emilia Romagna.[50] However, there are regions which, to date, in light of the abovementioned 'Guidelines for the promotion and improvement in the quality of the appropriateness of care measures in Pervasive Developmental Disorders (PDDs), with particular reference to autism spectrum disorders', are struggling to establish specific lines of operation. 'The current regional services for the problems of children and adolescents are affected by differences in the models and in the times for their planning and establishment that have been pursued by each Region. In recent decades, regional programmes seem to have moved towards addressing neurological, psychiatric and neuropsychological issues in childhood and adolescence by basically following two paths: in some regions, services are directed to the field of 'mother-child' health, in others towards psychiatric services for adults and thus to the *Dipartimenti di Salute Mentale* (Departments of Mental Health). Other regions have not yet precisely defined the organization and placement of services. However, in our legislative scenario, the coexistence of two Planning Objectives (POs) which address this issue should be considered. The PO *Tutela della salute mentale 1998-2000* (Protection of mental health 1998-2000) states that the organizational experience of mental health services for the adult population suggests that mental health activities dedicated to developmental age (child and adolescent) can be carried out on a departmental model, both structurally and technically functional, in a single direction, which ensures the unity of operations, continuity of care and the functional link between all departments involved in the protection of mental health, even when placed in different operational structures'.[51]

However, examining textual indications and proposals for legislative action programmes the necessary uniformity is not ensured, and also from the analysis of the guidelines for autism, emanating from different Italian regions (Abruzzo, Campania, Emilia Romagna, the Autonomous Province of Bolzano, to name but a few),[52] a uniform way in which to draw a univocal level of performance from their

[50] The data are taken from the records of workshop *Autismo che fare?* (What can we do about Autism?) Emilia Romagna, and comparing other Italian regions on the models of operation. Bologna, 17 January 2007.

[51] Decision by the regional council, 3 September 2008, no. 1384, *Linee d'indirizzo per la salute mentale* (Operational guidelines for mental health), excerpt.

[52] *La Società Italiana di Neuropsichiatria dell'Infanzia e dell'Adolescenza* (The Italian Society of Neuropsychiatry in Childhood and Adolescence) has taken steps to issue *Linee Guida per l'Autismo. Raccomandazioni tecniche-operative per i servizi di neuropsichiatria dell'età evolutiva* (Guidelines for Autism. Technical and operational recommendations for the services of developmental neuropsychiatry).

various situations does not emerge. This causes, on a regional level, a considerable gap between the levels of care exercised by the regions that generates, in turn, differentiation between the levels of performance, in apparent conflict with the principles of the formal and real equality of these constitutionally guaranteed individuals. So, from the picture that emerges between the different regional situations, there is no integrated coordination of issues that affects people with autism spectrum disorders.

The proposals of some Italian regions are summarised below.

6.1 Draft Laws and Regional Regulatory Developments in the Theme of Autism

6.1.1 The Region of Basilicata

Regional legislation identifies the *Servizi di Neuropsichiatria Infantile* (Child Neuropsychiatry Services), which are part of a single internal department of regional significance (DINPEE), divided into a single regional operating hospital unit, local operating units in each ASL (local health authority), and protected facilities for daycare and residential rehabilitation and recovery throughout the region. The plan for PSSR 2010–2012 envisages the creation of a 'regional centre of reference for infantile autism' and, by the second year of the plan, the development of a 'Day Centre for Autism' for each ASL.

6.1.2 The Region of Calabria

Calabria has not adopted specific rules relating to autism, but it is included as one of the diseases treated by the *Dipartimento della Salute Mentale* (Department of Mental Health). Through the guidelines and the organization of health activities, the establishment of centres for the prevention, treatment and rehabilitation of specific disorders, including autism is envisaged. Regional regulation no. 13 of 2009, relating to regulations and manuals for the accreditation of the regional health system, identifies organizational, structural and technological centres for extensive daycare rehabilitation for autism outside the hospital. These centres carry out rehabilitation daycare activities for adults, while for children with autism or similar disorders at different levels of gravity, which may require intensive and/or extensive care in the nature of rehabilitation and social rehabilitation, the aim is to develop their potential and their acquisition of the greatest independence possible.

6.1.3 The Region of Campania

The Campania region has adopted specific *Linee guida per il trattamento del disturbo dello spettro autistico* (Guidelines for the treatment of autism spectrum disorder),[53] with particular reference to the pediatric age (in 2003 and 2009), in full harmony with SINPIA recommendations and the document produced by the *Tavolo nazionale di lavoro sull'autismo* (National Working Table on Autism), 2008. Nevertheless, there are no specific rules relating to adults and their inclusion in an employment context, but these can be referred to in the discussion on the decisions prepared by the Department of Mental Health. The *Autismo-University* project, prepared jointly by the *Centri Servizi per la Disabilità* (Centres for Disability Services) of the Universities of Bologna, Catania and Naples, with the collaboration of associations ANGSA Campania and *Autism Aid Onlus*, is also worth mentioning. This school-university project defines learning objectives related to training, in strict accordance with the Dublin descriptors, as regarding the expected knowledge, skills and abilities and/or transferable skills in life and work contexts. In more detail, it is designed to provide students with Autism Spectrum Disorders and their families with tools to ensure a more conscious relationship with daily life, also from the perspective of improving and rationalizing interactions between educational institutions, local government, associations and families.[54]

6.1.4 The Region of Emilia Romagna

Emilia Romagna offers generous legislation for people with autism, including the *Programma Regionale Integrato per l'assistenza alle persone con disturbo dello spettro autistico-ASD* (Integrated Regional Programme for Assistance to People with Autism Spectrum Disorders-ASD) (PRI-A), and a support network of more articulated levels. The overall objective of the PRI-A project is to provide relevant hubs to which interested parties in the province can refer, to structure integrated pathways of the care system; this project involves an organization in a 'hub' and 'spoice' network model (reference centres covering large areas are 'hubs' and connected centres are 'spoices'). There are not, however, significant and explicit references to the condition of adults with autism, in view of ongoing education and vocational training.

6.1.5 The Region of Friuli Venezia Giulia

Friuli Venezia Giulia has addressed issues related to taking integrated charge of people with disabilities, who include individuals with Autism Spectrum Disorders,

[53] No. 21 of 2011, compiled by the *Istituto Superiore della Sanità* (National Institute of Health).

[54] National Project MIUR-CNUD 2009–2010. The national coordinator is Prof. Andrea Canevaro.

and placing them in the context of the regional social and health plan 2010–2012.[55] At this stage, the network of services works closely with the voluntary and third sector network, in particular with the *Fondazione Bambini e Autismo ONLUS* (Children and Autism Foundation NPO), a private non-profit institution, based in Pordenone, accredited and part of the Regional health care service, which provides network services for autism from infancy to adulthood. The venture includes building a diagnostic centre, a rehabilitation centre, a daycare centre and a work centre for adults. The main strategy, in a wider regional socio-health context, is to build a path of access, taking care of people with disabilities with a view towards a different relationship between the citizen and the welfare system. 'Taking integrated charge' is understood as the set of measures (health and social services firstly, but also educational, active labour market policies and the education system) and the legal and organizational conditions which, for the entire life span of a person with disabilities, guarantees a constant and comprehensive assessment of their operation resulting from the interaction between the person and the environment in which he lives. From this perspective, the concrete realization of regional health and social welfare reform requires systematic and consistent commitment necessitating adjustment and modifications in organizational and managerial legislation.

6.1.6 The Region of Lazio

The Lazio region approved the *Autismo ed Educazione Speciale* (Autism and Special Education) project[56] with the intention of engaging in a continuous exchange of information and direct communication between institutions, scientific researchers and users. With Regional Law no. 2 of 2009,[57] the *Centro di accesso unico alla disabilità* (Centre of single access to disability) was established, in order to guarantee that all citizens had access to the necessary information, in terms of assistance and guidance, and to ensure efficient management of the treatments and services for people with disabilities and their families. The centre also promotes, supports and coordinates actions and services within a single integrated health and social care access point. The region, on the basis of the service network, has also allocated some resources for public and non-profit organizations whose activities are aimed at people with autism; in the province of Rome, in particular, there are specific plans for patients with disorders of the autism spectrum. In contrast, however, there is no indication that there will be widespread and significant

[55] The objective of the plan is to obtain integrated control with different instruments, the first of which is the adoption of a common instrument for the multidimensional assessment of need and the definition of a personalized care plan, such as the ICF biopsychosocial model (International Classification of Functioning, Disability and Health) World Health Organization (2001).

[56] Regional Resolution no. 924, 26 October 2006. Innovative projects aimed at improving the lives of families who take care of autistic people at home.

[57] Founding of the *Centro di accesso unico alla disabilità* (CAUD).

legislative initiatives in favour of adults with autism, relating to higher education and vocational training.

6.1.7 The Region of Liguria

The Liguria region is very active in the field of autism; in fact it has promulgated, over a long period, several projects in collaboration with specialized centres and *Associazioni dei familiari* (family associations).[58] The region approved specific guidelines for autism, especially in Resolution no. 1555, 12 December 2004, *Approvazione indirizzi in materia di autismo* (Approval of guidelines on autism), adopted on the application of the 3-year plan for social services and community health, which defined the network of services for childhood, adolescence and adulthood. In addition, the *Gruppo Regionale Autismo* (Regional Group for Autism) was established, through which detailed regulations for the transition in care, from adolescence to adulthood were laid down.[59] In 2009, Liguria approved a regional agreement[60] aimed at the adoption and implementation of the *Linee di Indirizzo Nazionali per la Salute Mentale* (National Guidelines for Mental Health) which include, among other points, the implementation of treatment programmes in the area of autistic spectrum disorders, in accordance with the final document of the *Tavolo nazionale di lavoro sull'autismo* (National Working Table on Autism), 2008.[61]

[58] More proactive synergies were activated, in particular with the association ANGSA Liguria and the GROUP ASPERGER-Liguria.

[59] Precisely due to this delicate transition, it is expected that the maternal-infant sector (NOAC), which was in charge of the patient, report the case to the district of expertise. In the individual ASLs (local health authorities), adult patients with autism are supported by the *Unità operativa assistenza disabili* (Operational Unit Support Centre for the Disabled) (UOAD).

[60] Regional Resolution no. 739.

[61] Among other regulatory guidance in the region, there is: the Decree of 17 October 2002, no. 2147, *Progetto Autonomia per Minori e Giovani Adulti con Problemi Relazionali.* (Autonomy Project for Children and Young Adults with Relationship Problems), a regional contribution to the setting up of ANGSA—Liguria—*Associazione Nazionale Genitori Soggetti Autistici* (National Association of Parents of Autistic Subjects), Regional Law no. 15/2000, *Norme ed Interventi in Materia di Diritto all'Istruzione e alla Formazione* (Rules and Measures relating to the Right to Education and Training) (Chapter II: Regional Measures), Decree of 7 July 2006, no. 2106 *Progetto di Interesse Regionale in Materia di Autismo* (Project of Regional Interest in the Field of Autism), Regional Council Resolution, 27 October 2006, no. 1118, *Soggetti Autistici per una Presa in Carico Integrata* (Integrated Care for Autistic Subjects) jointly between the Genoese ASL 3 and the Istituto David Chiossone.

6.1.8 The Region of Lombardy

The Lombardy Region has approved, over the years, various projects for autism; in 1996, it activated the *Osservatorio autismo della Regione Lombardia* (Autism Observatory of the Lombardy Region) and since 1998, experimental points of convergence for autism have been put into action. In addition, in resolution no. 8/6861, 19 March 2008, the *Linee di indirizzo regionale per la neuropsichiatria dell'infanzia e dell'adolescenza* (Regional Guidelines for Neuropsychiatry in Childhood and Adolescence) were approved in the realisation of the PSSR 2007–2009. In 2008, in view of the results of the research *La Famiglia davanti all'autismo* (The Family Facing Autism) in 2005, the *Direzione regionale famiglia e solidarietà sociale* (Regional Directorate of Family and Social Solidarity) launched a tender for the financing of 3-year projects on autism. The Lombardy Region also approved a *Bando per la promozione di iniziative sperimentali per sviluppare una rete di interventi e opportunità a favore delle persone autistiche e delle loro famiglie* (Call for the Promotion of Experimental Initiatives to Develop a Network of Measures and Opportunities for People with Autism and their Families),[62] which aims, in fact, to implement policies in support of families, financing projects through local partnerships, also with a view to the possibility of increasing existing connections between different parts of the system of services for people with autism and their families. As a result of this announcement, the region has financed three projects carried out in respective ASLs (local health authorities) with the involvement, for about 2 years, of more than 300 families with autistic children aged 3–21 years.[63]

6.1.9 The Region of Marche

With the approval of the Regional Health Plan 2003–2006 and the Regional Law no. 13, 20th June 2003 for the reorganization of the health service, some elements for social and health integration of great importance were introduced into the regional system of Marche.[64] Among the most significant of these is the *L'Autismo nella regione Marche- verso un progetto di vita* (Autism in the Marche region—towards a life plan), a project which has put into action important expertise in support of family members.

---

[62] Regional Resolution no. 6635, 20 February 2008.

[63] ORMA project, *Organizzazione della Rete e del Modello di Sostegno per l'Autismo nella ASL di Cremona,* (Organization of the Network and the Support Model for Autism in the Local Health Authority of Cremona), Networking: the contribution of all towards the integration and continuity of measures for people with autism and their families in the ASL (Local health Authority) Monza-Brianza, *Rete Autismo* (Autism Network) at ASL Milano 1.

[64] The Marche Region, as mentioned above, is the first in Italy to have approved, on 7 October 2014, a specific regional law on autism.

6.1.10 The Region of Molise

In the Region of Molise there is no specific legislation on autism; the main legislative reference is Regional Law no. 30, 2002[65] and the relevant implementing regulation no. 1, 2004. The Regional Health Plan 2008–2010 envisages the empowerment of services for mental health care, especially the construction of residential medium and low complexity care: daycare and outpatient and home care, as well as activities for social and labour inclusion. It should be emphasized that the University of Molise has started, with Aurora Aid NPO, scientific collaboration and support for university education, relating to the theme of autism.

6.1.11 The Autonomous Province of Bolzano

In the Autonomous Province of Bolzano guidelines for autism have been adopted in the German language, which, however, have not been included in a Act. References to legislation, in fact, relate to the tutelage of mental health. In Alto Adige, people with autism can rely on an extensive network of services in all four districts that comprises the only health authority, providing care and support to both individuals with autism and their families. There are, in addition, some active projects in conjunction with the University of Bolzano, which has an established tradition of inclusive education.

6.1.12 The Autonomous Province of Trento

The Autonomous Province of Trento has set up specific centres for autism, which operate in close collaboration with families and the school. Thanks to the directives of the provincial health services for the provision of additional health benefits for the years 2007–2009, the Province has envisaged a financial contribution, by way of contributions to the cost of rehabilitation, for the benefit of patients with autism, childhood psychosis or cerebral palsy.

6.1.13 The Region of Puglia

In Puglia the main point of reference is the Regional Health Plan for 2008–2010[66] which identifies new targets for the prevention and treatment of disabilities, to be achieved through an integrated network of health and social workers, families and the school. The Plan highlights the lack of social and rehabilitative structures for some pathologies, among which is autism.[67]

---

[65] Implementing Regulation, pursuant to Article 13.

[66] Regional Law no. 23, 19 September 2008.

[67] However, some centres of excellence operate in the region, such as: the *Centro Nostra Famiglia* (Our Family Centre) in Ostuni, the *Centro di Riabilitazione Padre Pio* (Father Pio Rehabilitation Centre) in San Giovanni Rotondo, the Osmairm in Laterza, and the *Centro di Riabilitazione dei Padri Trinitari* (Rehabilitation Centre of the Trinitarian Fathers) in Gagliano del Capo.

6.1.14 The Region of Sardinia

With Regional Resolution (DGR) no. 44/10 of 31 October 2007, the *Programma straordinario di interventi per l'autismo e gli altri disturbi pervasivi dello sviluppo* (Extraordinary Programme of Measures for Autism and other Pervasive Developmental Disorders) was approved, underling the measures in the *Piano Regionale dei Servizi Sanitari 2006–2008 per la Neuropsichiatria Infantile e dell'Adolescenza (NPIA)* (Regional Plan of Health Services from 2006 to 2008 for Child and Adolescent Neuropsychiatry). This special programme is aimed at overcoming the current organizational, logistical and training deficiencies in the specific field of autism and pervasive developmental disorders, and covers several areas, including the reorganization of services for autism and other pervasive developmental disorders, as well as including and integrating the activities of the *Centro per l'assistenza a bambini e adolescenti con disturbi pervasivi dello sviluppo* (Centre for the care of children and adolescents with pervasive developmental disorders),[68] within the network of NPIA services, strengthening the supply of local services and NPIA hospitals and training the operators involved in the network of services.

6.1.15 The Region of Sicily

In Sicily, on 22 December 2005, a specific rule of law was promulgated stating that: 'The Regional Councilor of Health is authorized to issue a decree, within one hundred and eighty days from the date of publication of this Act, for a uniform regional programme for autism. This decree envisages that every local public health unit company of the Sicilian Region activates a centre for autism and pervasive developmental disorders'.[69] In 2007, guidelines for autism were published, with the aim of strengthening the currently patchy network of services in each ASL. However, to date, in Sicily there remains a shortage of specialist services, including dedicated services, as the document guidelines have only been partly realized. In fact, even if regional centres of excellence and good services operate, there are not enough to cover their needs.[70] An interesting activity has been realised by the *Fondazione siciliana per l'autismo* (Sicilian Foundation for Autism) (FSA),

---

[68] Regional Resolution no. 39/61, 10 December 2002. Special action programme for autism and other pervasive developmental disorders.

[69] Article 25(8).

[70] For example, *IRCCS Maria Santissima di Troina,* NPIA and territorial ASLs have promoted and prepared Units in each District, coordination with the Hospital, involvement of associations of parents and the school (with specific training of support teachers), courses for the adoption of an observation method for suspected diagnosis for paediatricians, and learning skills training and coherent taking charge, according to TEACCH and TED methodologies.

founded in June 2007 by a group of families, headed by ANGSA-Sicilia, who promoted a project pivoting on the development of the person with autism and the protection of his rights, including his right to an adult life.

6.1.16 The Region of Tuscany

The Regional Health Plan 2008–2010 includes specific goals for improving the network to ensure, in particular, a passage between the *Unità Funzionali Salute Mentale Infanzia Adolescenza* (Mental Health in Childhood and Adolescence Functional Units) and those for adults. In implementing the Plan, the region has adopted guidelines for early diagnosis and taking charge of multi-spectrum autistic disorders,[71] governing the system of services, as well as through the establishment of semi-residential (day care centres) and residential buildings, such as:

a) day centres, which must ensure qualified rehabilitation to accommodate the disease at different stages of life;
b) residential structures, articulated in several modules, which ensure the continuity of the care pathway, both for long and for limited periods of time, in relation to the clinical situation and the needs of the family;
c) highly specialized referral centres, supporting interdisciplinary teams, for children, adolescents and adults.

Therefore, the integrated network of services includes highly specialized reference centres, interdisciplinary business work groups and organizations of mutual aid. The region promotes various projects and initiatives on issues of assistance to people with autistic spectrum disorders (ASD). One, in particular, the *Osservatorio Regionale Autismo* (Regional Autism Observatory)[72] is active with scientific representatives and experts to monitor the management of the integrated network services.

6.1.17 The Region of Umbria

Umbria has developed an interesting and detailed plan of action by means of the *Progetto per la promozione della salute dei minori affetti da autismo* (Project for the promotion of the health of children affected by autism). In 2009, moreover, a *Centro di Riferimento regionale per l'autismo* (Regional Reference Centre for Autism), was established by the Regional Health Plan with the task, among others, to promote a trial on the use of innovative strategies to ensure better continuity of the care extended at the age of adolescence and adulthood, actively supporting social inclusion and appropriate forms of protected residence and job placement. In

[71] Regional Board Resolution no. 1066, 3 December 2008.
[72] Regional Resolution no. 6904, 29 December 2009.

this local context, the ANGSA[73] Association, founded on the stimulus of some parents who in 1985 wanted to give a future to people affected by autism, assumes a proactive decisive importance in supporting families. Even today, the Association holds significant importance in the region and throughout Italy, especially since, in 1989, it became part of Autism-Europe for its exchange of good practices of care and integration on an international scale. The Regional Social Plan also envisages SAL, services aimed at promoting tools and pathways (apprenticeship training, grants for work, ILSA, oriented in favour of vulnerable groups). The *Dipartimento di salute mentale* (Department of Mental Health) (DSM), together with the *Deliberazione di Giunta Regionale* (Regional Council Deliberation) no. 21, 12 January 2005, in particular, have developed ‘training programmes and job placement in support of therapeutic pathways’. However, even though the Umbrian experience has demonstrated an increasing use of specific tools in the work area, it is very patchy and unstable in the face of ever-increasing difficulty in employment.

6.1.18 The Region of Valle d’Aosta

The Valle d’Aosta has no specific legislation on autism, but the care network is framed within the operating model of assistance for mental health care, *Piano Regionale per la Salute e il Benessere Sociale 2006–2008* (Regional Plan for Health and Social Welfare 2006–2008)[74] and for people with disabilities (Regional Law no. 14, 18 April 2008). The Plan recognizes the function of mutual help groups between family members, patients and social cooperatives, for the purpose of employment. The Regional Law cited above is significant as it concerns an integrated system of measures and services for people with disabilities defining a *Progetto individuale per la persona con disabilità* (Individual Project for the Person with a Disability); this includes, in addition to a diagnostic and functional assessment, the performance of care and treatment and rehabilitation, as well as education, instruction, training and job placement in the perspective of social integration.[75] The region recognizes the modality for certifying skills according to the school curriculum as a means of correlation and connection between the worlds of education and work; it also supports attendance on routes to university

[73] The ANGSA Umbria Region was established in 2000.

[74] The Plan is responsible, together with the municipalities, for health and social integration and states that the services have been established for the protection of mental health, an operational model for regional assistance for the mentally ill, based in the area, albeit at different degrees of fulfilment.

[75] The Law also envisages that the region promotes the education process, both scholastic and training, covering all phases of the life of the person with disabilities from birth up to the age of the 64 years of age.

education by promoting specific initiatives for education[76] in order to foster strategies to support lifelong learning.

6.1.19 The Region of Veneto

The Region of Veneto is largely characterized by its legislation to protect the rights of persons with disabilities, promoting measures in favour of those with autism, programming initiatives, research projects and training programmes, carried out in collaboration between the region, universities, non-profit organizations, health-care professionals and social workers. The *Piani Locali della Disabilità* (Local Disability Plans) trace routes of treatment with home care and residential facilities, based on multidimensional assessment, by means of the *Scheda di valutazione per le persone disabili* (Assessment Form for People with Disabilities) (S.Va.M.Di.).[77] The Veneto Region, with DGR no. 3792, 2 December 2008 *Approvazione progetti di sostegno al sistema di offerta per persone non autosufficienti e disabili* (Approval of projects that support the supply system for dependent persons and the disabled), supports the project *Centro educativo pomeridiano per il trattamento dei disturbi pervasivi dello sviluppo di tipo autistico* (Afternoon education centre for the treatment of pervasive developmental disorders in the autistic spectrum).[78] Moreover, since 2006, the regional government annually approves and assigns resources for the creation of innovative structures for disability, including centres for autism.[79] The objective of these initiatives is to enhance services for people with disabilities and to promote opportunities to improve inclusion in education and employment. For people with autism, in particular, there is a need to implement the network of accessible specialist services, evenly spread throughout Veneto, and a need can be seen for stronger links between health, social and education areas.

7 From Legislation to Good Practice: National and European Autism Projects

In the individual Italian regions, there are several important specific initiatives of different nature and content aimed at achieving systematic action plans in relation to autism. 'We have to clarify, however, that the picture that emerges is in no way

[76] They are presented by the *Centro Territoriale Permanente di Istruzione e Formazione in Età Adulta* (Permanent Territorial Centre for Education and Training in Adulthood) (CTP), established by decree by the Superintendent of Education of the Autonomous Region of Valle d'Aosta, 21 February 2005, no. 7438.

[77] The Assessment Form was approved by Regional Resolution no. 331, 13 February 2007. Multidimensional assessment of persons with disabilities according to the ICF, subsequently integrated into Regional Resolution no. 2575, 4 August 2009.

[78] This project was presented by the company ULSS no. 10 and envisages the implementation of an afternoon workshop for children with autism.

[79] Regional Resolution no. 2333, 28 July 2009.

homogeneous regarding both the general profile, referring to the whole country, and local measures that cannot be assimilated with each other from the point of view of content'.[80]

In the Marche Region, the *Sotto-Progetto per l'istituzione di servizi per adolescenti ed adulti con disturbi autistici* (Sub-Project for the establishment of services for adolescents and adults with autistic disorders)[81] aims to promote the social integration of adolescents and adults with autism and focuses on adapting existing socio-educational day centres[82] and youth groups.[83] The project consists of the following points: characteristics of services for adolescents and adults, methodology of operation, training personnel, regional initiatives, the stages of implementation of the project, assessment and cost analysis. The prospect is to facilitate, through the implementation of socio-educational daycare centres and youth groups, opportunities to experience as normally as possible, a social life for individuals with autism, in a proper interaction with a real-life environment.

These centres are open at least 7 h a day, at least 5 days a week, 11 months a year. Moreover, a Management Committee with political, technical and users' families representation has been established, and a one-to-one relationship between social worker and user is guaranteed. In the project, the specific characteristics required of

---

[80] Giofrè (2010), p. 55.

[81] This is an integral part of the project *L'autismo nella regione Marche-verso un progetto di vita* (Autism in the Marche region—towards a life project) (Bollettino ufficiale regionale no. 121, 29 October 2002). The coordination group for the project consists of: Dr. Piero Feliciotti, psychiatrist for ASL no. 9 of Macerata (representing the technical-professional area), Prof. Lucio Cottini, Lecturer in Special Education at the University of Urbino (for the psycho-pedagogical and social area), Dr. Vinicio Alessandroni, manager at UMEA ASL no. 13 of Ascoli Piceno (for the area of operations). The project coordinator is Prof. Lucio Cottini.

[82] For more knowledge about this issue, see Articles 13 and 13*bis* of Regional Law no. 18, 4 June 1996, *Promozione e coordinamento delle politiche di intervento in favore delle persone in situazione di handicap* (Promotion and coordination of intervention policies in favour of people with disabilities), modified by Regional Law no. 28, 21 November 2000. In Article 13 (Socio-educational centres) the following is included:

1. In order to promote the development of personal autonomy and the process of social integration of people with serious disabilities who have finished their schooling, the Region supports and regulates the activation and operation of day structures.
   1*bis*. The socio-educational daycare centres are integrated local services open to the local community for the functions of day reception, integrated socio-educational and rehabilitative support and socialization, to increase and maintain appropriate levels of functional autonomy, to counteract regression and promote employment routes through job training and supported employment. [. . .].
2. The socio-educational daycare centres can be equipped to ensure forms of residential facilities for people with disabilities who are without family support.
3. The region contributes towards financing in favour of single municipalities and their associates or to the Mountain Communities for the management of socio-educational centres. Article 13*bis* (Residential Facilities) l. The region contributes to finance in favour of local bodies for the establishment and operation of small residential facilities housing people with severe disabilities, lacking family support, permanently or temporarily and in cases of emergency.

[83] They are regulated by Regional Law no. 46 of 28 March 1995. *Nuove norme per le assegnazioni e per la determinazione dei canoni degli alloggi di edilizia residenziale pubblica* (New rules for assigning and levying charges for accommodation in public housing).

centres welcoming adolescents and adults with autism relate to the structure, recommended activities and staff. The facilities must provide space for the performance of individual or cooperative activities, and must include: a room for work structured for specific types of learning (autonomy, cognitive skills, use of computer technology, communication activities, pre-employment activities, and so on), a room (or at least a private space) for the self-employed, classrooms and laboratories for work in small groups, a room used as a gym for physical activity (or possibly attendance at gyms outside the centre) and an open space.

'It's very important that the centres are located within the community context. The initiatives of the "farm community" cannot be considered satisfactory, unless as moments of a job which must always prioritise activities of interaction within a normal town environment'.[84] As far as the activities are concerned, the project draws on a multi-faceted model, organizing work open to the social context and related to six main life areas linked to activities: personalized cognitive and communicative, for autonomy, social, motor and expressive, lab (pre-professional), and leisure. It is envisaged that the services activate synergies with the employment centres in order to develop projects to start working, even protected work, for those who show sufficient skill. The project is divided into four stages of implementation, for a total of 3 years. The *Sotto-Progetto per l'istituzione di un servizio residenziale per soggetti con disturbi autistici* (Sub-Project for the establishment of a residential service for people with autistic disorders) is part of that same project, including initiatives related to sea or mountain trips and activities to support the family, as well as the establishment of a *Numero Verde Autismo* (toll-free number). The *Attività previste per i genitori* (Planned activities for parents)[85] are also of great interest and are developing in two specific directions: a *Progetto sollievo* (Relief Project) to provide specialized assistance at particular times, and specific training courses (for parents), through which it is hoped to be able to set up local mutual-help groups, stimulated and coordinated by parents who have attended these courses.

[84] Regional Resolution no. 1891, 29 October 2002 *L'autismo nella regione Marche-verso un progetto di vita* (The Autism Project in the Marche region—towards a life project).

[85] 'Predicting activities of family support means not only trying to supply help in situations of great difficulty, but also laying the foundations to ensure that the family itself becomes a resource of fundamental importance in the integration process of the child. Many research projects have revealed that the family certainly needs to be helped and supported in this direction, and the level of adaptation that it is possible to achieve in many cases is generally extremely positive in the sense that they can do a lot for their children, for themselves and for the services of the community. These families are really great resources, the ideal partners for all educational and rehabilitation services, and references to other families who find themselves in similar conditions. Parents' associations in Italy have effectively compensated for the deficiencies of support services to the family, playing a supporting role in many highly significant cases. So, the equation according to which a family with an autistic child is almost inevitably destined to have a crisis and collapse is by no means a foregone conclusion. The risk, however, exists and is valid, especially if systemically organized aid procedures, in which the whole community is involved (e.g., community care) are not brought into the field'. (Ibid).

The purpose of the relief project is to establish a fund to finance the presence of teachers and other specialized assistants who can take care of people with autism, adolescents and adults, for limited periods of time (a week or two), so as to allow family members to deal with personal needs (medical, work activities, periods of hospitalization, etc.), or to indulge in short holidays/days/evenings to cultivate personal interests. The parent training courses are training courses consisting of ten training units, divided into three interconnected modules. The Autism toll-free number is important for obtaining different types of information about autism, which may include the following: the location, characteristics, and activities conducted by the services, contact persons for possible specialist check-ups, the opportunity to take advantage of planned initiatives on a regional level, and so on. In addition, the Autism toll-free number is also aimed at teachers and professionals in this field so that they are able to obtain more specific information. The service is free and active for 4 days a week, alternating with the presence of technicians, social workers and parents.

In Tuscany, the 'Community Farm' project[86] sponsored by the Agrabah Association[87] in 2009, aims to achieve, in fact, a farming community in the province of Pistoia, at Gello to be precise, with the idea of providing adults with autism with the tools to develop essential skills for working in nurseries. Users are selected according to: pathology, chronological age (over 18 years), residence (Pistoia, and the province of Pistoia), and are engaged in work for 5 days a week. They are joined by a group of expert workers (specialists in horticulture) and professionals from workshops in various sectors; in fact, the work involves professional training through a variety of: workshops (sports, theatre, autonomy, communication, culinary), activities (carpentry, market, assemblies, equestrian and/or pet therapy, ceramics, découpage, music, orchestra) and field trips for the selection and purchase of materials for these activities. In the same region, the *Autismo e lavoro agricolo* (Autism and agricultural work) project[88] at the *Casa di Ventignano* (CdV) (Ventignano House), was set up in February 2003. The *Piano di lavoro 2014* (2014 Work Plan) envisages the Project 'Autism and agriculture', aimed at five youths with autism, 4 days a week (for a total of 10 h) in activities related to: work in the garden, harvesting and cleaning vegetables for crates,[89] and choosing and

[86] The project is achieved through productive collaboration between the Association of Agrabah and the Department for the Mental Health of Adults, ASL 3 of Pistoia, which guarantees the presence of two psychiatrists who follow the planning and therapeutic evolution of the 18 users.

[87] It is an Association of Parents for Autism NPO.

[88] Approved by the *Dipartimento di Salute Mentale* (Department of Mental Health), the *Associazione Autismo Toscana* (Tuscan Autism Association) and the Cooperativa Sinergic@.

[89] The strategy followed by the cooperative working in the project was to produce market vegetables through buying groups, 'according to the principles of environmentally sustainable and ethically short chains, seasonality and the wholesomeness of the products, as well as respect for the rights of workers'. (*Piano di lavoro 2014 del sottoprogetto 'Autismo e lavoro agricolo'*, 2014 Work Plan of the subproject 'Autism and agricultural work') at the Casa di Ventignano (CDV).

placing them in the crates. Work activities are carried out in the greenhouse and on the land adjacent and behind it, and are recorded in the *Agenda con immagini* (picture diary) of each user.

In the Emilia Romagna Region, in Reggio Emilia to be precise, a bridge project called 'Job trainer disability' was established[90] to support individuals with autism in practical ways in the delicate transition from school to work. The methodology involves the formation of a 'simplifier', an innovative profile that could form a 'bridge' in the transition to the world of work. 'All the reports that come to us from other countries indicate that tutor social workers do not feel prepared and equipped to meet the challenges that educational support to the disabled, especially intellectual support, requires', explained the creator of the project, Silvia Fontanesi, Cspmi European project designer.[91] Hence, there was the need to develop the skills of trainers, thanks to funding from the Province of Reggio Emilia, together with the *Aut Aut* Association, the ASL of Reggio, the Municipality of Reggio and the provincial education system. 'Job trainer disability' [...] is a 'path to distinguish their CV, highlighting their talents and their abilities to develop those soft skills recommended in the guidelines of the European Community and to focus and realize their projects and their dreams'.[92] In 2012, 11 teachers, 11 autistic children and as many companies and cooperatives were involved in a pilot experiment conducted in the area with encouraging results: the creation of a new professional job profile and the involvement of some of the users in working activity. In the same experiment the 'Leonardo project' was founded, which lasts 2 years (November 2013–November 2015) and which will transfer the knowledge and methodology of the job trainer to partner countries; in Reggio Emilia they are starting up the expansion of the project to people with dyslexia, Down syndrome, physical disabilities, etc.. To guarantee objectivity, this project is monitored by an external body, which is the Greek company Cyberall Access, based in Athens, which will make use of scientific collaboration from Autism-Europe. In the end, there will be about 60 newly-trained Job Trainers or Facilitators, throughout Europe.

In Friuli Venezia Giulia there is another encouraging activity, promoted by *L'Officina dell'arte* (The Art Workshop), a workshop for people with autism which is part of the Pordenone services network, set up by the *Fondazione Bambini e Autismo ONLUS* (Children and Autism Foundation NPO), which involves the active participation of all those involved in their care and welfare. The initiative for inclusion in employment is set up as a life pathway in which work, social life and residency are integrated in the context of environment and coherent organization, and includes the art workshop and the residential path, *Vivi la città* (Enjoy the city) projects. In the first, mosaic experts train the workers in the processing techniques

[90] Achieved by the *Centro servizi piccole-medie imprese* (Center services SMBs) (Cspmi), it has received the approval of the European Community and funding for exporting to other EU countries, such as Austria, Malta, Spain and Turkey.

[91] http://www.corriere.it/salute/13_ottobre_18/così-autistici-trovano-lavoro.

[92] www.job.trainer.it/info.

of mosaic for the manufacture of quality, useful and salable products, and the teachers themselves are, in turn, trained in the most appropriate ways to interact with people with autism, also helping them to learn social skills. The working environment is tailored for users. In fact, it is characterized by: sensory cleaning, communication support, step-by-step directions, predictability, the presence of 'co-workers', not 'assistants', the integration of the centre with other services in the network and locally. At the end of the working day the *Vivi la città* programme starts, which offers the opportunity to develop personal and domestic autonomy, by experiencing the city and making several choices: leaving or staying at home, going to the cinema, theatre or the pub, cooking, shopping, doing sports activities, meeting colleagues outside work, etc.

In the Region of Lazio, the recent founding of an association called 'Insettopia', deserves mention. It has the characteristics of a non-profit social organization, and has its headquarters in Rome. Its founder, journalist Gianluca Nicoletti, father of an autistic boy, has designed a format by which a group of seven to eight families of autistic people[93] organize themselves like a small business, pooling public and personal resources and any possible available property and educational staff, in order to implement a large community aimed at creating an 'ideal city for autism', profitably employing technologies that allow interaction between physical and digital objects. In essence, Insettopia has the aim of becoming a mediator for concrete and effective projects between the family associations and the institutions, the tangible possibility for research, design, adapting the intended primary use of each electronic device, computer, or application, system or 'emotional prosthetic', which can facilitate the lives of people with autism spectrum disorders, offering them concrete opportunities: job placement and training, social interaction and independent living. Insettopia relies on the technology platform Snappin, developed by start-up FWR,[94] which in a short time has been able to obtain the confidence of important Italian and foreign companies.

An absolute novelty in the Veneto region, is the *Centro Multisistemico per l'autismo* (Multisystemic Centre for Autism) project, sponsored by *ViviAutismo* in Padua relating to the period 2013–2014. The objectives of the Centre (CSMA) are, among other things, to promote the inclusion of people with autism spectrum disorder into the world of work since their coming of age through carrying out concrete and sustainable activities, whether held in a protected environment or not. One of the structures which is a subject of employment resource is Roncajette Park, an environmental reserve that requires a full and better use by the citizens, where users are involved in its redevelopment and where there are premises and planned specific and economically-viable activities.

[93] Selecting the households follows a policy of specific characteristics referring to the same age group of children with autism and to a similar level of disability.

[94] FWR is technological start-up aimed at developing a platform where information (digital media, services, animation) converge, engaging and involving homogeneous sets of users.

The *Start Autismo-Sistema territoriale per l'Autonomia e la realizzazione dei talenti di persone con autismo* project (Area System-Autism Start for Autonomy and the realization of the talents of people with autism) is typical of activities from the Abruzzo Region. It is sponsored by the Foundation *Il Cireneo onlus per l'autismo* (The Cireneo NPO for autism) and the *Focolare Maria Regina Onlus* (Maria Regina Home NPO). It is funded by the European Social Fund and is networked with Italian and European partners.[95] It aims to promote a positive evolutionary transition from childhood to adulthood, favouring full social inclusion and employment. Among the main activities planned for 2012–2014, there are 20 customised projects for work training, based on pilot testing at the *Centro per l'Autismo* in Penna di Sant'Andrea, according to an inclusive model of operation based on assessment and on the provision of services: guidance, training, job matching, coaching, mentoring and job placement, on the design and implementation of a social enterprise, the exchange of experience and dissemination of good practice in networking with European and national centres, through a digital platform.[96]

In concluding this brief survey, it seems appropriate to mention two good practice projects in the international arena, namely 'Education and Professional Training (IFTS): policy and school practices for special educational needs' and the 'European Project Ispectrum'.[97] The first project was launched by the European Agency for Development in Special Needs Education, and focuses on the education and training of students with disabilities between the ages of 14 and 25 years, with the intention of promoting good practices and improvement in job opportunities and employment. The project involved more than 50 experts from 26 European countries[98] and analyzed the curricula with a view to assessing the results in relation to the labour market. From this analysis, a model for vocational education and training was developed, and some recommendations were put forward. This project, which was presented and discussed at the Cyprus Conference (November 2012), sought to identify the similarities and differences between school systems, highlighting, in particular, the factors that facilitate academic success and those that hinder it.

---

[95] The Project relies on the collaboration of the following organizations: National Autistic Society in London (United Kingdom), *Specialisterne of Ballerup* (Denmark), *Cascina Rossago* in Pavia; Faculty of Psychology, University of L'Aquila, *Centro Regionale di Riferimento Autismo* (Regional Centre for Autism Referral) in the Abruzzo region, *Fondazione Papa Paolo VI onlus* (Pope Paul VI Foundation NPO) in Pescara, Don Carlo Gnocchi Foundation, Milan, Social cooperative type B *Volentieri* in Casoli (Ch), Ascot Srl in Florence, *Centro Terapeutico Europeo* (European Therapeutic Centre) in Rignano sull'Arno (FI).

[96] *Comunità di Pratiche sull'inserimento lavorativo dei soggetti autistici* (Community of Practices in employment inclusion of people with autism).

[97] http://www.ispectrum.eu/index.php/en/network.

[98] Austria, Belgium, Cyprus, Denmark, Estonia, Finland, France, Germany, Greece, Hungary, Iceland, Ireland, Latvia, Lithuania, Luxembourg, Malta, Netherlands, Norway, Poland, Portugal, the Czech Republic, Slovenia, Spain, Sweden, Switzerland and the United Kingdom.

The second project, the 'European project Ispectrum'[99] aims to improve social interaction abilities in people with autism and other special needs in the workplace by using virtual working environments that help them increase their chances of finding a job.[100] In detail, in the project's 'Module 3', there is a simulated 3D work environment, based on three different virtual working environments (an IT department, a shop and a nursery), where the autistic adult can launch a Web Quest to create a concept and outline the design for his own Serious Game, have experience in using a serious 3D game, find out how this has developed and develop his own design.

8 Conclusions

'The removal of barriers to learning and the participation of all stakeholders at school and in social life is the cornerstone of inclusive education, whose guiding principles, rooted in the fight against discrimination, inequality and exclusion from education of the most vulnerable, in particular, are intended to guide policies and socio-cultural and economic strategies in different countries to make education for all a reality. Since 2000, 'Education for All' (EFA) is one of the central objectives among those identified as part of the Millennium Development Goals and defined during the Millennium Summit, following the adoption of the United Nations Millennium Declaration'.[101] From this assumption, it can be seen that the sensitivity of the institutions and the public towards people with autism has increased over time. However, it seems necessary to continue to encourage the promotion and development of vocational training initiatives aimed at teenagers and adults, and effective support to their families, as well as opportunities for social development, through the provision of organized services, and the design of routes towards work orientation, stimulating at the same time ways to manage leisure and recreational time, based on a project of development training for the person.

In fact, 'if [...] on the one hand, autism spectrum disorders can drastically reduce the chances of a spontaneous encounter and comparison with others, on the other, they can also enhance some features that are particularly important in some areas of work: the ability to be repetitive and systematic (sometimes invaluable in activities that require a high degree of organization and precision), attention to detail (which can help locate items of information that often escape the attention of most people)'.[102]

It is important to remember that, at the end of the seventh annual World Autism Awareness Day, celebrated on 2 April 2014, in Italy there was a request for a law

---

[99] Bulgaria, Italy, Germany and United Kingdom.

[100] 'Serious Game'—Module 3.

[101] Chiappetta Cajola (2013).

[102] Pontis and Fadda (2013), pp. 9–10.

determining uniform national regulations on the rights of persons with Autism Spectrum Disorders, a condition that involves the communicative, as well as the behavioral and social aspect. A few days before the approval of the *Legge Regionale sull'autismo* (Regional Autism Law) in Italy[103] some regions filed motions for law in Parliament, calling for the adoption of the Guidelines of 2011, promulgated by the National Institute of Health, and the Guidelines approved in the State-Regions Conference in 2012. It thus seems clear that '[...] the challenge of the third millennium is to make sure that autism does not produce great disability in different areas of development. Because it is not so much autism that prevents inclusion in a normal life, but the disability produced by it to prevent it, a disability which depends on education, learning and skills'.[104]

References

Alessandroni V (2010) Che cosa succede dopo. La gestione dell'età adulta. In: Cottini L (ed) L'autismo. La qualità degli interventi nel ciclo di vita. FrancoAngeli, Milano

Billstedt E, Gilbert IC, Gillberg C (2010) Aspetti della qualità della vita negli adulti con diagnosi di autismo in età pediatrica. Retrieved from: http://www.sagepublications.com/

Censis (2014) I disabili, più diseguali nella crescita delle diseguaglianze sociali. Press Release. Roma

Chiappetta Cajola L (2013) Per una cultura didattica dell'inclusione. In: Chiappetta Cajola L, Ciraci AM (eds) Didattica inclusiva. Quali competenze per gli insegnanti? Armando editore, Roma, pp 15–124

Chiappetta Cajola L (2014) Indagini quantitative negli studi delle disabilità e dei DSA: problemi e prospettive in ambito nazionale e internazionale. ECPS J. doi:10.7358/ecps-2014-009-chia

Corcella R (2014) Serve una legge per le persone autistiche. Corriere della sera/Neuroscienze. http://www.corriere.it/salute/neuroscienze/14_marzo_31/serve-legge-nazionale-le-persone-autistiche-5e5b5dee-b8bb-11e3-917e-4c908e083af6.shtml. Accessed 31 Oct 2014

Cottini L (ed) (2010) L'autismo. La qualità degli interventi nel ciclo di vita. FrancoAngeli, Milano

Giofrè F (2010) Autismo. Protezione sociale e architettura. Alinea Editrice, Firenze

Howlin P, Goode S, Hutton J, Rutter M (2004) Adult outcome for children with autism. J Child Psychol Psychiatry 45(2):212–229

Matson JL, Smith KRM (2008) Current status of intensive behavioral interventions for young children with autism and PDD-NOS. Res Autism Spectr Disord 2:60–74

McGovern CW, Sigman M (2005) Improvement in cognitive and language skills from preschool to adolescence in autism. J Autism Dev Disord 35(1):15–23

Pontis M, Fadda R (2013) Introduzione. In: Pontis M (ed) Autismo e bisogni educativi speciali. FrancoAngeli, Milano, pp 9–10

---

[103] Regional Authority for Marche (2014), *Disposizioni in materia di disturbi dello spettro autistico* (Provisions for Autism Spectrum Disorders).

[104] Corcella (2014).

Raffin C (2010) Autismo Oggi. Available via Fondazione ARES. http://www.fondazioneares.com. Accessed 31 Oct 2014

Seltzer MM et al (2004) Trajectory of development in adolescents and adults with autism. Ment Retard Dev Disabil Res Rev 10(4):234–247

Uccelli di Nemi S, Barale F (2010) L'autismo nell'età adulta: profili evolutivi e modi di cura. In: Cottini L (ed) L'autismo. La qualità degli interventi nel ciclo di vita. FrancoAngeli, Milano, pp 196–197

Lucia Chiappetta Cajola is Professor of Special Education and Pedagogy at University Roma Tre, Rome, Italy.

Article 27 of the CRPD and the Right of Inclusive Employment of People with Autism

Marco Fasciglione

1 Introduction

According to global estimates, persons with disabilities constitute some 15 % of the world's population. Between 785 million and 975 million of them are of working age (15 years or older)[1] and most live in developing countries where the informal economy employs a substantial proportion of the labour force. The labour force participation rate of persons with disabilities is low in many countries. Recent figures for members of the Organization for Economic Co-operation and Development indicate that slightly less than half of working-age persons with disabilities were economically inactive compared to one in five persons without disabilities of working age.[2] While it is difficult to draw comparisons between countries on rates of unemployment due to national differences in definitions on disability and statistical methodology, it is clear that an employment gap exists across countries and regions. As far as the EU, unemployment rate of persons with disabilities in the 2011 was at 17.4 %, a data lower than 2010 (when it was at 18.0 %), but however very far from the unemployment rate of persons without disabilities for the same year (at 10.2 %).[3]

Indeed, when persons with disabilities are employed, they are more likely to be situated in low-paying jobs, at lower occupational levels and with worst working conditions than their colleagues. More often than their peers, they are in part-time jobs or temporary positions, often with few possibilities for career development.

[1] See World Health Organization and the World Bank (2011), p. 261. For all websites, last access 30 October 2014.

[2] Ibid., p. 237.

[3] Data are drawn by the Report on the implementation of the UN Convention on the Rights of Persons with Disabilities (CRPD) by the European Union, SWD(2014) 182 Final, p. 62.

M. Fasciglione (✉)
Institute for International Legal Studies (ISGI-CNR), Naples, Italy
e-mail: marco.fasciglione@cnr.it

V. Della Fina, R. Cera (eds.), *Protecting the Rights of People with Autism in the Fields of Education and Employment*, DOI 10.1007/978-3-319-13791-9_6

The obstacles that such persons face in this regard are often related to negative attitudes or opinions, deeply rooted stigma and stereotypes and lack of interest of governments, employers and the general population. Lack of access to education and training in skills relevant to the labour market are also major barriers. Persons with disabilities are often seen as unfit for working life, incapable of carrying out tasks, as required in the open labour market, or better off in protected environments such as sheltered workshops. Worst data there exist as to the specific category of persons with autism spectrum disorder (ASD). Indeed, less than 10 % of people with ASD can get a job compared with 45 % of those with a disability, and 65.8 % of people without a disability.

2 The Right to Work and to Employment of Persons with Disability: Article 27 of the CRPD

The protection of the rights of persons with disabilities is since long a challenge for international community, and at the very least, as far as the employment sphere, since the International Labour Organization (ILO) Convention no. 159 concerning Vocational Rehabilitation and Employment of Disabled Persons (1983). However, it is only with the United Nations Convention on the Rights of Persons with Disabilities (hereinafter CRPD) that a coherent and complete protection of rights of persons with disabilities has been foreseen. Article 27 of the Convention sets out the right to work of persons with disabilities: it constitutes one of the most detailed provisions of the Convention, establishing the legal framework for State obligations in relation to work and employment of persons with disabilities.[4]

Article 27 (1) of the Convention obligates States parties to recognize the right of persons with disabilities to work, on an equal basis with others. It develops the provision of Article 23 of the Universal Declaration of Human Rights and employs similar language to that of Article 6 of the International Covenant on Economic, Social and Cultural Rights.[5] It states that the right of persons with disabilities to work includes the right to the opportunity to gain a living by work freely chosen or accepted in a labour market and work environment that is open, inclusive and accessible to persons with disabilities and sets out a non-exhaustive list of appropriate steps for States parties to take, including through legislation, to safeguard and promote the realization of the right to work, including for those who acquire a disability during the course of employment.[6]

[4] The Convention was adopted by the United Nations General Assembly on 13 December 2006 and entered into force on 3rd May 2008 together with its Optional Protocol. The CRPD is the first United Nations human rights treaty to be adopted in the twenty-first century and is reputed to be the most rapidly negotiated ever. On the Convention, see Hendricks (2007), Lawson (2007), Kayess and French (2008), and Flynn (2011).

[5] See the Committee on Economic, Social and Cultural Rights' general comments No. 5 (1994) on persons with disabilities and No. 18 (2005) on the right to work.

[6] See Convention on the Rights of Persons with Disabilities, Article 27 (1) (a) to (k).

The right of persons with disabilities to work involves an obligation on the part of States parties to create an enabling and conducive environment for employment, in both the public and private sectors.

Article 27 of the Convention guides States parties in the implementation of the right of persons with disabilities to work by setting forth some basic rules: (a) *non-discrimination*, as the persons with disabilities have the right to work on an equal basis with others; (b) *accessibility*, as the right of persons with disabilities to work includes the opportunity to gain a living in a work environment that is accessible to persons with disabilities, identifying and removing barriers that hinder persons with disabilities from carrying out their work on an equal basis with others[7]; (c) *reasonable accommodation*, as with a view to facilitating access of persons with disabilities to work on an equal basis with others, States parties must ensure that reasonable accommodation is provided to persons with disabilities who request it, and should take effective steps, including through legislation, to ensure that the denial of reasonable accommodation constitutes discrimination; (d) besides a duty to impose obligations on private-sector employers, States should adopt *positive measures* to promote employment opportunities for persons with disabilities.

These standards, therefore, impose different levels of obligations on States: more in particular from one side States are obliged to abstain from infringing rights of persons with disabilities, and from another side the Convention requires them to adopt positive measures to promote employment opportunities for persons with disabilities and this especially with regard to private-sector employers.

Amongst the implementation measures that States parties should take on the basis of the Convention a pivotal role is played by the duty of aligning national standards and practice to the Convention. In this respect, Article 4 (1) (a) and (b) of the Convention imposes two general obligations on States parties; namely: (a) to adopt all appropriate legislative, administrative and other measures for the implementation of the rights recognized in the Convention related to work and employment; (b) to take all appropriate measures, including legislation, to modify or abolish laws, regulations, customs and practices that constitute discrimination against persons with disabilities in the areas of work and employment.

[7] According to the Committee '[p]ersons with disabilities cannot effectively enjoy their work and employment rights, as described in article 27 of the Convention, if the workplace itself is not accessible. Workplaces therefore have to be accessible, as is explicitly indicated in article 9, paragraph 1 (a)' and '[a] refusal to adapt the workplace constitutes a prohibited act of disability-based discrimination' (see the CRPD Committee, General Comment No. 2 (2014), *Article 9: Accessibility*, UN DOC. CRPD/C/GC/2, 22 May 2014, para 41).

2.1 The Prohibition of Discrimination in the Workplace

The general principle of non-discrimination applies to employment as to all other sphere of life and the prohibition of discrimination against persons with disabilities is one of the main pillars of the CRPD. Indeed, discrimination on the basis of disability is defined in Article 2 of the Convention as 'any distinction, exclusion or restriction on the basis of disability which has the purpose or effect of impairing or nullifying the recognition, enjoyment or exercise, on an equal basis with others, of all human rights and fundamental freedoms in the political, economic, social, cultural, civil or any other field...'. According to this provision this definition 'includes all forms of discrimination, including denial of reasonable accommodation'. From this perspective, while the full realization of economic, social and cultural rights, including the right to work, is subject to the principle of the progressive realization,[8] the prohibition of discrimination on the basis of disability is an obligation with immediate effect. States parties have an obligation to prohibit discrimination on the basis of disability and must ensure that persons with disabilities are protected from discrimination,[9] including with regard to all matters concerning all forms of employment[10] as in any other area.

What is important to stress here is the circumstance that the protection of discrimination covers all forms of employment: in the open labour market as well as in sheltered or supported employment schemes. In effect, the prohibition of (both *de jure* and *de facto*) discrimination should cover all aspects of employment, including, but not limited to, the following: recruitment processes such as advertising, interviewing and other selection processes; review of hiring standards to remove indirect discrimination that places persons with disabilities at a disadvantage; recruitment decisions; terms and conditions of employment such as remuneration rates, work hours and leave; promotion, transfer, training or other benefits associated with employment, or dismissal or any other detriment, such as demotion or retrenchment; benefits related to the (non-discriminatory) termination of employment; victimization and harassment; safe and healthy working conditions.

[8] See Article 4 (2) of the Convention echoing the content of Article 2 (1) of the International Covenant on Economic, Social and Cultural Rights. As far as the application of the progressive realization principle and the necessity to assuring that economic constraints do not involve infringements of basic economic social and cultural rights of marginalized and less favoured individuals of the society see Fasciglione (2014).

[9] See Article 5 (2).

[10] See Article 27, para 1 (a).

2.2 Accessibility to Workplace

It is well-established that accessibility is both a general principle and a substantive provision of the CRPD[11] and applies to workplaces (both public-sector workplaces and private-sector employers) as to all other spheres of life. States are required to take steps towards ensuring a fully accessible workplace: this obligation is crucial for removing the various barriers—physical, attitudinal, information-, communication- or transport-related—that prevent persons with disabilities from seeking, obtaining and maintaining work. Physical barriers such as inaccessible public transport, housing and workplaces are often among the main reasons why persons with disabilities are not employed. The simple fact that a workplace is not accessible does not justify the failure to employ persons with disabilities.[12] States have to inform employers—irrespective of size or sector—about their positive obligation to identify barriers to equal access to the workplace by persons with disabilities and to take appropriate steps towards removing such barriers. Good practices to this end include awareness-raising efforts among employers on the need to implement regulations relating to the creation of a barrier-free, disability-friendly environment, and the development of guidelines on accessibility and universal design for employer.

2.3 The Principle of Reasonable Accommodation as a General Rule of the CRPD and as a Specific Standard to Be Applied in the Workplace

The Convention includes the duty to provide reasonable accommodation,[13] as defined in Article 2. According to this definition 'reasonable accommodation' has to be meant as the 'necessary and appropriate modifications and adjustments not imposing a disproportionate or undue burden, where needed in a particular case, to

[11] See Article 9 of the Convention.

[12] State practice reveals that many countries have taken steps to make workplaces accessible for persons with disabilities, including through legislative and policy measures. Most countries have taken action towards promoting physical accessibility, including through building ramps, accessible toilets, elevators providing sign language interpretation for deaf applicants in interviews, or legislating at national level that accessibility must be ensured in both private and public sector workplaces with more than a certain number of employees.

[13] The concept of reasonable accommodation was introduced in the United States of America 1968 Civil Rights Act and subsequently applied in the Americans with Disabilities Act of 1990; comparable legislation in the United Kingdom of Great Britain and Northern Ireland and in Australia uses the term 'reasonable adjustment'. European Union Council Directive 2000/78/EC states that reasonable accommodation for disabled persons shall be provided in the area of employment (Article 5). Examples of what constitutes reasonable accommodation are included in the WHO (2011), cit., p. 74.

ensure to persons with disabilities the enjoyment or exercise on an equal basis with others of all human rights and fundamental freedoms'. Furthermore, what is important to underpin is the circumstance that according to the CRPD the denial of reasonable accommodation constitutes a discrimination on the basis of disability. It follows that States *must ascertain* that the duty to ensure reasonable accommodation is introduced in their legislation and anti-discrimination legislation should define denial of reasonable accommodation as a form of discrimination.[14] The abovementioned provision is reinforced by Article 5(3), which also requires States 'to take all appropriate steps to ensure that reasonable accommodation is provided'. The incorporation of a State obligation to ensure that reasonable accommodations are adopted to facilitate the exercise by persons with disability of CPRD rights is perhaps the most fundamental instrumental element of the Convention. Indeed, such a broad scope to reasonable accommodation sets the Convention apart from its predecessors in international law, directly linking the absence of reasonable accommodation to the perpetuation of discrimination and inequality; furthermore, it affords to State parties the onus to take *all appropriate steps* to meet the reasonable accommodation requirement. Nevertheless, its formulation, very far from the optimal, may be narrow interpreted and unduly restrict the scope of application of the States' obligations. In effect, the obligation ceases at the point where the adjustment required constitutes a 'disproportionate or undue burden'. In the second place, the terms 'disproportionate' and 'undue burden' have been drafted as additive, effectively creating a two element test that may allow the obligation to be evaded at the lower of either threshold (which may vary according to context). In the third place, the thresholds themselves appear insufficiently challenging to penetrate to the core of exclusionary practices affecting persons requiring significant structural adjustments. They appear more likely to produce results for persons who require relatively marginal changes to the prevailing social environment. Finally, it should be also observed that the terminology 'undue burden' is far from being opportune in that it activates precisely the construction of persons with disability as 'burdens' on the community: an approach that the CPRD otherwise attempts to overcome.

[14] Since the beginning of its mandate, the CRPD Committee has consistently urged States parties to establish, including in legislation, that denial of reasonable accommodation constitutes discrimination. As for instance, in its first concluding observations with regard to Tunisia, the Committee instructed the State party to, 'incorporate the definition of reasonable accommodation in national law and to apply it in accordance with article 2 of the Convention, in particular by ensuring that the law explicitly recognises the denial of reasonable accommodation as a disability based discrimination' and that the State party 'act with urgency to include an explicit prohibition of disability-based discrimination in an anti-discrimination law, particularly those governing elections, labour, education and health, among others' (see Committee on the Rights of Persons with Disabilities, *Concluding observations: Tunisia*, Fifth session 11–15 April 2011, CRPD/C/TUN/CO/1, 13 May 2011, paras 12–13).

2.3.1 The Reasonable Accommodation in the Workplace and Its Implementation

The most prominent application of the reasonable accommodation requirement remains in the field of work and employment. Article 27 of the CRPD requires States Parties to safeguard and promote the realisation of the right to work of persons with disabilities by taking appropriate steps to ensure that reasonable accommodation is provided to persons with disabilities in the workplace. Under the Convention, employers have a legal obligation to provide reasonable accommodation to persons with disabilities. Legislation must stipulate that both public- and private-sector employers are responsible for providing reasonable accommodation to individual employees with disabilities. Governments, hence, should develop policies aimed at promoting and regulating flexible and alternative work arrangements that reasonably accommodate the individual needs of employees with disabilities. Such policies should include, *inter alia*, adjustment and modification of machinery and equipment, modification of job content, working time and work organization, and adaptation of the work environment to provide access to the workplace, in order to facilitate the employment of individuals with disabilities. The implementation of the principle of reasonable accommodation in national disability-related legislation has been slow in many countries; this is due usually to several factors. In the first place, from the national law level, the notion of reasonable accommodation (an individual requirement) is often confused with accessibility measures (a general requirement) or with positive measure schemes. In the second place, this may be due to the reluctance of employers to recruit persons with disabilities determined by the fear of having to make expensive workplace adjustments. Indeed, a general misconception that all persons with disabilities will need reasonable accommodation or that accommodations will be too costly or difficult to provide, there exists.[15] With a view to correcting misconceptions, States have the responsibility to inform employers of their duties to provide reasonable accommodation, to raise awareness on the concept among employers, trade unions and persons with disabilities, and to provide technical assistance on how to transform the provision into practice. The determination of what constitutes 'appropriate measures' is essential for the effective implementation of the duty to provide reasonable accommodation. It can be argued that measures are appropriate if they facilitate access to and participation in working life, job advancement and training on an equal footing with others for a person with disabilities requesting them. The identification of appropriate measures must be made on the basis of an individual assessment of the specific job, the needs of the person with a disability and a realistic assessment of what the employer is capable

[15] However, many persons with disabilities do not need reasonable accommodation and many accommodations can be provided at little or no cost. Even where required, only accommodation that is reasonable, necessary, appropriate and which does not impose disproportionate or undue burden, is mandated.

of providing. This process should be interactive and participatory to be effective, and all information related to the reasonable accommodation request should be handled with confidentiality.

2.4 *Positive Measures to Promote Employment of Persons with Disabilities*

Besides having a duty to impose obligations on private-sector employers, States have an obligation to take positive measures to increase employment of persons with disabilities in the private sector. The Convention establishes that States parties shall undertake measures to employ persons with disabilities in the public sector, and to promote the employment of persons with disabilities in the private sector through appropriate policies and measures, which may include affirmative action programmes, incentives and other measures (Article 27(1)(h), also (e), (i) and (k)).

Usually, the most common employment promotion scheme tends to be the use of quotas. Most countries have legislation on the percentage of positions in the public-sector for persons with disabilities, and some also have quotas for the private sector, providing for sanctions for non-compliance.[16] Existing quota systems can be divided into two main categories: strict quotas and flexible quotas. Strict quotas refer to schemes in which a person with a disability is treated preferentially irrespective of whether he or she is as qualified as other applicants. With flexible quotas, an applicant with a disability is treated preferentially only if he or she has equal merits and qualifications as another applicant. States are facing challenges in establishing effective positive measures that adequately advance equal possibilities for persons with disabilities to participate in working life. One concern is that they might send a (negative) message that persons with disabilities are hired solely on the basis of their disability, which can lead to reinforcement of stigma and negation of their role as professionals. For this reason, States are recommended to design

[16] In Italy Act n. 68 of 12 March 1999 obliges both public and private employers with at least 15 workers, to hire disabled workers in accordance with reserve quota (see Article 3). This mandatory hiring, limited to new workers and valid for technical/executive staff only, also concerns political parties, trade unions and no-profit associations operating in the field of social solidarity, assistance and rehabilitation. For police services, civil protection and national defence, the placement of persons with disabilities only concerns administrative services. The quota system is enforced also in Austria, Belgium, Cyprus, Ireland, Luxemburg, Malta, France, Germany, Greece, Spain, Romania, and Portugal. Bulgaria and Hungary have a quota system but do not foresee any sanction or penalties as to its enforcement. Norway and the Netherlands do not have any specific recruitment and dismissal rules for people with disabilities. Outside the European regional level, Mauritius has introduced quota system with the Training and Employment of Disabled Persons Act of 1996. The Act requires workplaces with 35 or more employees to set aside at least 3 % of their positions for persons with disabilities. Any employer who contravenes this provision is liable to a compensatory payment payable to the Training and Employment of Disabled Persons Board or to imprisonment (see International Labour Organization 2004, p. 5).

positive measures in such a way that the potential negative element is minimized. The focus of these programmes should be on increasing recognition of the value of diversity in the workplace and equal career development for all. Programmes focusing on promoting employment of persons with disabilities should extend to all persons with disabilities, with a special focus on women and youth with disabilities, persons with intellectual or psycho-social disabilities and other potentially vulnerable groups.

3 The Implementation of Article 27 CRPD Within the European Regional System

3.1 The EU Rights-Based Approach

The EU accession to the CRPD in 2010[17] ensured that the rights enshrined within the CRPD became part of EU law, albeit only to the extent that the EU has competence in the relevant field. The CRPD is now situated between primary and secondary law in the hierarchy of EU legislation, creating new standards of protection for persons with disabilities for the EU and its Member States. Therefore, the implementation of the rules on work and employment of persons with disabilities fall within European Union competence under two main aspects, at the very least. The EU has shared competence with member States with respect to the implementation of the right to employment and exclusive competence as regards the compatibility of State aid with the common market and the Common Customs Tariff.

As far as the first area of analysis, by the 1990s, the European Commission's Communication on *Equality of Opportunity for People with Disabilities: A New European Community Disability Strategy* puts the focus firmly on the barriers facing persons with disability, noting that 'our societies are, in many ways, organised for an "average" citizen without any disability, and, therefore, a great number of citizens are excluded from the rights and opportunities of the vast majority'.[18] It also recognised the need to address disability discrimination far beyond employment, to cover education, mobility and access, housing and welfare systems. Amsterdam amending the Treaty on European Union (Amsterdam Treaty) marked a breakthrough in disability non-discrimination law, enshrining the

[17] The CRPD and its Optional Protocol are the first UN human rights treaties to be signed by the European Union. Under Article 44 of the CRPD and Article 12 of its Optional Protocol the European Union may act on behalf of its members in relation to the treaties to the extent of its mandate, which must be the subject of a formal declaration, deposited with the Secretary-General. While the European Union may also ratify the treaties, only the direct ratifications of its member States count towards the treaties coming into force. As far as the history and the process of the European ratification of the CRPD, see Waddington (2009).

[18] European Commission (1996) *Communication of the Commission on equality of opportunity for people with disabilities*: A new European Community disability strategy, COM(96) 406 final, 30 July 1996.

principle of non-discrimination on the grounds of disability in primary legislation. Specifically including disability in the general non-discrimination Article 13, the Treaty expressly gave the European Community competence in the disability field for the first time. The non-discrimination approach in the field of disability was further embedded by Council Directive 2000/78/EC establishing a general framework for equal treatment in employment and occupation (Employment Equality Directive). It sets out broad equality and non-discrimination objectives—specifically including disability—in the field of employment and, crucially, calls on Member States to 'put into effect' the principle of equal treatment. Disability rights protection was strengthened when the Charter of Fundamental Rights of the European Union (hereinafter 'the Charter'), became legally binding with the adoption of the Lisbon Treaty in December 2009. Albeit limited to the areas of EU competence, the EU Charter of Fundamental Rights went beyond the Amsterdam Treaty in inserting Article 26 on the integration of persons with disabilities, reflecting core social model values of inclusion and equal opportunity, Article 21 by introducing a general prohibition of discrimination (explicitly mentioning the disability as one of the grounds of discriminations) and Article 15 on the protection of the freedom to choose an occupation and right to engage in work.[19] The Charter also protects ancillary rights, such as the worker's right to information (Article 27), the right of collective bargaining (Article 28), the right of access to placement services (Article 29), the right to protection in the event of unjustified dismissal and the right to just and favourable working conditions (Article 30). All such rights, obviously, do apply to persons with disability.

As far as the compatibility with EU State aid rules, the General Block Exemption Regulation (GBER) exempts from notification obligations aid for the recruitment of disadvantaged workers and aid for the employment of disabled workers totalling, respectively, up to EUR 5 million and EUR 10 million per undertaking per year.[20] The GBER covers aid for additional costs of employing disabled workers, such as the costs of adapting premises and equipment to disabled workers' needs and the costs of employing staff to assist disabled workers (Article 42). Aid in the form of wage subsidies for employing disabled workers may cover up to 75 % of the wage costs and aid for up to 100 % of eligible additional costs of employing disabled workers. For the purposes of the GBER, a 'disabled worker' is defined as a person who has 'a recognised limitation which results from physical, mental or psychological impairment' or is recognised as a disabled worker by national law (Article 2(20)). The GBER may apply to support for the habilitation and

[19] Article 15 of the European Charter on Fundamental Rights recognizes that everyone has the right to engage in work and to pursue a freely chosen accepted occupation; states that every citizen of the Union has the freedom to seek employment, to work, to exercise the right of establishment and to provide services in any Member State; and by entitles nationals of third countries, who are authorised to work in the territories of the Member States, to working conditions equivalent to those of citizens of the Union.

[20] Commission Regulation (EC) No 800/2008 of 6 August 2008 declaring certain categories of aid compatible with the common market in application of Articles 87 and 88 of the Treaty (General block exemption Regulation), Articles 40 and 41.

rehabilitation of workers with disabilities, where such support constitutes State aid. In 2012, with its Communication on State aid Modernisation (SAM), the Commission launched a broad review of State aid rules. State aid enforcement should facilitate sustainable, smart and inclusive growth, focus on cases with the biggest impact on the single market, streamline the rules and provide for faster, better informed and more robust decisions. The reviewing process of the GBER has been completed in 2014 and the new GERB mechanism puts forward new ways of supporting the training and employment of workers with disabilities through the inclusion of new categories of eligible cost. It applies the term 'worker with disabilities' and adapts its definition to that in the CRPD.[21]

Lastly, another way in which Member States are permitted by EU law to favour disabled workers is through the use of disability considerations in public procurement processes. The revised public procurement Directives, adopted in 2014[22] and replacing pre-existing legislation have broadened the possibility to reserve public contracts to certain economic operators. This will concern not only sheltered workshops, but also economic operators whose main aim is the social and professional integration of disabled or disadvantaged persons.

3.2 *The 2000/78/EC Employment Equality Directive*

Within the European legislation, specific legal discipline is provided by Council Directive 2000/78/EC (the so-called 'Employment Equality Directive'); the Directive requires Member States to prohibit, *inter alia*, discrimination on the grounds of disability in the fields of employment, occupation and vocational training. According to the Directive, Member States are required to prohibit direct discrimination, indirect discrimination,[23] harassment, victimisation and instructions to discriminate on the grounds, *inter alia*, of disability.

---

[21] Commission Regulation (EU) No 651/2014 of 17 June 2014 *declaring certain categories of aid compatible with the internal market in application of Articles 107 and 108 of the Treaty*, see point (54) of the Preamble.

[22] Directive 2014/24/EU of the European Parliament and of the Council of 26 February 2014 on *public procurement and repealing Directive 2004/18/EC*; Directive 2014/25/EU of the European Parliament and of the Council of 26 February 2014 on *procurement by entities operating in the water, energy, transport and postal services sectors and repealing Directive 2004/17/EC*.

[23] Direct discrimination is considered to occur where one person is treated less favourably than another is, has been or would be treated in a comparable situation. Indirect discrimination is considered to occur where an apparently neutral provision, criterion or practice would put persons with a particular religion or belief, a particular disability, a particular age, or a particular sexual orientation at a particular disadvantage as compared with other persons, unless: (1) that provision, criterion or practice is objectively justified by a legitimate aim and the means of achieving that aim are appropriate and necessary; or (2) the employer, or any person or organisation to whom the Directive applies, is obliged under national legislation to take appropriate measures in line with the principles of 'reasonable accommodation for disabled persons' in order to eliminate disadvantages entailed by such provision, criterion or practice.

As far as the CRPD 'reasonable accommodation' principle is concerned, Article 5 of the Directive deals with its implementation at EU level and requires that 'reasonable accommodation' be provided to guarantee compliance with the principle of equal treatment in relation to persons with disabilities. This means that employers and providers of vocational training must take appropriate measures, where needed in a particular case, to enable a person with a disability to have access to, participate in, or advance in employment, or to undergo training, unless such measures would impose a disproportionate burden on the employer. This burden is not regarded as disproportionate when it is sufficiently remedied by existing measures under the disability policy of the Member State concerned.[24] The duty of employers to adjust reasonable accommodation for disabled people is a key element of protection of persons with disabilities under the Directive. Employers must provide reasonable accommodation to enable a person with a disability to have access to employment and advance in it; however, Member States may decide whether to make exceptions as regards disability and age when it comes to employment in the armed forces: the EU reservation on Article 27 CRPD[25] follows the logic of Article 3(4) of the Directive.[26]

The Commission has rigorously monitored the correct transposition of the Directive in national laws[27] and initiated several infringement procedures against Member States for incorrect implementation. Indeed, it is the Commission's role to scrutinise whether a complaint reveals incorrect transposition or application of the

[24] From this perspective, the preamble to the Directive states that appropriate measures should be provided to adapt the workplace to the disability, for example by adapting premises and equipment, patterns of working time, the distribution of tasks or the provision of training or integration resources. The preamble also states that, to determine whether the measures in question give rise to a disproportionate burden, account should be taken in particular of the financial and other costs entailed, the scale and financial resources of the organisation or undertaking and the possibility of obtaining public funding or any other assistance. As for instance, EU health and safety legislation has been used as a means of requiring adaptations of the work environment for employees with disabilities. Thus, the 1989 Safety and Health Directive requires that workplaces are organised to take account of disabled workers, if necessary, in particular as regards doors, passageways, staircases, washbasins, lavatories and workstations used or occupied directly by handicapped persons.

[25] See Council Decision 2010/48/EC concerning the conclusion, by the European Community (now European Union), of the United Nations Convention on the Rights of Persons with Disabilities, containing in Annex III a reservation with respect to Article 27(1) of the CRPD, O.J. L 23/35 (2010).

[26] See, as for instance, the UK's reservation to the Directive in respect of service in the Armed Forces. Service in the Armed Forces was exempt from the employment provisions of the Disability Discrimination Act (DDA) 1995, on grounds that Armed Forces personnel must be combat effective in order to meet a worldwide need to deploy, and to ensure that military health and fitness remain matters for Ministry of Defence Ministers based on military advice, not the courts. The continuing need for this exemption was reviewed when the Equality Act 2010 was developed, and it was concluded that it is still required. The reservation reflects this position.

[27] National provisions communicated by the Member States concerning Council Directive 2000/78/EC are available at: http://eur-lex.europa.eu/legal-content/EN/TXT/?qid=1401876783757&uri=CELEX:32000L0078.

Directives by the Member State concerned. At the moment, two non-conformity infringements cases[28] and three complaint-based cases under Directive 2000/78/EC are currently pending.[29] In 2014 the Commission published a report on the implementation of the Directive according to which, while all Member States have transposed EU rules in national law, further efforts are needed to apply them in practice, in particular through policy action, awareness-raising and training.[30]

3.3 The Notion of 'Disability' of the Directive and ASD: The Judicial Enlargement Performed by the Case-Law of the CJEU and Its Effects on National Laws

Differently than Article 1 of the CRPD, the Directive does not define disability and therefore does not clarify which groups of persons are protected from discrimination. In particular, it does not expressly indicate whether persons with ASD are included. Indeed, it appears from the research's findings that there is still a lack of clarity in European national legislations regarding the definition of disability and in particular whether it includes persons with ASD.[31] In the majority of countries, the legislation transposing the Employment Equality Directive either does not define the term disability or provides language open to interpretation as to its exact scope of application. This highlights the importance of interpretation when applying such legislation and its capacity to confirm that the scope of protection extends to persons with ASD. There is thus the risk that narrower interpretations of the concept of disability in national legislation and in judicial case law may limit the scope of the protection offered by the Directive excluding certain groups, notably persons with social interaction, communication, and understanding impairments (this risk, therefore, main involve persons with ASD).[32]

---

[28] Non-conformity infringement cases concern Belgium and Romania.

[29] Two cases concern Greece and discriminatory age limits in public service, one case concerns the Czech Republic and insufficient protection from discrimination for disabled persons seeking employment.

[30] See Report from the Commission to the European Parliament and the Council, *Joint Report on the application of Council Directive 2000/43/EC of 29 June 2000 implementing the principle of equal treatment between persons irrespective of racial or ethnic origin ('Racial Equality Directive') and of Council Directive 2000/78/EC of 27 November 2000 establishing a general framework for equal treatment in employment and occupation ('Employment Equality Directive')*, COM (2014) 2 final, 17 January 2014 available at the following website http://ec.europa.eu/justice/discrimination/files/com_2014_2_en.pdf.

[31] On this aspect see the chapter by V. Della Fina, in this volume.

[32] As for instance, Denmark legislation uses the term 'handicap'. A person with a handicap is described in the 2008 Civil Act no. 1349 on the Prohibition of Discrimination in the Labour Market a person with a 'physical, psychological or intellectual impairment who must be compensated in order for that person to function on an equal level with other citizens in a similar situation.' Whether this definition of disability is broad enough to live up to Danish obligations under the

The CJEU case law has filled this gap by giving some landmark rulings on the ground of disability.

In the first place, in the 2006 case *Chacòn Navas v. Eurest Collectividades SA*, the Court by ruling that the concept of 'disability' 'should be given an autonomous and uniform interpretation', made a distinction between 'sickness' and 'disability' and concluded that whereas the latter is protected by the Directive the former is not automatically afforded protection.

In second place, in 2008, in the *Coleman v. Attridge Law and Steve Law* judgement,[33] the ECJ Court has enlarged the scope of application *ratione personae* of the Directive by stating that it includes also the protection against situations of 'discrimination by association' protecting victims of discrimination who do not themselves have a disability. According to the Court of Justice point of view, Directive 2000/78/EC protected a mother of a disabled child from harassment and discrimination in employment, when the problems were due to the fact that the mother needed extra time off to take care of her child.

Finally, in 2013 decision in the case *HK Danmark*[34] the Court, while admitting that the concept of disability can in certain circumstances also include conditions caused by incurable or curable long-term illnesses, ruled that disability '. . .results in particular from physical, mental or psychological impairments which in interaction with barriers may hinder the full and effective participation of the person concerned in professional life on an equal basis with other workers, and the limitation is a long term one. . .'.[35] In sum, with such decisions the Court has upheld the position of the Advocate General Geelhoed who, in his Opinion on the case *Chacòn Navas* concluded that the concept of disability 'must be interpreted autonomously and uniformly throughout the Community legal system'[36] but acknowledged the difficulties in finding a definition, as the concept of disability is 'undergoing fairly rapid evolution' and may be interpreted differently in different contexts.[37] He argued, therefore, that we should not endeavour to find more or less exhaustive and fixed definitions of the term 'disability',[38] and made a proposal that has inspired the Court in the *HK Danmark* judgment. At para 37 of the *HK Danmark*

Employment Equality Directive and to include ASD is matter of big controversy: in 2012 a case concerning a child-minder who claimed to be discriminated against on grounds of the disability of her son, who suffered from Asperger's syndrome, was held before the Danish Equal Treatment Board who concluded that any possible impairments suffered by the complainant's son in the long run could not be deemed with sufficient certainty to constitute disability within the meaning of the Anti-discrimination Act. In other words, according to the Board, ASD did not constitute a disability and the complainant had not therefore faced discrimination because of her son's disability (see Decision No. 275/2012 of 9 May 2012).

[33] See *Coleman v. Attridge Law and Steve Law*, Case C-303/06, judgment of 17 July 2008.

[34] See, joined Cases C-335/11 and C-337/11, *HK Danmark*, judgment of 11 April 2013.

[35] Ibid., para 1 of the grounds of the decision.

[36] Opinion of Advocate General Geelhoed, ECJ, C-13/05, *Chacón Navas v. Eurest Colectividades SA*, 16 March 2006, para 64.

[37] Ibid., para 58.

[38] Ibid., para 67.

judgment, in effect, the Court noted how, after the judgment in *Chacón Navas* had been delivered, the European framework in this field changed due to the entry into force of the CRPD for the European Union.[39] Consequently, the European Union is bound by the Convention within the limits of its competences[40] and Directive 2000/78/EC must, as far as possible, be interpreted in a manner consistent with the Convention and with its principles.[41] Among these principles the Court noted how the CRPD acknowledges in recital (e) that 'disability is an evolving concept and that disability results from the interaction between persons with impairments and attitudinal and environmental barriers that hinders their full and effective participation in society on an equal basis with others'; the Court went on noting also that in the second paragraph of Article 1 the CRPD states that persons with disabilities include 'those who have long-term physical, mental, intellectual or sensory impairments which in interaction with various barriers may hinder their full and effective participation in society on an equal basis with others'.

At the end of the game, the extensive approach adopted by the CJEU has allowed the same Court to interpret discrimination on the grounds of disability in line with the spirit of the CRPD. The notion of disability developed by ECJ case law include three cumulative requirements: there must be a limitation which results in particular from physical, mental or psychological impairments; the limitation must hinder the participation of the person concerned in professional life; and it must be probable that the limitation will last for a long time.

ASD is consistent with this three-tiered test[42]; therefore ASD fall within the scope of application of the EU legislation in this field area. At the end of the game, persons with ASD may receive protection under member States' domestic legislation transposing the Directive, in two ways. In the first place, States may enact legislation, or amend already existing legislation, by which ASD is expressly included in the domestic legislative notion of disability.[43] In the second place,

[39] The European Union signed the Convention on 30 March 2007 and the Convention entered into force with respect to the EU on 22 January 2011. The CRPD is the first legally binding international human rights instrument to which the European Union has become a party. EU's first periodic report on the implementation of the UN Convention on the Rights of Persons with Disabilities has been delivered in June 2014.

[40] These are illustrated in Annex II to Council Decision 2010/48/EC of 26 November 2009 concerning the conclusion, by the European Community, of the United Nations Convention on the Rights of Persons with Disabilities, OJ L 23 of 27.1.2010, p. 35.

[41] See paras 28–37 of *HK Danmark* judgment.

[42] As far as international accepted medical standards encompassing ASD see WHO's *International Classification of Diseases and Related Health Problems*, which concerns Mental and Behavioural Disorders (ICD-10), disposable online at the following site www.apps.who.int/classifications/icd10/browse/2010/en.

[43] As for example, in Ireland Section 1 of the 2012 *Autism Bill* amended the definition of disability in the *Employment Equality Act* 1998 to include reference to autism; Section 2 introduced similar provision in the *Equal Status Act* 2000. Similarly, North Ireland the *Autism Act* 2011 amended Schedule 1 to the *Disability Discrimination Act* 1995 (c. 50) with the same objective. England *Autism Act* 2009 enacted similar provisions with the aim that 'definitional issues will be dealt with

absent an explicit inclusion of ASD within legislative notion of disability, its up to the domestic courts, through their judicial interpretation activity, to render domestic law consistent with Directive's and international standards by enlarging the scope *ratione personae* of domestic provisions on disability to persons with ASD. Lacking an action by domestic courts it is up to supra-national bodies of control (i.e. the CJEU in this case) to assure the full and correct transposition of the European principles.[44]

3.3.1 Article 5 of the Directive and the Duty to Provide Reasonable Accommodation in the Field of the Employment

Provision of reasonable accommodation for disabled persons by the employer is one of the key elements of the Directive and the Commission has rigorously monitored its correct transposition in national laws.[45] In effect, Member States use different terminology to refer to the term 'accommodation' as set forth in the Employment Equality Directive. While many Member States chose to use the terminology of the Directive, others have replaced the word 'accommodation' with alternative terms such as 'adjustments', 'steps' or 'measures'.[46] Furthermore, the comparative analysis of the national legislation transposing the Directive further reveals that the meaning of the term 'reasonable' has been interpreted by Member States in two different ways. While some Member States have interpreted the term 'reasonable' to refer to an accommodation which does not result in excessive costs,

in the autism strategy, which, as it has to be kept under continual review, will allow for changes to be made much more quickly in response to new developments than if the definition were to be included in primary legislation' (see commentary to Section 1 of the 2009 Autism Act). In other situations States enact domestic legislation, which, without making reference to the ASD, apply a wide-ranging notion of disability that is consistent with benchmarks fixed in the CRPD. As for instance, new Croatian Social Care Act of 2012 defines a person with a disability as a person with long-term physical, mental, intellectual or sensory impairments that, in interaction with various barriers, may hinder her full and effective participation in society on an equal basis with persons without disabilities.

[44] This is what happened as far as the already cited *HK Danmark* case before the CJEU. The definition of disability provided with the Denmark Act on the *Prohibition against Discrimination in the Labour Market*, was excessively narrow and was not in line with Denmark's obligations under the Directive.

[45] Article 5 of the Directive includes a duty to provide reasonable accommodation for persons with disabilities. It requires employers, in certain cases, to take appropriate measures to enable persons with disabilities to have access to, participate in, or advance in employment, or to undergo training, unless such measures would impose a disproportionate burden on the employer.

[46] In the United Kingdom the domestic legislation requires the making of reasonable "adjustments"; Finnish law refers to "steps"; the Irish Employment Equality Act 1998–2004 and the French Labour Code, drawing their inspiration from Recital 20 to the Directive, define a reasonable accommodation as an "appropriate measure"; this term is also found in the Lithuanian Law on Equal Treatment of 2005 and the Slovakian Act on Equal Treatment in Certain Areas and Protection Against Discrimination of 2004.

difficulties or problems for the employer,[47] others have associated the term 'reasonable' to the quality of the accommodation, meaning that the accommodation must be effective in terms of allowing an individual with a disability to carry out a particular set of employment-related tasks.[48]

However, a number of Member States initially had problems in respect to the implementation of Article 5 of the Directive and were addressees of infringement procedures.[49]

In the great majority of EU Member States, non-discrimination legislation contains a duty to provide reasonable accommodation for persons with disabilities. As for instance, the Estonian Equal Treatment Act, transposing the Employment Equality Directive, requires employers to 'take appropriate measures, where needed in a particular case, to enable a person with a disability to have access to, participate in, or advance in employment, or to undergo training, unless such measures would impose a disproportionate burden on the employer'.[50] Similar provisions, as part of the transposing legislation, may be found, for example, in Finland,[51] Poland,[52] Spain,[53] Sweden[54] and the United Kingdom.[55] From this side, it may be argued that in a majority of countries, the scope of the transposing legislation that provides for reasonable accommodation can be interpreted to include persons with ASD. However, in some Member States, even though the transposing legislation provides for reasonable accommodation it does not contain a definition of disability, which

[47] This approach has been incorporated, as for instance, in the Finnish Non-Discrimination Act 21/2004, which obliges employers and trainers to 'take any reasonable steps to help a person with disabilities to gain access to work or training, to cope at work and to advance their career.' According to the Act 'In assessing what constitutes reasonable [sic], particular attention shall be devoted to the costs of the steps, the financial position of the person commissioning the work or arranging the training, and the possibility of support from public funds or elsewhere towards the costs involved'.

[48] A leading example of a jurisdiction which has transposed Article 5 of the Directive in this way is the Netherlands. The Dutch Act on Equal Treatment on Grounds of Disability or Chronic Illness 2004 provides that the prohibition of making distinction '[...] also includes the duty for the person to whom the prohibition is addressed, to make effective accommodations in accordance to the need for this, unless doing so would constitute a disproportionate burden upon her.' The Dutch statute, therefore, does not require a "reasonable accommodation", but instead establishes a duty to make 'effective accommodations.'

[49] Belgium, Estonia, Cyprus, Italy, Latvia, Lithuania, Hungary, Poland and Slovakia. Some Member States had been criticised for interpreting the Directive as limiting the duty of reasonable accommodation to existing workers, thus wrongly excluding both applicants and trainees. The majority of infringement procedures have been closed by now.

[50] Estonia, Law No. 315 of 11 December 2008 on Equal Treatment, para 11.

[51] See Section 5 of the Finnish Non-discrimination Act 21/2004 and its successive amendments.

[52] See the 1997 Act on Vocational and Social Rehabilitation and Employment of Persons with Disabilities, Article 23a.

[53] See Law 51/2003 on Equal Opportunities, Non-Discrimination and Universal Access for Persons with Disabilities, Article 7.

[54] See the 2008 Discrimination Act, Chapter 2, Section 1.

[55] See 2010 Equality Act, Section 20.

makes assessing whether the duty to provide reasonable accommodation also applies to persons with ASD rather difficult. Only a judicial or quasi-judicial decision could clarify the situation. For example, in Greece, Article 10 of the transposing legislation closely follows the wording of the Employment Equality Directive, but as Law No. 3304/2005 does not provide any definition of disability, and there is, to date, no national case-law to provide guidance, it is unclear whether persons with ASD could benefit from the reasonable accommodation provision.

This situation may be perceived also in other EU countries in which the scope of the duty to provide reasonable accommodation is not the same as the scope of the prohibition of discrimination on the grounds of disability. For instance, in France, the obligation to provide reasonable accommodation is subject to an additional requirement to those laid down in the definition of disability under Article L 114 of the Social Policy and Family Code. Articles L 5212-13 and L 5213-6 of the Labour Code use a different and more limited definition of disability which stipulates that only individuals who are officially recognised as disabled can claim an accommodation. Therefore, 'non-registered' disabled people, along with all others not falling within the requirements laid down in Article L 5212-13 of the Labour Code, are not covered by the obligation of reasonable accommodation.

In Germany, the General Treatment Act, which transposes the directive, refers to the definition if disability in Article 2(1) of the Social Code Book. However, the duty to provide reasonable accommodation, according to Article 81(4) and (5) of the Social Code Book IX, applies to persons with a severe disability, defined in Article 2(3) of the Social Code Book IX as persons with a degree of disability of more than 50 %, or between 30 and 50 %, if they would be unable without equal rights provisions to find or keep suitable employment.

Persons with ASD may therefore only benefit from reasonable accommodation provisions insofar as they have a degree of disability of at least 30 %. The European Commission initiated infringement proceedings against Germany for incorrectly implementing its obligation to include regulations on reasonable accommodation under Article 5 of the Employment Equality Directive. Legal proceedings were closed in October 2010, after Germany presented draft laws implementing national case law which secured compliance with the Directive's requirements.

One Member State (Italy) has been found to be in breach of the Directive by the CJEU on 4 July 2013 due to failure to correctly transpose the provision by not comprehensively covering all disabled persons. Indeed, while Legislative Decree No. 216/2003, which transposed the Employment Equality Directive, did not contain a reasonable accommodation clause, the national authorities argued that reasonable accommodation was provided for by measures in other pieces of legislation, such as Law No. 104/1992 and Law No. 68/1999. However, on 6 April 2011, the European Commission referred Italy to the Court of Justice of the European Union pointing out that Italy had not completely transposed Article 5 of the Employment Equality Directive. The European Commission considered that Italian law did not provide for a general rule of reasonable accommodation for persons with disabilities in all aspects of employment. On 4 July 2013 the Luxemburg Court upheld the position of the Commission and condemned Italy which has been obliged to amend its own legislation.[56] Quite all the remaining infringement procedures have been closed by now.

3.3.2 The Gaps of the Directive as to the Notion of 'Reasonable Accommodation'

The Directive does not further define the concept of reasonable accommodation; in particular, it does not state, while CRPD does, whether denial of reasonable accommodation is a form of discrimination. Nevertheless, some guidance as to the meaning of the 'appropriate measures', which are required under the duty to provide reasonable accommodation is provided in Recital 20 of the Preamble, while Recital 21 elaborates on the concept of 'disproportionate burden'.

National laws, however, should define closely what is meant by reasonable accommodation, so that misinterpretation is avoided and employers clearly understand what they must do. As for example, in the United States, the obligation to make a reasonable accommodation is to be found in the Americans with Disabilities Act 1990. Reasonable accommodation, hence, is understood to mean any change in the work environment or in the way a job is performed that enables a person with a disability to enjoy equal employment opportunities. There are three categories of reasonable accommodations: changes to a job application process, changes to the work environment or the way a job is usually done, and changes that enable an employee with a disability to enjoy equal benefits and privileges of employment, such as access to training. Furthermore, in other countries, including Australia,[57] New Zealand[58] and South Africa[59] legal provisions stipulating that the failure to provide a reasonable accommodation constitutes a form of discrimination there exist. This is consistent with provisions of the CRPD which stipulates that this failure be considered as a form of discrimination.

However, even in this circumstance the CJEU case law has played a vanguard role enlarging the scope of the protection afforded by the Directive. In its first decisions on the implementation of the Directive, indeed, the CJEU has also clarified what the notion of 'reasonable accommodation' has to be meant in the light of the CRPD standards. Under a first perspective in the 2013 *Commission v. Italy* case (C-312/11, decision 4 July 2013), the Court has clarified that mere support and incentives measures are not sufficient for assuring the fair and effective transposition of the directive; according to the Court, indeed:

---

[56] See Article 9, 4ter, of the Law decree no. 76/2013, converted in Law 99/2013, which has added the Article 3bis into the law of transposition of Equal employment Directive (i.e. Legislative Decree 216/2003). The normative amendment is currently under examination by the Commission.

[57] See Australia's Disability Discrimination Act of 1992.

[58] See Human Rights Act of 1993.

[59] See Employment Equity Act No. 55 of 1998.

> il ne suffit pas, pour transposer correctement et pleinement l'article 5 de la directive 2000/78, d'édicter des mesures publiques d'incitation et d'aide, mais il incombe aux États membres d'imposer à tous les employeurs l'obligation de prendre des mesures efficaces et pratiques, en fonction des besoins dans des situations concrètes, en faveur de toutes les personnes handicapées, portant sur les différents aspects de l'emploi et du travail et permettant à ces personnes d'accéder à un emploi, de l'exercer ou d'y progresser, ou pour qu'une formation leur soit dispensée.

Under a second perspective, *i.e.* which are the appropriate measures that the employer is required to take in order to enable a person with a disability to have access to, participate in, or advance in employment, in the *HK Danmark* Judgment, the Court has underpinned, and despite the contrary opinion of the national employers, that as recital 20 in the preamble to Directive 2000/78 and the second paragraph of Article 2 of the CRPD envisage 'not only material but also organisational measures, and the term 'pattern' of working time must be understood as the rhythm or speed at which the work is done, it cannot be ruled out that a reduction in working hours may constitute one of the accommodation measures referred to in Article 5 of that Directive' (para 55).

3.4 The Council of Europe Standards on Reasonable Accommodation

Council of Europe standards do not make reference to the terminology 'reasonable accommodation' as such, instead using the term 'reasonable adjustment'. Article 15 (2) of the European Social Charter (revised) calls on Parties to 'adjust the working conditions to the needs of the disabled' and Article 15(3) urges them to promote social integration and participation in the life of the community 'through measures, including technical aids, aiming to overcome barriers to communication and mobility and enabling access to transport, housing, cultural activities and leisure'. Case law delivered on this issue by the European Committee on Social Rights has confirmed the duty of States to provide reasonable accommodation under Article 15(2) of the revised Charter and has also concluded in several occasions for non-conformity with this provision[60] demonstrating to considering the duty of reasonable accommodation as a crucial requirement in non-discrimination legislation in the area of disability. As for instance, in its 2003 Conclusions on France, the Committee specifically asked France to provide further information 'on how the concept of reasonable accommodation is incorporated in the legislation'.[61]

---

[60] See Council of Europe, European Committee of Social Rights, Conclusions (2008)—Articles 1, 9, 10, 15, 18, 20, 24, 25, Armenia p. 58, Belgium p. 131, Cyprus pp. 201–204; available at www.coe.int/t/dghl/monitoring/socialcharter/Conclusions/ConclusionsYear_en.asp.

[61] See Council of Europe, European Committee of Social Rights, Conclusions (2003) France, p. 68, available at: www.coe.int/t/dghl/monitoring/socialcharter/Conclusions/State/France2003_en.pdf.

As far as the European Convention on human rights, the ECtHR case law has also reinforced member States' duty to provide reasonable accommodation, and by adopting a wide approach to its interpretative activity has derived the duty to accommodate from some provisions of the Convention in some cases. In the case of *Glor v. Switzerland*, where the Court found a violation of Article 14 in conjunction with Article 8 of the ECHR, it suggested that people in the applicant's situation might be offered the possibility of alternative forms of service in the armed forces that entailed less physical effort and were compatible with the constraints of a partial disability. Moreover, for the first time the Court's judgment makes explicit reference to the CRPD as an example of the existing European and universal consensus on the need to protect persons with disabilities from discriminatory treatment.[62]

Turning to the CoE Committee of Ministers, the Recommendation No. Rec (2006)5 containing the Action Plan to promote the rights and full participation of people with disabilities in society: improving the quality of life of people with disabilities in Europe 2006–2015 (hereinafter the Action Plan)[63] refers to the need for 'reasonable adjustments' in order to achieve the objective of full participation of persons with disabilities. More in particular, Action line No. 5 on employment, vocational guidance and training asks Member States to make reasonable adjustments. States must 'ensure that people with disabilities have access to vocational guidance, training and employment-related services at the highest possible qualification level, and making reasonable adjustments where necessary'.[64] States must also encourage employers to employ people with disabilities by, for example, 'making reasonable adjustments to the workplace or working conditions, including telecommuting, part-time work and work from home, in order to accommodate the special requirements of employees with disabilities'.[65]

[62] See, *Glor v. Switzerland*, application No. 13444/04, judgment of 30 April 2009, para 53.

[63] Council of Europe, Committee of Ministers (2006) Recommendation Rec(2006) on the Council of Europe Action Plan to promote the rights and full participation of people with disabilities in society: improving the quality of life of people with disabilities in Europe 2006–2015, 5 April 2006.

[64] Ibid. section 3.5.3, iii.

[65] Ibid. section 3.5.3, v

4 The Impact of the Financial and Economic Crisis on the Implementation of Art 27 Rights and the Progressive Realization of Economic, Social and Cultural Rights

Some final remarks are required as to the relationships amongst the State duty to assure the right to employment of persons with ASD, the contemporary economic crisis and the principle of progressive realization of rights in the field of ESC rights. Indeed, the full implementation of Article 27 rights requires that adequate resources be allocated to this goal by States. However, the available resources may be increasingly limited, and the resource allocation undermined, by the contemporary financial crisis and economic recession, as well as by anti-crisis measures to be adopted by States for the alleviation of their debt and debt-service burdens. Such measures, in fact, usually apply structural adjustment policies aimed at curbing public expenditures for social welfare, or involve measures of privatization of the economy and, consequently, oblige States to re-allocate resources with the view of ensuring strict compliance with the commitments derived from international agreements on foreign debt. This occurs even at the cost of reducing the allocation of resources for realizing other international obligations, such as those prescribed by international human rights and, especially, by economic, social and cultural rights.

In sum, States might pretend that as every other ESC rights, the full realization of right to employment of persons with ASD too should be subject to progressive realization and, therefore, be implemented only within the extent permitted by available resources. Realization of this right could be hampered by a lack of resources and be achieved only over a period of time. States, in the second place, might pretend to be legitimized to derogate from respecting their duties in the field of the employment of persons with disabilities in response to the exceptional and emergence situations such as the global financial crisis and to the debt restructuring mechanisms.[66] As far as the first aspect, there are some duties deriving from Article 27 CRPD which States may not derogate. Indeed, even if the principle of

[66] This situation is perfectly illustrated, *mutatis mutandis*, by the review before the European Committee of Social Rights of the Greek national measures adopted to redress the effects of economic crisis in the recent *GENOP-DEI and ADEDY v. Greece* cases (see ESC/C, Complaint No. 65/2011, *General Federation of Employees of the National Electric Power Corporation (GENOP-DEI) and Confederation of Greek Civil Servants' Trade Unions (ADEDY) v. Greece*, 23 May 2012, para 17; and ESC/C, Complaint No. 66/2011, *General Federation of Employees of the National Electric Power Corporation (GENOP-DEI) and Confederation of Greek Civil Servants' Trade Unions (ADEDY) v. Greece*, 23 May 2012, para 13). The government in both cases has made some preliminary statements aimed at underpinning the fact that challenged measures were 'part of an overall package of initiatives adopted as a response to this crisis'. Such observations, albeit without mentioning Articles G and F of the Revised European Social Charter, seem to constitute an attempt to justify any eventual impact that the adoption of these measures might have had on the rights guaranteed by the Charter, with the exceptional economic and financial situation that Greece has to face.

progressive realization describes a pivotal aspect of States' obligations in connection with economic, social and cultural rights under international human rights treaties, and even if this principle is well-established in these treaties, included the CRPD's Article 4,[67] the CRPD Committee has recently clarified in its Concluding Observations on Spain that 'the duty to provide reasonable accommodation is immediately applicable and not subject to progressive realisation'.[68] From this perspective it might be argued that the duty to provide reasonable accommodation may be seen as a kind of 'minimum core obligation' under CRPD. As far as the second aspect, who is writing has already demonstrated[69] that even in situations of financial crisis and recession—perhaps, especially in such situations—States are not completely boundless with regard to economic, social and cultural rights because these rights may not be considered to be at States' complete discretion. On the contrary, even in these dramatic circumstances, States are requested not to distribute the burden of the rigour unequally among social groups, omitting to afford protection to vulnerable and disadvantaged groups that make up the at-risk categories during such circumstances. Furthermore they bear the immediate due diligence duty to strike a fair balance between obligations arising from their external debt objectives, for example, the implementation of austerity measures for consolidating public spending, and the obligations enshrined in international human rights law: in these circumstances, striking the fair balance requires that austerity measures be enforced by avoiding any discrimination amongst individuals or amongst groups of individuals and be consistent with the principles of reasonableness and proportionality. This applies also to the enforcement of the principle of reasonable accommodation in the field of the employment of persons with disability or with ASD.

5 Conclusions

Individuating best practices as far as implementation of Article 27 CRPD and the degree of employment inclusion of persons with ASD is a hard task. Several requirements have to be assessed from this perspective: from the existence of an enabling legal environment, enhancing accessibility and addressing

[67] See CRPD Article 4: 'With regard to economic, social and cultural rights, each State Party undertakes to take measures to the maximum of its available resources and, where needed, within the framework of international cooperation, with a view to achieving progressively the full realization of these rights, without prejudice to those obligations contained in the present Convention that are immediately applicable according to international law'.

[68] UN, Committee on the Rights of Persons with Disabilities (2011b) Consideration of reports submitted by States parties under article 35 of the Convention: Concluding observations of the Committee on the Rights of Persons with Disabilities (Spain), CRPD/C/ESP/CO/1, 23 September 2011.

[69] See Fasciglione (2014) cit., pp. 42–45.

misunderstandings concerning people with disabilities to the presence of vocational and skills training opportunities for persons with disabilities. Moreover, the level of protection of employment rights of autistic persons in each country depends by several factors including social, cultural and economic circumstances: these factors may change on the basis of countries concerned. From this perspective, according to our point of view, there is no a one size-fit-for-all approach in the normative implementation employment rights of persons with ASD, but different *régimes* may be enforced, on a case by case basis, with the aim of striving at maximum Article 27 rights.

However, what emerges from the analysis performed is the circumstance that disability-related legislations to be adopted at national level in this field area have to rely on two 'normative principles', at the very least. In the first place, the adoption of a normative definition of disability sufficiently wide in order to include ASD cases and, in the second place, the avoidance of national legislations ambiguous about whether failure to provide reasonable accommodation is to be treated as a form of unlawful discrimination.[70] These two principles have to be regarded as benchmarks to be applied by national States in implementing legislations.

As far as the notion of disability the new Croatian Social Care Act of 2012 may be cited. The 2012 Act adopts the definition of disability provided by the UN CRPD and defines a person with a disability as a person with long-term physical, mental, intellectual or sensory impairments that, in interaction with various barriers, may hinder her full and effective participation in society on an equal basis with persons without disabilities: a definition that, as we have seen before, is sufficiently broad and may be interpreted as including also ASD.

Other countries have preferred to include explicitly ASD in normative definition of disability at national level, by adopting specific provisions in this sense. In Ireland, the 2012 Autism Bill aims to provide for an autism strategy to provide a coherent and national framework for addressing the specific needs of adults with ASD. Its Section 1 amends the definition of "disability" in the Employment Equality Act 1998 to include specific reference to autism. Section 2 makes similar provision in the Equal Status Act 2000.[71] Similarly, in UK, who enacted in 2009 a specific legislation in the field of autism (the 2009 Autism Act), the Section 6 of the 2010 Equality Act provides with a wide-range definition of disability, consistent with the CRPD, as a physical or mental impairment which has a substantial and adverse long-term effect on the person' ability to carry out normal day-to-day activities. What is important to stress here is the circumstance that according to the 'Guidance on matters to be taken into account in determining questions relating

[70] This is the case, for instance, of the Hungarian See Act on the Rights of Persons with Disabilities and the Guaranteeing of their Equal Opportunities, and Latvian Labour Law.

[71] Moreover, Sect. 3 creates an obligation to produce an autism strategy. Section 4 sets out a duty to implement the strategy. On national autism plans and strategies see the chapter by V. Della Fina, in this volume.

to the definition of disability' for the purposes of the 2010 Act the notion of 'impairments' have to be interpreted as including ASD.[72]

As far as the need for treating the failure to provide reasonable accommodation as a form of unlawful discrimination, in France, the failure to meet the duty constitutes unlawful discrimination, even if it is not specified whether this is classified as direct or indirect discrimination.[73] In Sweden, on the contrary, failure to provide reasonable accommodation is treated as direct discrimination in the fields of employment and education,[74] while failure to provide reasonable accommodation is treated as indirect discrimination in Austria and Denmark.[75] Furthermore, in the United Kingdom failure to provide reasonable accommodation is defined as a specific form of discrimination[76] and in the Netherlands as a prohibited form of distinction.[77]

Finally, other countries have chosen to adopt a broader approach to this issue. Interestingly, according to Slovakia law, failure to provide reasonable accommodation is regarded as a violation of the principle of equal treatment (which is broader than the prohibition of discrimination and its individual forms and also encompasses the duty to adopt measures to prevent discrimination) and it does not equate to direct or indirect discrimination. However, this does not mean that in specific situations the actions or omissions of an employer cannot at the same time also fall within definitions of the specific forms of discrimination defined by the Slovak Anti-discrimination Act: mainly direct or indirect discrimination or harassment.[78]

---

[72] Equality Act 2010, Guidance on matters to be taken into account in determining questions relating to the definition of disability, on the 'Meaning of impairments' p. 9. UK courts hearing employment cases have had no problems in accepting that ASD and other common physical and psychological disorders are 'disabilities' under the Equality Act 2010: ASD (in *Hewett v. Motorola*, UKEAT/0526/03, Employment Appeal Tribunal, 2004) Personality disorder (in *The Carphone Warehouse Ltd v Mr S Martin*, UKEAT/0371/12/JOJ, and UKEAT/0372/12/JOJ); Dyslexia (in *Price v Transport for London*, UKEAT/0005/11/JOJ); Mental impairment, personality disorder and major depression (in *Jennings v Barts and the London NHS Trust*, [2013] Eq. L.R. 326); Multiple Sclerosis (in *Burke v College of Law*, [2012] EWCA Civ 37; Post traumatic stress disorder (in *Abbey National Plc v Dutton*, UKEAT/0879/04/CK).

[73] See the Labour Code, Articles L 5212-2, L5212-13 and L5213-6. Race or ethnic origin. And the Law No. 2005 102 on Disability, Article 24 IV and 32.

[74] See Discrimination Act, Chapter 2, Section 1.

[75] See the Austrian Employment of People with Disabilities Act, paras 7c (4)–(6) and the Federal Disability Equality Act, paras 6(3), 6(4). As far as Denmark see the Act on Prohibition of Discrimination in the Labour Market, Article 2(a).

[76] See the 2010 Equality Act, Section 20.

[77] See the Disability Discrimination Act, Article 2. In the Netherlands, the word 'distinction' is used in the equal treatment legislation, instead of 'discrimination'. Although the Government is taking the stance that there is no substantive difference between these words, this choice of terminology has engendered a lot of criticism.

[78] See the Slovakian Act on Equal Treatment in Certain Areas and Protection against Discrimination, Section 7.

References

Fasciglione M (2014) The protection of economic, social and cultural rights of persons belonging to marginalized and vulnerable groups in times of financial crisis: how to reconcile the irreconcilable? Eur Yearb Minor Iss 11:1–47

Flynn E (2011) From rhetoric to action: implementing the UN Convention on the rights of persons with disabilities. Cambridge University Press, Cambridge

Hendricks A (2007) UN Convention on the rights of persons with disabilities. Eur J Health Law 14 (3):273–298

International Labour Organization (2004) Mauritius country profile. Employment of people with disabilities: the impact of legislation (East Africa). ILO, Geneva

Kayess R, French P (2008) Out of darkness into light? Introducing the Convention on the rights of persons with disabilities. Hum Rights Law Rev 8(1):1–34

Lawson A (2007) The United Nations Convention on the rights of persons with disabilities: new era or false dawn? Syracuse J Int Law Commer 34(2):563–618

Waddington L (2009) Breaking new ground: the implications of ratification of the UN Convention on the rights of persons with disabilities for the European Community. In: Arnardóttir OM, Quinn G (eds) The UN Convention on the rights of persons with disabilities: European and Scandinavian perspectives. Martinus Nijhoff Publisher, Leiden/Boston, pp 111–140

World Health Organization, The World Bank (2011) World report on disability. WHO, Geneva. http://whqlibdoc.who.int/publications/2011/9789240685215_eng.pdf?ua=1. Accessed 30 Oct 2014

Marco Fasciglione is Researcher at the Institute for International Legal Studies (ISGI-CNR), Naples.

Corporate Social Responsibility and the Right to Employment of Persons with Disabilities

Marco Fasciglione

1 Introduction

Access to employment is recognized as a fundamental human right in the United Nations Convention on the Rights of Persons with Disabilities (hereinafter CRPD). However, and as far as the European Union, which is a Party of CRPD, the proportion of persons with disabilities not participating in the labour market is at least twice as high as that of average EU citizens.[1] This situation increases their poverty risk that social benefits cannot compensate, especially in presence of severe economic crisis impairing the allocation of resources for public expenditures in welfare field area.

The adoption of the CRPD in 2006 has further strengthened the social model of disability and granted persons with disabilities with a wide spectrum of human rights including the right to employment based on the principles of equal treatment, accessibility and non-discrimination. Employment is considered one of the pivotal elements of social inclusion, that is especially important for the employment of persons with disabilities in the mainstream labour market. However, the official unemployment rates for persons with disabilities of working age in most of the developed countries are still reported at least twice low than for those with no disability. Since persons with disabilities are pronounced to be equal members of society by international institutions and are recognized as an important group of human diversity who have rights including the right to employment, their integration into employment sphere has been progressively included within the CSR

[1] See Grammenos (2011), p. 22.

M. Fasciglione (✉)
Institute for International Legal Studies (ISGI-CNR), Naples, Italy
e-mail: marco.fasciglione@cnr.it

V. Della Fina, R. Cera (eds.), *Protecting the Rights of People with Autism in the Fields of Education and Employment*, DOI 10.1007/978-3-319-13791-9_7

policy agenda at international[2] and at regional level[3] recognizing disability as a relevant item in CSR agendas. Nowadays, hiring persons with disabilities is increasingly recognized as a part of the philosophy of corporate social responsibility (CSR) and an essential dimension of the workforce diversity.

2 The Shift from the Medical Model to the Social Model of Disability and Its Impact on the Perception of the Role of Private Sector's Entities

At the international level, there has been significant evolution in the approach to persons with disability.[4] Historically, persons with disability have been treated as objects of pity and as burdens on their families and societies. According to this view, disability would be a 'personal tragedy' and persons with disability would be victims of great misfortune and perceived as socially dead or better off dead, as passively coming to terms with a condition that will forever limit their activities. According to this perspective the focus is on the 'affliction' caused by the particular condition or impairment and the provision of cure, treatment, care and protection to change the person so that they may be assimilated to the social norm. This is commonly referred to as the medical model of disability, which has probably been the most powerful influence on the conceptualisation of disability in modern history[5] and '... has guided and dominated clinical practice with the resulting assumption that both problems and solutions lie within people with disabilities rather than within society'.[6] This perception of disability not only has reinforced the idea that it is the impairment itself that causes the limitation, without recognising the role of the social environment in disabling persons with impairments, but has also influenced policy responses to persons with impairments, resulting in a disabling culture that perpetuates negative attitudes and discriminatory practices that ultimately oppress and exclude persons with impairments.

---

[2] See principle 6 of UN Global Compact concerning the elimination of discrimination in respect of employment and occupation, available at http://www.unglobalcompact.org. For all websites, last access 30 October 2014.

[3] See the European Commission's new Communication, A renewed EU strategy 2011–2014 for Corporate Social Responsibility (COM(2011) 681 final, 25.10.2011), pp. 10 and 14.

[4] As far as the evolutions of approached and policies dealing with disability, see, among the others, Shakespeare (2006), Bickenbach (1999), and Oliver (1996).

[5] The medical model views disability as a deficiency or deviation from the norm, located in the individual, and carries an action implication to treat or change the person so that they can conform to existing social processes and structures. This treatment is typically provided in service systems and settings isolated from the general community. The medical model is not confined to the health domain, but for many persons with disability, has pervaded all areas of life. Examples include institutional residential services, special education systems and sheltered employment.

[6] French (1994), p. 4.

On the contrary, the social model of disability[7] locates the experience of disability in the social environment, rather than in the impairment, and carries with it the inference that problems of disability have to be located squarely within society by noting that it is not individual limitations which are the cause of the problem but society's failure to provide appropriate services and adequately ensure the needs of persons with disabilities are fully taken into account in its social organisation. This model involved disability activist academics reinterpreting 'disability' as social oppression,[8] and radically refocusing the agenda away from cure, treatment, care and protection to acceptance of impairment as a positive dimension of human diversity, and to the problematisation and rejection of a social norm that results in exclusion. The social model has had an enormous influence in the development of the CRPD and is continuing to evolve; furthermore this shift of paradigms has contributed in highlighting the role played by all the actors of society in preventing and fighting discrimination against person with disability, included business entities. From this perspective, the focus on the contribution of the private sector has matched the emerging debates at international level as to the responsibility for human rights of private sector entities and on the challenges posed to the full and effective realization of human rights by their activities.

3 The Rise of the Role of Business Actors Within Human Rights Protection Field Area

International human rights treaties generally do not impose direct legal obligations on business enterprises. Legal liability and enforcement for the infringement by businesses of international human rights standards are, therefore, defined largely by national law.[9] However, in the last decades the demand that business sector demonstrate a commitment to conducing its operations in a manner that takes into account of human rights of individuals that might be impaired by these operations and of the level of vulnerability of workers, has increased. The rising of public concerns as to the need for constraints on corporate conducts for human rights protection purposes, have become more pronounced with the current wave of globalization, expansion in international trade, and explosive growth in certain developing countries in the areas of manufacturing, mining, oil and gas, forestry, etc. Also well-established is the circumstance that according to international legal system on human rights, States bear the legal obligation to respect, protect and fulfil

[7] The social model of disability is a generic term for a broad theory of disability that began to emerge from the mid 1960s principally from within the disability rights movement in the United Kingdom.

[8] See Quinn (1999), p. 281.

[9] As to the literature on general human rights see Cushman (2012), Rehman (2010), Hunt (2007), and Ishay (2008).

the human rights set out in the international human rights conventions they ratify.[10] More in particular, the obligation of States to respect human rights means that they must refrain from interfering with or curtailing the enjoyment of human rights. Their obligation to protect human rights requires them to protect individuals and groups against human rights abuses, including by business enterprises. Their obligation to fulfil human rights means that States must take positive action to facilitate the enjoyment of basic human rights. As far as the obligation to protect, nowadays is well-established in international human rights law the duty of States to protect against non-State human rights abuses within their jurisdiction. This duty not only extends to the protection against abuses by business entities; also, it has been included within the core United Nations human rights treaties as elaborated by the treaty bodies, and is also generally agreed to exist under customary international law. What is interesting is the fact that treaty bodies unanimously affirm that this duty requires steps by States to regulate and adjudicate abuses by all social actors including businesses. However, the earlier United Nations human rights treaties, such as the International Convention on the Elimination of All Forms of Racial Discrimination (ICERD), the International Covenant on Economic, Social and Cultural Rights (ICESCR), and the International Covenant on Civil and Political Rights (ICCPR), do not specifically address State duties regarding business. They impose, on the contrary, generalized obligations to ensure the enjoyment of rights and prevent non-State abuse. For examples, ICERD requires each State party to prohibit racial discrimination by 'any persons, group or organization' (Article 2.1 (d)). And some of the treaties recognize rights that are particularly relevant in business contexts, including rights related to employment, health and indigenous communities.

What is worth noting, here, is the circumstance that these treaties, generally, in conceding to States discretion regarding the modalities for regulating and adjudicating non-State abuses, emphasize legislation and judicial remedies. Furthermore, the treaty bodies monitoring fair enforcement of these international conventions, have widely elaborated upon the duty to protect. General Comment No. 31 of the Human Rights Committee (HRC) may be seen as confirming the paradigm of such approach. According to the General Comment, indeed, under the ICCPR 'the positive obligations on States parties to ensure Covenant rights will only be fully discharged if individuals are protected by the State, not just only against violations of Covenant rights by its agents, but also against acts committed by private persons or entities'.[11] The General Comment further clarifies that States could breach Covenant obligations where they permit or fail 'to take appropriate measures or

[10] As far as the tripartite division see Eide (1984). A fourth level partition (obligations of respect, protect, ensure and promote) has been proposed by Van Hoof (1984). More recently, a scheme consisting of five levels of obligations (respect rights of others; create institutional machinery essential to realization of rights, protect rights/prevent violations; provide good ad services to satisfy rights; promote rights) has been proposed by Alston and Steiner (2000).

[11] HRC, General Comment No. 31, *Nature of the General Legal Obligation on States Parties to the Covenant*, U.N. Doc. CCPR/C/21/Rev.1/Add.13 (2004), para 8.

to exercise due diligence to prevent, punish, investigate or redress the harm caused by such acts by private persons or entities'. Therefore, the case-law of all main human rights treaty bodies has started to express concern about State failures to protect against business abuse most frequently in relation to the right to non-discrimination, indigenous peoples' rights, and labour and health-related rights. This duty to protect applies to all substantive rights and the monitoring bodies tend not to specify the precise content of required State action, but generally recommend regulation through legislation and adjudication through judicial remedies, including compensation where appropriate. An identical evolution may be perceived at regional human rights systems; also regional mechanisms, in effect, have recognized the State duty to protect against non-State abuse, and established similar correlative State requirements to regulate and adjudicate corporate acts.[12]

In sum, the State duty to protect against non-State abuses is part of the very foundation of the international human rights regime: this duty requires States to play a key role in regulating and adjudicating also abuses by business enterprises risking to breach their international obligations.

4 The State Duty to Protect from Private Actors' Violations of the CRPD in the Employment Field Area

The duty on States to protect individuals from infringements occurring within the framework of business operations is also at the heart of the CRPD system and hence applies, as far as Article 27 of the Convention, to private sector employers. According to the Convention States parties bear the general obligation to promote, protect and ensure the full and equal enjoyment of all human rights and fundamental freedoms by all persons with disabilities and to promote respect for their inherent dignity. As far as the duty to protect the rights of persons with disability within the employment field area, Article 5 of the Convention obliges State Parties to prohibit all discrimination on the basis of disability and guarantee to persons with disabilities equal and effective legal protection against discrimination on all grounds. Furthermore, in order to promote equality and eliminate discrimination, States Parties are requested to take all appropriate steps to ensure that reasonable accommodation is provided. Finally, under Article 27 of the Convention, which recognizes the right of persons with disabilities to work on an equal basis with others in work freely chosen and in a work environment that is open, inclusive and accessible, State parties are bound to safeguard and promote the realization of the right to work for such category of individuals *by taking appropriate steps including legislation*. From this perspective member States are expected, if necessary, to review and amend their domestic workplace laws and policies in order to prohibit

[12] For an overview of regional human rights mechanism approach see Clapham (2006) and Udombana (2004).

discrimination, protect rights, promote the employment in the private sector through policies and measures such as affirmative action, incentives, etc.

The right of persons with disabilities to employment involves, therefore, an obligation on States parties to create an enabling and conducive environment for employment, in both the public and private sectors. Accordingly, Article 27 of the Convention guides States parties in the implementation of such right by setting forth some basic rules: (a) *non-discrimination*, as the persons with disabilities have the right to work on an equal basis with others; (b) *accessibility*, as the right of persons with disabilities to work includes the opportunity to gain a living in a work environment that is accessible to persons with disabilities, identifying and removing barriers that hinder persons with disabilities from carrying out their work on an equal basis with others; (c) *reasonable accommodation*, as with a view to facilitating access of persons with disabilities to work on an equal basis with others, States parties must ensure that reasonable accommodation is provided to persons with disabilities who request it, and should take effective steps, including through legislation, to ensure that the denial of reasonable accommodation constitutes discrimination; (d) besides a duty to impose obligations on private-sector employers, States should adopt *positive measures* to promote employment opportunities for persons with disabilities.

These standards, therefore, impose different levels of obligations on States; more in particular according to a first perspective, State are obliged to abstain from infringing rights of persons with disabilities; from a second perspective the Convention fixes a duty to protect rights of persons with disability stemming from Article 27. In achieving this goal States bear several positive obligations including the duty to promote employment opportunities for persons with disabilities and this especially with regard to private-sector employers.[13] Amongst the implementation measures that States parties should take on the basis of the Convention, a pivotal role is played by the duty of aligning national standards and practice to the Convention. In this respect, Article 4, para 1 (a) and (b) of the Convention imposes

[13] There are several examples of government-driven initiatives enforcing such State duty. In Belgium the Federal Government developed in 2005, in cooperation with the regions, a new Equality-Diversity label for enterprises in respect of employment and promotion of diversity. In 2006, a pilot project was launched, with the enterprises concerned making an active commitment to further diversity and equality within their organizations in order to obtain the label. So far, 15 of the enterprises involved in the project have been awarded the label. As far as Germany is concerned, the 'Diversity Charter', a corporate initiative under the patronage of Federal Chancellor Angela Merkel, launched in 2006, seeks to create a corporate culture that is typified by fairness and respect. The signatories undertake to create a working environment which is free of prejudices and marginalisation in which each worker experiences respect, regardless of gender, race, nationality, ethnic origin, religion or philosophical creed, disability, age, sexual orientation and identity. More than 900 enterprises and public facilities all over Germany have so far subscribed to the Charter. In Luxemburg the 2003 law *relative aux personnes handicapées* of 12 September 2003 and successive amendments has introduced the 'disability management' approach, a qualified form of case-management pursuing the goal of support job retention of employees who due to a decrease in their ability to work may become inactive.

two general obligations on States parties; namely: (a) to adopt all appropriate legislative, administrative and other measures for the implementation of the rights recognized in the Convention related to work and employment, and (b) to take all appropriate measures, including legislation, to modify or abolish laws, regulations, customs and practices that constitute discrimination against persons with disabilities in the areas of work and employment.

5 From the State Duty to Protect to the Corporate Duty to Respect: Corporate Social Responsibility Standards and Disability

Internationally recognized CSR standards and guidelines addressing disability, usually focus their attention on the principles of non-discrimination and equality. As for instance, the latest 2011 amendments to these OECD Guidelines (2011)—the fifth since 1976—require that enterprises comply with the principles of non-discrimination and respect the human rights of specific categories of individuals, including persons with disabilities. The Guidelines address enterprises to recruit persons with disabilities from local communities and invest in their training and lifelong learning.

At the United Nations level, the Global Compact launched in 1999, involves corporations from all over the world to voluntary advance ten principles that address human rights, labour, the environment, and anti-corruption policies.[14] According to principle 6 of the Compact, 'businesses should uphold the elimination of discrimination in respect of employment and occupation'. With this aim, discrimination in employment and occupation has to be interpreted in the sense of treating people differently or less favourably because of characteristics that are not related to their merit or the inherent requirements of the job. In international and national law, these characteristics commonly include: race, colour, sex, religion, political opinion, national extraction, social origin, age, disability, HIV/AIDS status, trade union membership, and sexual orientation; however, Principle 6 allows companies to consider additional grounds where discrimination in employment and occupation may occur. The different forms of discrimination can arise in a variety of work-related activities, including access to employment, to particular occupations, promotions and to training and vocational guidance. Moreover, discrimination can occur with respect to the terms and conditions of the employment, such as: recruitment, remuneration, hours of work and rest/paid holidays, maternity protection, security of tenure, job assignments, performance assessment and advancement, training and opportunities, job prospects, social security, occupational safety and health. For example, the UN Global Compact, hailed as 'the world's largest corporate citizenship and sustainability initiative', has an existing membership of

[14] As to the Global Compact see Rasche and Kell (2010).

only 8,000 participants, with approximately 6,000 being businesses situated across 135 countries. While these numbers may appear impressive at first glance, even the UN Secretary-General has labelled the initiative's current participation rate inadequate, insofar as it reflects only a small percentage of the estimated 70,000 multinationals and millions of small businesses. Moreover, already more than 2,400 companies have faced expulsion from the Global Compact's esteemed membership 'for failing to report to their stakeholders on [human rights-related] progress they have made'.[15]

The idea that business has to play a more prominent societal role also occupies an important part of the European Union's debates on Union policy developments. The Green Paper of the European Commission of 2001 articulates the importance of going beyond compliance to legislation and investing into human capital, environment and stakeholders such as business partners and suppliers, customers, public authorities and local communities organizations.[16] In the 2002 follow up document, the European Commission pronounces such aspects of CSR as provision of quality employment, lifelong learning and equal opportunities and considers integration of persons with disabilities an important aspect to be addressed by CSR strategies. In this respect, enterprises are encouraged to exchange CSR experiences and to act in a socially responsible manner towards people with disabilities in relation to promoting equal employment opportunities, developing designed-for-all products and improving accessibility to assistive technologies.[17] The recently 2011 Communication of the Commission setting forth a renewed EU strategy 2011–2014 for CSR, articulates hiring persons with disabilities an important social responsibility issue recognized as a part of the business CSR philosophy.[18]

6 The Corporate Duty to Respect: The 2011 United Nations Guiding Principles on Business and Human Rights and the 'Protect, Respect and Remedy' Framework

The work of Professor John Ruggie, appointed in 2005 as the Special Representative of the UN Secretary-General (hereinafter, SRSG) on the issue of human rights and transnational corporations and other business enterprises, represents a

---

[15] UN Global compact, *Secretary-General Urges Companies to Join Global Compact*, available at http://www.unglobalcompact.org/news/134-06-21-2011.

[16] See European Commission *Green Paper: Promoting a European Framework for Corporate Social Responsibility*. Brussels, 18.7.2001.

[17] See European Commission *Communication from the Commission Concerning Corporate Social Responsibility: A business contribution to Sustainable Development* COM(2002) 347 final Brussels, 2.7.2002.

[18] See European Commission *Communication from the Commission A renewed EU strategy 2011–2014 for Corporate Social Responsibility* COM(2011) 681 final Brussels, 25.10.2011.

milestone as to the relevance of business in the advancement of human rights and, obviously, it has great relevance as far as the enforcement of CRPD's Article 27 right to employment of persons with disability by corporate actors. It is well-know that the SRSG work has been crystallized in the 2011 Guiding Principle on Business and Human Rights[19] which sets out guiding principles for addressing the relationship between business and human rights. The justification for this focus flows from the fact that Ruggie's effort, encompassing a lengthy and inclusive consultation process, has garnered UN endorsement and therefore stands as the most internationally authoritative statement in this area.

The Guiding Principles are the product of 6 years of research commissioned by former UN Secretary General Annan in July 2005. In June 2008, Professor Ruggie presented a report titled 'Protect, Respect and Remedy: a Framework for Business and Human Rights to the UN Human Rights Council' (the 'Framework'). The Framework consists of three core principles: (1) the duty of States to protect against human rights abuses by third parties, including business enterprises; (2) the corporate responsibility to respect human rights; and (3) the need for greater access by victims to effective judicial and non-judicial remedies. The UN Human Rights Council welcomed the Framework and requested that Professor Ruggie offer 'concrete and practical recommendations' for its implementation. In November 2010, Professor Ruggie responded by issuing a draft of the 'Guiding Principles on Business and Human Rights' ('Draft Principles'). The Draft Principles were open for comment for 3 months and received approximately 90 submissions from the business community, NGOs, international organizations, academics, and governments. After considering these written submissions and engaging in consultations with various stakeholders, Professor Ruggie submitted the revised and final text of the Guiding Principles to the Human Rights Council in March 2011, endorsed on 16 July 2011 by Human Rights Council with a specific resolution.[20]

The Guiding Principles do not aspire to create binding international law or impose obligations on TNCs. Rather, its 'normative contribution lies ... in elaborating the implications of existing standards and practices for States and businesses; integrating them within a single, logically coherent and comprehensive template; and identifying where the current regime falls short and how it should be improved'.[21] They, also, do not aim to offer a plug-and-play tool kit for identifying corporate human rights responsibilities. On the contrary, the Principles offer a sliding-scale approach for corporate actors, based on their size and, ostensibly, their location. In the words of the SRSG 'when it comes to means for implementation ... one size does not fit all'.[22]

[19] Special Representative of the Secretary-General on the Issue of Human Rights and Transnational Corporations and Other Business Enterprises *Guiding Principles on Business and Human Rights: Implementing the United Nations "Protect, Respect and Remedy" Framework*, U.N. Doc. A/HRC/17/31, 21.03.2011 (hereinafter Guiding Principles).

[20] See Human Rights Council, *Human rights and transnational corporations and other business enterprises*, Resolution A/HRC/RES/17/4.

[21] See Guiding Principles, para 5.

[22] Id.

As far as responsibility for human rights infringements is concerned, the Guiding Principles aim to 'clearly differentiate the respective roles of businesses and governments and make sure that they both play those roles'.[23] In other words, according to the Guiding Principles while governments retain the exclusive responsibility for protecting and fulfilling human rights obligations, the litmus test for corporations under the Guiding Principles only inquires whether business enterprises respect human rights. Indeed, the Guiding Principles are intended to elaborate on the implications of existing standards and practices for States and businesses, rather than create new international law obligations. As with the Framework, they represent 'soft' rather than 'hard' law (but with the possibility, as with any such instrument, they may evolve over time into hard law or otherwise inform standards of care). The Principles track the structure of the Framework, with each substantive section addressed to one of the three pillars; accordingly as far as the first Pillar, the Principles reiterate the State's core duty to protect human rights (Principle 1), recommending, *inter alia*, that States should address any gaps in laws and policies requiring businesses to respect human rights, provide guidance to businesses on how to respect human rights, and encourage or require reporting by businesses on their human rights performance (Principle 3), exercise adequate oversight with respect to contractual relationships and ensure respect for human rights by State-controlled enterprises (Principles 4–6), promoting human rights through multilateral institutions dealing with business-related issues (Principle 10), etc.

As far as the second Pillar, the Principles calls on business enterprises to respect human rights. In particular, businesses must avoid infringing on human rights and address adverse human rights impacts with which they are involved (Principle 11). To do so, businesses should adopt a clear human rights policy statement approved at the most senior levels and embedded in the organization through operational procedures (Principles 15–16) and most important, conduct on-going human rights 'due diligence' process to identify, prevent, mitigate and account for how they address their impacts on human rights (Principles 17–21), engage in remediation where they have caused or contributed to adverse human rights impacts (Principle 22), explore ways to respect human rights regardless of the domestic enforcement context (Principle 23b); and treat the risk of contributing to gross human rights abuses through human rights violations as a matter of legal compliance wherever they operate (Principle 23c).

As far as the third Pillar, the Principles call for effective State-based and non-State-based remedial mechanisms for those affected by business-related human rights harms. In particular States should ensure access to State-based judicial and non-judicial grievance mechanisms and facilitate access to non-State-based grievance mechanisms (Principles 25–28); Businesses should establish or participate in non-State-based, operational-level grievance mechanisms to identify, track, and address adverse human rights impacts from their activities (Principle 29).

[23] Id.

Grievance mechanisms should be legitimate, accessible, predictable, equitable, transparent, rights-compatible, a source of continuous learning, and—in the case of operational-level mechanisms-based on dialogue and engagement (Principle 31).

From a substantial point of view, Guiding Principles also include the corporate duty to respect human rights of persons with disabilities in the employment sphere. Indeed, principle 12 acknowledges that '[t]he responsibility of business enterprises to respect human rights refers to internationally recognized human rights – understood, at a minimum, as those expressed in the International Bill of Human Rights and the principles concerning fundamental rights set out in the International Labour Organization's Declaration on Fundamental Principles and Rights at Work'. The Commentary to Principle 12 goes further, admitting that, depending on circumstances, business enterprises may need to consider additional standards and, as for instance, enterprises should respect the human rights of individuals belonging to specific groups or populations that require particular attention, where they may have adverse human rights impacts on them. This include United Nations instruments that have elaborated further on the rights of indigenous peoples, women, national or ethnic, religious and linguistic minorities, children, as well as persons with disabilities.

7 The Legal Enforcement of the Corporate Duty to Respect the Right to Employment of Persons with Disabilities

From this last perspective, compliance with the legislation in force is a main requirement for all the companies, moreover when they pretend to be defined as socially responsible. In the area of employment of persons with disabilities, this means mainly three things: in the first place, compliance with existing national legislation on employment quotas for persons with disabilities, where this legislation exists; in the second place, compliance with equal treatment legislation which forbids all discrimination on grounds of disability among others; and, in the third place, the setting forth of reasonable accommodations to ensure persons with disabilities the enjoyment on equal basis with others of all human rights and fundamental freedoms. As a result of the European Directive 2000/78/EC on equal treatment in the workplace,[24] and of the entry into force of CRPD, enacting

[24] The Directive 2000/78/EC *establishing a general framework for equal treatment in employment and occupation* (Employment Equality Directive), sets out broad equality and non-discrimination objectives—specifically including disability—in the field of employment and, crucially, calls on Member States to 'put into effect' the principle of equal treatment. The Directive requires Member States to prohibit, *inter alia*, discrimination on the grounds of disability in the fields of employment, occupation and vocational training. According to the directive, Member States are required to prohibit direct discrimination, indirect discrimination, harassment, victimisation and instructions to discriminate on the grounds, *inter alia*, of disability.

such type of legislation is binding for all member States and, in effect, it has been enforced in the majority of the European countries. Most countries have legislation on the percentage of positions in the public-sector for persons with disabilities, and some also have quotas for the private sector, providing for sanctions for non-compliance.[25] Through quota systems States establish an obligation for employers with more than a certain number of workers to employ a minimum percentage of people with disabilities (the range of quotas is normally between 2 and 5 %). Existing quota systems can be divided into two main categories: strict quotas and flexible quotas. Strict quotas refer to schemes in which a person with a disability is treated preferentially irrespective of whether he or she is as qualified as other applicants. With flexible quotas, an applicant with a disability is treated preferentially only if he or she has equal merits and qualifications as another applicant. States are facing challenges in establishing effective positive measures that adequately advance equal possibilities for persons with disabilities to participate in working life. In some countries quota obligation can be met by corporate actors through alternative options, which might include the payment of a compensation fee to a special fund for the employment of people with disabilities or the purchase of products and/or services from special companies (sheltered workshops) whose workforce is mainly composed of people with disabilities. As far as equal treatment legislation is concerned, such legislation prohibits all kind of direct or indirect discrimination on grounds of a person's disability in any of the stages of the labour market integration process (search, selection, hiring, professional promotion. . .). The obligation of equal treatment includes carrying out the necessary reasonable adjustments required by a person with disability to participate in any work activity on the same terms as all other employees. The legislation also includes the specific prohibition of harassment at work on grounds of disability and of discriminatory instructions, which means for instance that a company cannot ask a human resources company or temporary work agency to exclude people with disabilities from its recruitment processes. Finally, as far as the reasonable

[25] In Italy the Law 68/99 obliges both public and private employers with at least 15 workers, to hire disabled workers in accordance with reserve quota (art. 3). This mandatory hiring, limited to new workers and valid for technical/executive staff only, also concerns political parties, trade unions and no-profit associations operating in the field of social solidarity, assistance and rehabilitation. For police services, civil protection and national defence, the placement of persons with disabilities only concerns administrative services. Germany was among the first countries to adopt a quota-levy scheme in 1974. Under the Social Code, Book 9, of 2002, public and private employers with a workforce of at least 20 employees are required to ensure that 5 % of their workforce is made up of people with disabilities. Employers who do not meet their quota obligation are obliged to pay a fixed compensatory levy for every unfilled quota place. In France, the funds arising from non-fulfilment of the quota obligation may be used to fund vocational training of individuals with disabilities. The French quota law also provides other options for employers to partially meet their obligation under the law, such as by purchasing goods or services from sheltered workshops employing disabled people, or by implementing an agreement, negotiated between employers' and employee associations, aimed at the integration of disabled workers, though recruitment, training, job retention or adjustment to technological change.

accommodation principles is concerned, the provision of a reasonable accommodation by the employer is an individualized measure that does not need to be temporary in nature: in fact, it should be provided for an individual for the duration of his or her employment. Reasonable accommodation measures should be distinguished from affirmative action measures aimed at the favourable treatment of groups. Also, the duty to provide a reasonable accommodation should not be confused with the duty to comply with general accessibility and occupational health and safety standards. According to this duty, recognized both by Article 27 of the CRPD and Article 5 of the 2000/78/EC Directive, employers are required, in certain cases, to take appropriate measures to enable persons with disabilities to have access to, participate in, or advance in employment, or to undergo training, unless such measures would impose a disproportionate burden on the employer. In order to enforce this obligation disabled workers or job applicants claiming a reasonable accommodation should demonstrate that: they are (otherwise) qualified for the job; and the employer (or other party) was aware of their needs; and with an accommodation, they could (safely) perform the essential functions of that particular job. Employers are only exempted from this obligation in cases where they can prove that they were not aware of the need for an individual accommodation, or an effective accommodation, enabling the disabled worker/job applicant to perform the essential functions of a job, is not available, or the requested accommodation imposes a 'disproportionate burden' on the employer.

The disproportionate burden 'defence' for not accommodating a disabled person needs to be drafted carefully. Otherwise, unscrupulous employers might make recourse to this defence in order to avoid any obligation. Much litigation might ensue. The fact that the workplace or work schedule would be inconvenienced clearly does not amount to a 'disproportionate burden'. In practice, the question as to what constitutes a disproportionate burden very much depends on the context of the case concerned, and is not merely dependent on the financial costs of an accommodation or financial compensation schemes. It depends on such factors as its practical implications, effects on the overall work process, number of disabled workers already employed and length of the envisaged employment contract.

8 Operationalizing Corporate Due Diligence Principle as to the Right to Employment of Persons with Disabilities

If amongst corporate responsibilities in the field of the employment of persons with disabilities there is the duty to enforce legal norms on quotas, on reasonable accommodation, on non-discrimination, applicable to such category of workers, the question raises on how private entities should enforce these corporate obligations. The 2011 UN Guiding Principles, and the abovementioned evolution of international standards on corporate responsibility, have demonstrated that avenues for enforcing such corporate responsibilities should be found in the corporate due diligence duty.

The due diligence concept is an important development as it offers a general principle of corporate action that can form the basis of corporate obligations to act in a socially responsible manner. In particular this concept may lead to the development of corporate duties of care where due diligence is inadequately carried out and consequential loss is suffered by third persons whose interests are thereby harmed. Guiding Principles 17–21, discussing the practical steps that business enterprises should take to discharge this responsibility, appear under the heading 'Human rights due diligence'. These steps include having a human rights policy; assessing human rights impacts of business activities; integrating those values and findings into corporate cultures and management systems; and tracking as well as reporting performance. Also, the notion of due diligence is defined by the UN as follows: such a measure of prudence, activity, or assiduity, as is properly to be expected from, and ordinarily exercised by, a reasonable and prudent [person or enterprise] under the particular circumstances; not measured by any absolute standard, but depending on the relative facts of the special case. In the context of the Guiding Principles, human rights due diligence comprises an on-going management process that a reasonable and prudent enterprise needs to undertake, in light of its circumstances (including sector operating context, size and similar factors) to meet its responsibility to respect human rights.[26]

Furthermore, extremely interesting is the circumstance that such a duty appears to be complementary of the international human rights legal obligation of due diligence in relation to the actions of non-state actors,[27] and the general voluntary business practice of due diligence.[28]

From this last perspective, the notion of due diligence in corporate governance environment, indeed, has emerged since long, across many industries and business activities such as mergers and acquisitions (M&A), initial public offering (IPO), real estate, technology, human resources, supplier evaluation or private banking customer identification. In this field area due diligence (also known as due care) is essentially understood as a way of preventing damage or unnecessary harm to either party involved in a transaction or business decision. Failure to make this effort is considered negligence fault. In a financial transaction (M&A, IPO) context, therefore, activating due diligence processes means carrying out an investigation or audit of a potential investment serving as a confirmation of all material facts in regard to a transaction. Hence, due diligence is a review of financial records including anything deemed material to the transaction, sell- or buy-side (financial capacity, honesty, reputation, management quality, ownership, etc.). Risk can materialize at various levels, e.g. via direct cost increase, revenue decrease, unmet expectations related to market access and growth, as swell as damaged brand value and reputation.

[26] UN Human Rights Office of the High Commissioner (2012).

[27] The leading case in this area is *Velasquez Rodriguez v. Honduras*, (1989 28 ILM 294).

[28] See, e.g., Perry and Herd (2004).

Moreover, materialized risk at one level may impact at the other levels as well through cascading effects. For example, damaged brand value may reduce market access, leading to revenue decrease etc. A due diligence analysis, therefore, aims at identifying intangible factors responsible for undetected, and therefore unmanaged, risks leading to a common decision base in multi-actor situations facing intangibles and complexity.[29] Just from this perspective, the SRSG has noted how '[b]usinesses routinely employ due diligence to assess exposure to risks beyond their control and develop mitigation strategies for them, such as changes in government policy, shifts in consumer preferences, and even weather patterns. Controllable or not, human rights challenges arising from the business context, its impacts and its relationships, can pose material risks to the company and its stakeholders, and generate outright abuses that may be linked to the company in perception or reality. Therefore, they merit a similar level of due diligence as any other risk'.[30]

If companies are to carry out due diligence, what is its scope? The process inevitably will be inductive and fact-based, but the principles guiding it can be summarized succinctly. The key goal of the procedure is to identify the materiality in risk areas, which usually are seen as merely intangible. The task is how to identify, measure and describe environmental and social performance of industrial activities in an aggregated form. The outcome should not only give specific risk information, it should also enable intra-organization benchmarking and management system development of corporate responsibility. The gained information and drawn conclusions then serve to take decisions on: whether or not engaging into a business transaction due to the level of identified new facts or potentially impacting effects which costs are or would be acceptable or inacceptable; what will be the resources needed for risk mitigation, i.e. to reduce economic impacts to an acceptable risk level; and what will be the costs of maintenance for the necessary and targeted quality of risk management. The described methodology involves three distinct phases: (1) a pre-investigation about the relevance of social or environmental topics in the given situation; (2) if the indication of relevance is strong enough, an initial screening is carried out; (3) followed by in depth investigation. Finally, as an option: follow-up of risk management activities.

Tasks to be performed within these three main phases may be summarized as follows. The first phase involves the screening of the business landscape of the sector in question for relevant and significant social risk areas. The relevance explains the level of potential risks a company has to face due to the type of sector it is in (like supply chain for toys manufacturing). The significance results from the analysis of the client's value chain: where and how strong might a potentially relevant issue impact the economic success factors. This first phase aims at giving a clear picture for the management whether or not there is a need for immediate action (e.g. immediate withdrawal from the deal) or for further investigation. Equally important is the ability of the company to have an independent external

[29] See Gorman et al. (2005).

[30] SRSG Report to UN Human Rights Council UN Doc. A/HRC/11/13 (April 22, 2009).

view which allows to investigate for example critique from NGOs or other stakeholders like customers, joint venture partners, law enforcement bodies or investors. The second phase includes an in-depth investigation of critical issues and business activities for detailed risk assessment in a particular area of its value chain: supply, manufacturing, distribution, use and follow-on responsibilities like 'take-back' obligations. Based on the results from the first phase, on-site audits are carried out wherever necessary to enable a fact-based analysis of perceived risks and, if the case allows it, a fact-based stakeholder dialogue is performed. This gives the possibility to immediately investigate options to mitigate the risks: de-selection of suppliers, contractual obligations and review processes, direct management influence or even labelling of CSR-quality by a third-party. By providing the issue landscape and the economic implications mapping the method allows to deal with CSR-topics in the usually most pressing, financially relevant and by all management levels hopefully accepted way. It is the development from issue-management to integrated sustainability management at all levels of corporate responsibility: the board, the top-management, the value chain management, the specialist functions and the personnel in general. Finally, the third phase includes management activities performed to cope with evaluating the performance of singular remediation action, surveying the implementation steps of management quality improvements and assessing whether or not, for example, management information systems (MIS) follow also in economic terms the different anchoring procedures.

It follows that due diligence may be approached as a container concept. Every professional will first think of due diligence in his own field of expertise, depending on the scope and purpose of the project or of the corporate policy decisions which experts will be engaged for the due diligence process. For a full due diligence investigation, many different experts can be involved. Multidisciplinary teams will work on: business issues (this work will typically be performed by commercial lawyers and the company's commercial staff); financial position and forecast (the company's financial staff, investment bankers, accountants); technical aspects (in-house and external technical experts); tax risks (tax lawyers); corporate structure and legal liabilities (lawyers and notaries); real estate (notaries; real estate agents' valuation experts); pension issues (lawyers, tax lawyers, accountants and actuaries); IT issues (IT consultants); environmental issues (environmental law and administrative law specialists, technical environmental consultants); insurance issues (insurance or actuarial experts); and fraud and corruption (forensic accountants).

The abovementioned analysis demonstrates, also, how the perspective of due diligence is very much one of risk management, with the twist that the harm may occur outside the company, but then rebound to it in terms of reputational loss. The major advantage of human rights due diligence is that its outcomes can be fed into the existing system of corporate risk control. It becomes, in sum, embedded, rather than an 'add on' that can be quickly put to one side. However, as it has been argued 'the human rights due diligence assessment may not sit easily with the corporate aim of profit maximization' particularly since the basis of corporate law remains 'rooted in the prioritization of enhancing shareholder value'[31] or as noted in the literature 'some key ways of placing rights related elements on the corporate radar (e.g. socio-ethical risk assessment) involve mind-sets and skills that are still non-conventional in many board rooms'.[32]

In addition, and with specific regard to the employment of person with disabilities issue, due diligence in relation to labour rights remains quite a blunt instrument that has not fully thought through what it means in relation to the enterprise's own workers or workers of enterprises linked to it in the supply chains, as contrasted to other individuals, groups or communities affected by their operations. Workers are not 'stakeholders' in the same way as persons or groups external to the enterprise's production of value added. It will therefore be very important to see how due diligence processes will be carried out in relation to employment of persons with disabilities. Due diligence processes in such situations need to take into account the structure of firms and their business relationships, the information relied upon, and the broader culture within an enterprise. As a general matter, the Guide for integrating Human Rights into Business Management, developed by BLIHR, the Office of the UN High Commissioner for Human Rights and the UN Global Compact, sets out a series of processes for situating human rights considerations within standard business practices, from strategy to measuring impact and auditing and reporting.[33] The due diligence process itself identifies the steps to be taken in carrying it out. However, other factors will need to be taken into account. One is better identification along the supply chain as well as in the company of who is responsible for what. Another step would be setting out some criteria for assessing the reliability of information relied upon and the transparency about its sources. When businesses carry out due diligence in relation to other types of risks, they rely on internal and external sources. In the now more regulated financial services sector, due diligence is reported as being regularly undertaken in relation to prospective clients, prospective employees and prospective investors. Information comes from public and private sources, and pose the challenges of verification, timeliness, multiplicity of sources, and cost, particularly from commercial databases.[34] The commentary to Principle 21 suggests that business reporting should include 'indicators concerning how enterprises identify and address adverse impacts on human rights'. The most likely scenario is that they will seek out existing indicators. Here we find a number of competing sources, of variable quality and accessibility of data. Multiple, non-transparent and non-comparable firm-based indicators would not be particularly helpful. But more importantly, there is always the risk of reductionism, that the indicator becomes not a proxy for the right, but a reduced notion of the right itself. Context and nuances that can be critical in the

[31] See Muchlinski (2012), p. 177.

[32] See Horrigan (2010), p. 330.

[33] The Guide may be accessed at the following website: http://www.integrating-humanrights.org/about_all_steps.

[34] Ainsworth (2007), pp. 250–251.

enjoyment of human rights in the context of labour risk being lost through an over-reliance on indicators. Last but certainly not least, the overall environment in which human rights due diligence is carried out also matters. Muchlinski has warned, 'unless a corporate culture of concern for human rights in instilled into the officers, agents and employees of the company, due diligence could end up missing the very issues it is set up to discover. At worst it could degenerate into a 'tick-box' exercise designed for public relations purposes rather than a serious integral part of corporate decision-making. It is here that the ethical duty to respect human rights is key. The acceptance of such a duty may be said to 'constitutionalise' concern over human rights impacts in the corporate psyche and culture. The due diligence process then allows this concern to be put into operation'.[35]

Finally, even if the Guiding Principles are only recommendatory and even if due diligence is a voluntary process, the application of due diligence approach in these situations may be used as a shield against legal actions. In effect, notwithstanding the fact that the 2011 Guiding Principles contain the caveat that 'nothing in these Guiding Principles should be read as creating new international law obligations....', at the same time, a concern about possible legal consequences relating to non-respect for human rights, surfaces from time to time in the SRSG's reports and are certainly on firms' radar screens. Principle 23, indeed, in the context of remediation, recognizes that in all contexts, business enterprises should 'treat the risk of causing or contributing to gross human rights abuses as a legal compliance issues wherever they operate'. Furthermore, the commentary to Principle 17 closes with this remark: 'Conducting appropriate human rights due diligence should help business enterprises address the risk of legal claims against them by showing that they took every reasonable step to avoid involvement with an alleged human rights abuse. However, business enterprises conducting such due diligence should not assume that, by itself, this will automatically and fully absolve them from liability for causing or contributing to human rights abuses'. With proper documentation, however, evidence of having engaged in human rights due diligence could certainly help a business entity make its case in some circumstances. Civil law offers far greater potential application of such due diligence scheme: Canada due diligence has already 'developed beyond a simple commercial risk assessment process into a basic element of complying with a wide range of environmental, health, safety and other regulations involving strict liability offences, becoming analogous to the 'reasonableness' element in civil tort cases'.[36] The same Special Representative in his 2010 interim report pointed to examples of national legislation from the Netherlands, Singapore and the United States that he saw as widening the responsibilities of directors when considering the duties owed to their firms.[37]

[35] Muchlinksi (2012), cit., p. 156.

[36] Muchlinksi (2012), cit., p. 157.

[37] SRSG, Corporate Law Project: Overarching Trends and Observations, p. 14.

9 Corporate Social Responsibility and Disability: Going Beyond Strict Legislation

Both States and corporate employers are obligated by the CRPD and, as far as the EU level, by the 2000/78/EC Directive, to protect the right of people with disabilities to work. However, business sector may employ people with disabilities not only to fulfil legal and moral obligations, but also for economic reasons. Indeed, hiring persons with disabilities makes economic sense from several perspectives. In the first place, persons with disabilities are high quality and reliable employees: indeed many workers with disabilities have equal or higher performance ratings on the job than workers without disabilities. Secondly, many workers with disabilities have higher job retention than non-disabled workers. In the third place, persons with disabilities may have underutilized talents and perspectives that can assist in developing new products and broaden the consumer base of your company. From this side, they may bring abilities to a position due to the affect of their disability, for instance an unusual degree of creativity, high level of accuracy, or attention to detail. In the fourth place, persons with disabilities may enhance corporate business culture, employee morality and business reputation: in these situations indeed, non-disabled employees may feel more positively about their company and its contribution to their community; corporate managerial staff may come to feel that they are better able to learn the needs of their staff and to improve their communication with the general workforce. Finally, most reasonable accommodations do not carry any significant cost, and non-disabled employees commonly require accommodations. Accommodations that involve physical modifications also benefit consumers and non-disabled employees by creating a universally friendly environment. For example, a ramp that benefits a wheelchair-using employee also benefits customers with prams and non-disabled employees who transport inventory. There are 'ripple effects' that emanate from reasonable accommodations. These include higher productivity, greater dedication, and more widespread use by workers without disabilities of efficiency-enhancing technologies previously used only by their peers with disabilities.

Upholding legal and moral responsibilities so that people with disabilities can claim their right to work is an important step in fighting against stereotypes falsehood. A significant cultural myth is the idea that people with disabilities are unable to be effective workers. By employing a person with a disability corporate actors may help to erode prejudices and misconceptions regarding this group. Employment is a hallmark of true citizenship for it enables individuals to participate meaningfully in society. The workplace is where meaningful conversations occur, where meaningful relationships form, and where loyalty to co-workers is forged. Being a part of this community is a crucial way for people with disabilities to be full members of society, and to be deemed as such. Probably the best example of the fallaciousness of this stereotype is represented by those corporate best practices concerning the access to employment of persons with autism spectrum disorder (ASD). Danish corporation Specialisterne, which is a socially innovative company where the majority of employees have a diagnosis on the ASD and work as business consultants on tasks such as software testing, programming and data-entry for the public and private sectors, is perhaps the most well known example. The Specialisterne model, where enterprises outsource some processes and also outsource the responsibility for ASD people working on these processes, although already in place since 2005, is innovative.[38] Pilot projects conducted by Specialisterne confirmed that this model could potentially work across the EU, other projects of Specialisterne are expected to demonstrate that they work worldwide.[39]

Other examples of employment's integration of persons with autism involve the case of Passwerk, a Belgian software testing company, which has developed strategies to handle social and communication skills difficulties that employer with autism usually experience in the workplace. Passwerk provides training and job coaching for its employees with autisms not only in professional development, but also in social skills development, tailored to each employee's individual needs. In addition, when an employee is unable to carry out a particular task, due to the limitations of their autism, a 'job coach' will step in to assist. Passwerk has one job coach for every seven employees with autism. The job coaches work closely with the employees with autism, acting as a first point of contact for both employees and customers. As in most workplaces, each employee's skills are put to use in the most appropriate and efficient way possible, so that together the team gets the job done well.

In the United States, a small farming business called Green Bridge Growers is succeeding to grow produce all year-round, primarily using a method called 'aquaponics' where fish and vegetables grow in harmony. The company now employs a number of individuals with ASD and finds that the scheduling, precision and monitoring required in aquaponics perfectly match with their skills. Green Bridge Growers was founded to deal with a problem that highly intelligent adults with autism often face. Successful initiatives designed to employ people with autism may be found also at the level of large international companies willing to achieve social as well as business goals and create a more diverse workforce. In 2007, Walgreens, a chain of pharmacies in the United States, opened a new distribution centre where more than 40 % of its staff has some disabilities, including autism. An on-site training facility helps those with special needs become prepared for the job and all employees, with and without disabilities, meet the same productivity goals. Walgreens aims to fill 10 % of its distribution centre production jobs

[38] Other examples include software giant SAP, who recently announced plans to hire 650 new employees with autism, Auticon in Germany, and Apiritech and Semperical in the US, which have followed Specialisterne's example. These organizations structure workplace environments that enable individual value creation, or focusing training programs on bringing out and developing exceptional abilities, or establishing performance-management systems that de-emphasize conformity and instead focus on removing obstacles to higher performance.

[39] See European Commission, Results of four pilot projects on employment of persons with autism, vp/2010/017, p. 15.

with people with disabilities, and is already more than halfway towards reaching this goal. Finally in Italy, cosmetic company L'Oréal has started a long-term project to facilitate the employment of people with autism throughout the company. The company has created training for employees with autism, other staff and managers and designated specific staff members to act as coaches for employees with autism. L'Oréal also has a policy to ensure they employ people with disabilities in at least 2 % of positions within the company.[40]

In conclusion, companies which aim to be socially responsible on disability, should set themselves a series of objectives to pursue independently from the circumstance that the company is bound by quota legislation, or not. It should have to establish concrete employment targets for people with disabilities and an action plan to achieve these targets; it should have to employ persons with disabilities working at all company levels and to fix for this category of employees concrete targets facing additional challenges to being included in the labour market, like women with disabilities, people with more severe disabilities and elderly people with disabilities.

10 Conclusions

Human rights corporate responsibility goes beyond core company activities and donations to charity, and is understood as an integrated part of doing business, based on corporate values included in strategy and daily operations. Moreover, the current financial crisis has shown how business activities solely motivated by the desire for short-term profit can have serious global consequences, while in order to achieve sustainable practices, business need to be ethical and invest in local communities and economies. The importance to address disability as a part of CSR strategies is certainly becoming more visible in the practices of the MNEs and important part of successful CSR strategies and inclusive corporate culture. There is the need for more and more 'disability champions': business cases and best practices advocating strongly for hiring persons with disabilities Also, the importance of the issue is proved by the evolvement of special organizations and networks that aim to improve the underemployment of persons with disabilities and cooperate with enterprises (both public and private) in extending their CSR strategies.

This notwithstanding, 'disability' still remains a rather sensitive element of CSR for the companies and is addressed differently due to the different levels of understanding the importance and the benefits of such actions. The present analysis

[40] Aiming to integrate young adults in particular into their workforce, L'Oréal is working with Fondazione TEDA (an association for autism) to develop the project. Activities proposed to people with autism include administration tasks such as working with databases, updating files, data entry and archiving, as well as packaging cosmetics, quality checking, security and other tasks.

demonstrates that it is not sufficient that corporate entities address disabilities in their organizational norms and values; they have to incorporate this issue further into corporate culture, HR policies and work environment setting forth a system of corporate governance which take into account these concerns. Indeed, it is definitely a challenge for an enterprise not only to demonstrate attitude towards inclusion of persons with disabilities in CSR strategies, but to promote the implementation of these policies further into 'inclusive corporate culture and work environment'. Thus, to make the choice work, creative and diverse options are needed as not one solution does fit for all. Besides, dissemination of the positive examples for the larger number of companies to understand the benefits of engaging in such activities, is highly important.

References

Ainsworth M (2007) Complete compliance: due diligence on companies and individuals. Bus Inf Rev 24(4):250–251

Alston P, Steiner HJ (2000) International human rights in context, 2nd edn. Oxford University Press, Oxford/New York, pp 180–185

Bickenbach JE (1999) Models of disablement, universalism and the international classification of impairments, disabilities and handicaps. Soc Sci Med 48(9):1173–1187

Clapham A (2006) Human rights obligations of non-state actors. Oxford University Press, Oxford, pp 347–436

Cushman T (ed) (2012) Handbook of human rights. Routledge, London

Eide A (1984) The international human rights system. In: Eide A et al (eds) Food as a human rights. United Nations Publisher, Tokyo, pp 152–161

French S (1994) What is disability? In: French S (ed) On equal terms. Working with disabled people. Butterworth-Heinemann, Oxford, pp 4 ff

Gorman GG, Rosa PJ, Faseruk A (2005) Institutional lending to knowledge-based businesses. J Bus Venturing 20:793–819

Grammenos S (2011) Indicators of disability equality in Europe. ANED 2011 Task 4. www.disability-europe.net/content/aned/media/ANED%202011%20Task%204%20-%20Synthesis%20Report.doc. Accessed 30 Oct 2014

Horrigan B (2010) corporate social responsibility in the 21st century: debates, models and practices across government, law and business. Edward Elgar Publishing, Cheltenham

Hunt L (2007) Inventing human rights. A history. Norton, New York

Ishay M (2008) The history of human rights: from ancient times to the globalization era. University of California Press, Berkeley

Muchlinski P (2012) Implementing the new UN corporate human rights framework: implications for corporate law, governance and regulation. Bus Ethic Q 22(1):145–177

Oliver M (1996) Understanding disability: from theory to practice. Macmillan, Hampshire

Perry JS, Herd TJ (2004) Mergers and acquisitions: reducing M&A risk through improved due diligence. Strategy Leadersh 32(2):12–19

Quinn G (1999) The human rights of people with disabilities under EU law. In: Alston P, Bustelo M, Heenan J (eds) The EU and human rights. Oxford University Press, Oxford, pp 281 ff
Rasche A, Kell G (eds) (2010) The United Nations global compact: achievements, trends and challenges. Cambridge University Press, Cambridge
Rehman J (2010) International human rights law. Pearson, Harlow
Shakespeare T (2006) Disability rights and wrongs. Routledge, Abingdon
Udombana N (2004) Between promise and performance: revisiting states' obligations under the African Human Rights Charter. Stanford J Int Law 40:105–142
UN Human Rights Office of the High Commissioner (2012) The corporate responsibility to respect human rights: an interpretive guide. United Nations, Geneva, p 4
van Hoof GJH (1984) The legal nature of economic, social and cultural rights: a rebuttal of some traditional views. In: Alston P, Tomaševski K (eds) The right to food. Martinus Nijhoff Publishers, The Hague, pp 97–110

Marco Fasciglione is Researcher at the Institute for International Legal Studies (ISGI-CNR), Naples.

Conclusions

Valentina Della Fina and Rachele Cera

The protection of the rights of people with autism in the fields of education and employment is far from being uniform within the European Union. Among countries substantial differences exist with regard to the legal regimes in favour of persons with ASD and, currently, only few European countries have developed specific legislation or national plans and strategies on autism.

As flexible instruments addressing the needs of people with ASD, national autism plans and strategies set out adapted, life-long support and services to enable them to enjoy full inclusion and participation in relevant social fields. The national autism plans and strategies developed in the United Kingdom are good practices as they take into account the needs of people with autism from childhood to adulthood and are more respondent to the principles and rights enshrined in the CRPD. In particular, the Northern Ireland Autism Strategy (2013–2020) and its Action Plan (2013–2016) are modeled on the CRPD which is expressly recalled as a legal source to which their strategic priorities are conformed in order to reinforce the human rights of persons with autism in the domestic legal order.

While specific legislation in favour of people with ASD are generally lacking, some legislative measures in the fields of education, vocational training and life-long learning, and employment apply to people with autism.

In the field of education, the current tendency in EU Member States is to develop a policy towards inclusion of pupils with special educational needs. There are still countries with a selective rather than an inclusive education system, but some advancements have been put in place. On the contrary, some EU Member States, such as Italy or UK, have long been leaders in protecting the right to education of children with disabilities and their legislations have much to offer as implementing practice of Article 24 of the CRPD. However, many challenges remain reflecting

V. Della Fina (✉) • R. Cera (✉)
Institute for International Legal Studies, National Research Council (CNR), Rome, Italy
e-mail: valentina.dellafina@cnr.it; rachele.cera@cnr.it

V. Della Fina, R. Cera (eds.), *Protecting the Rights of People with Autism in the Fields of Education and Employment*, DOI 10.1007/978-3-319-13791-9_8

gaps in applying laws. While it is considered perhaps the most inclusive education system in the world, Italy serves as an important reminder about the many challenges of translating the language and values of law into practice.

Article 24 of the CRPD calls for an inclusive education system which should be flexible to meet the special needs of people with disabilities. Adjustments are especially needed to address ASD pupils' needs, for whom education cannot rely on centrally-determined curricula and teaching methodologies. Qualified by the OHCHR has a good example of support measures consistent with Article 24 (2) (d) of the CRPD, the IEPs should be intended, in order to meet the needs of pupils with ASD, as a global plan including didactic, rehabilitative, social and welfare aspects. Good examples in this regard are the PEI in Italy and the EHC plan in England.

Similarly, the sensitivity of the institutions and the public towards people with autism has increased over time in the field of vocational training and lifelong learning. However, it seems necessary to continue encouraging the promotion and development of vocational training initiatives aimed at teenagers and adults. A project of development training of persons with ASD should include the provision of effective support to their families, as well as opportunities for social development, through organized services, and the design of routes towards work orientation, stimulating at the same time ways to manage leisure and recreational time.

The implementation of Article 27 of the CRPD in the EU Member States shows that the level of protection of the right to work and employment of persons with ASD in each country depends by several factors including social, cultural and economic circumstances. From this perspective, there is no a one size-fit-for-all approach in the implementation of employment rights of people with autism at domestic level, but different regimes may be enforced, on a case by case basis, with the aim to achieve the objectives of Article 27. However, disability-related legislations to be adopted at national level in this field have to rely on two 'normative principles': in the first place, the adoption of a normative definition of disability sufficiently wide to encompass ASD and, in the second place, the avoidance of national legislations ambiguous about whether failure to provide reasonable accommodation is to be treated as a form of unlawful discrimination. These two principles have to be regarded as benchmarks to be applied by national implementing legislations.

In conclusion, the promotion of equal rights for people with autism, in the key areas of education and employment, should be high on the agenda of EU Member States in consideration of their commitments deriving from the CRPD. Being the overall aims of the Convention the inclusion and full participation of persons with disabilities in all aspects of life, the achievement of such goals for persons with ASD can be realized especially through education and employment, as highlighted by the UNGA Resolution 67/82 of 19 March 2013 and by the message of the UN Secretary General on the 2014 World Autism Awareness Day.

MIX
Papier aus verantwortungsvollen Quellen
Paper from responsible sources
FSC® C105338

If you have any concerns about our products,
you can contact us on
ProductSafety@springernature.com

In case Publisher is established outside the EU,
the EU authorized representative is:
Springer Nature Customer Service Center GmbH
Europaplatz 3, 69115 Heidelberg, Germany

Printed by Libri Plureos GmbH
in Hamburg, Germany